THE CHRISTIAN PLATONISM OF
SIMONE WEIL

Simone Weil — 1943

THE CHRISTIAN PLATONISM OF
SIMONE WEIL

EDITED BY

E. Jane Doering

Eric O. Springsted

University of Notre Dame Press   *Notre Dame, Indiana*

Frontis: Courtesy of Bibliothèque Nationale – Fonds Simone Weil

Library of Congress Cataloging-in-Publication Data
The Christian Platonism of Simone Weil / edited by E. Jane Doering and
  Eric O. Springsted.
      p.   cm.
   Includes bibliographical references and index.
   ISBN 0-268-02564-9 (alk. paper)
   ISBN 0-268-02565-7 (pbk. : alk. paper)
      1. Weil, Simone, 1909–1943.   2. Platonists—France—History—20th century.
3. Weil, Simone, 1909–1943—Religion.   4. Christianity—Philosophy—History—
20th century.   I. Doering, E. Jane.   II. Springsted, Eric O.
   B2430.W474C49   2004
   194—dc22

                                                             2004018963

∞ *This book is printed on acid-free paper.*

To André-A. Devaux,

founder of l'Association pour l'étude de la pensée
de Simone Weil, for his unflagging efforts to encourage
the study and discussion of Simone Weil's thought

CONTENTS

ACKNOWLEDGMENTS

The Christian Platonism of Simone Weil has come into being thanks to genial cooperation between the members of the American Weil Society and the members of the French Association pour l'étude de la pensée de Simone Weil. Undaunted by distance or language, both groups profited from numerous opportunities to discuss the challenging topic of Simone Weil and Christian Platonism.

Our students deserve special recognition: they have been a constant source of fresh insights into Simone Weil's thought. We thank them for giving us ever-renewed confidence in the future of Weil studies.

We offer heartfelt thanks to Chris Callahan and Bernard Doering. Their support was cheerful, imaginative, and generous. They unstintingly applied their gifts as wordsmiths to making the final English versions read as smoothly as the original French, and as the manuscript preparation became more demanding, they continued to offer more than was asked.

We thank all the many colleagues and friends who listened patiently to our plans and offered support and ideas.

Above all, this project could not have gotten started or come to fruition without the wholehearted endorsement and generous financial support of the University of Notre Dame's Institute for Scholarship in the Liberal Arts and the Florence Gould Foundation, dedicated to encouraging close affective ties between America and France. We are sincerely appreciative.

E. Jane Doering
Eric O. Springsted

ABBREVIATIONS: THE WORKS OF SIMONE WEIL

English

FLN   *First and Last Notebooks*. Trans. Richard Rees. London: Oxford University Press, 1970.

GG   *Gravity and Grace*. Trans. Emma Craufurd. London: Routledge & Kegan Paul, 1972.

IC   *Intimations of Christianity among the Ancient Greeks*. Trans. E. C. Geissbuhler. London: Routledge & Kegan Paul, 1957, 1976.

LOP   *Lectures on Philosophy*. Trans. Hugh Price. Cambridge: Cambridge University Press, 1978.

NB   *The Notebooks of Simone Weil*. 2 vols. Trans. Arthur Wills. London: Routledge & Kegan Paul, 1956, 1976.

NR   *The Need for Roots*. Trans. Arthur Wills. London: Routledge & Kegan Paul, 1952, 1978, 1987.

OL   *Oppression and Liberty*. Trans. A. Wills and J. Petrie. Amherst: University of Massachusetts Press, 1973.

SE   *Selected Essays 1934–43*. Trans. R. Rees. London: Oxford University Press, 1962.

SL   *Seventy Letters*. Trans. Richard Rees. London: Oxford University Press, 1965.

SN   *Science, Necessity, and the Love of God*. Trans. Richard Rees. London: Oxford University Press, 1968.

SWA   *Simone Weil: An Anthology*. Ed. Sian Miles. New York: Weidenfeld and Nicolson, 1986.

SWW   *Simone Weil: Writings Selected with an Introduction by Eric O. Springsted*. Maryknoll, N.Y.: Orbis Books, 1998.

WG   *Waiting for God*. Trans. Emma Craufurd. New York: Harper and Row, 1973.

French

AD   *Attente de Dieu*. Paris: La Colombe, 1950.

C II   *Cahiers* II. Paris: Plon, 1972.

C III   *Cahiers* III (nouvelle èdition). Paris: Plon, 1974.

CS   *La Connaissance surnaturelle*. Paris: Gallimard, 1950.

EHP   *Écrits historiques et politiques*. Paris: Gallimard, 1960.

EL   *Écrits de Londres et dernières lettres*. Paris: Gallimard, 1957.

IPC   *Intuitions pré-chrétiennes*. Paris: La Colombe, 1951.

LDP   *Leçons de philosophie de Simone Weil (Roanne 1933–1934)*. Paris: Plon, 1959.

LR   *Lettre à un religieux*. Paris: Gallimard, 1951.

OC   *Oeuvres complètes*. Paris: Gallimard, 1988– .

         OC I   *Premiers écrits philosophiques*

         OC II.1   *Écrits historiques et politiques: L'engagement syndical (1927–juillet 1934)*

         OC II.2   *Écrits historiques et politiques: L'Expérience ouvrière et l'adieu à la révolution (juillet 1934–juin 1937)*

         OC II.3   *Écrits historiques et politiques: Vers la guerre (1937–1940)*

         OC VI.1   *Cahiers (1933–septembre 1941)*

         OC VI.2   *Cahiers (septembre–février 1942)*

         OC VI.3   *Cahiers (février 1942–juin 1942)*

Oe   *Oeuvres*. Ed. F. de Lussy. Paris: Gallimard, 1999.

P   *Poèmes*. Paris: Gallimard, 1968.

PSO   *Pensées sans ordre concernant l'amour de Dieu*. Paris: Gallimard, 1962.

SG   *La Source grecque*. Paris: Gallimard, 1963.

SS   *Sur la science*. Paris: Gallimard, 1966.

Not long ago the only positive sense in which one might write about Christian Platonism was a historical one whereby the influence of Greek philosophy on Christian thinking could be laid out in a straightforward manner and then analyzed. Once that task was done, both philosophers and theologians stood back to take critical aim.

What philosophical interest there was in Plato chiefly concerned epistemology, metaphysics, and cosmology; his ethics was largely subordinated to the first two disciplines or seen as the forerunner of Aristotle's ethics. In the early years of the twentieth century the great Plato scholar F. M. Cornford could state flatly that the two linchpins of Plato's thought were the doctrine of ideas and the immortality of the soul. Philosophers examined other topics in Plato, of course, but by and large topics such as "God" and the ethical life that led to God, even assimilation to God, which loom large in the Christian tradition, were not pursued. They were considered irrelevant philosophically, even embarrassing.

Although Christian theologians might have had more interest in these topics, Platonism, except in a warmed-over Hegelian version, generated little interest or perhaps hostility. For the past century and a half, Platonism has tended to be a bête noire of Western religious thought, a strain of religion, particularly in Christianity, that many thought needed exorcizing. In part this view was the result of an overzealous but otherwise well-intended effort to restore Hebrew thought to its rightful place in early Christianity. In part it was linked to a larger effort to rid Western philosophy of metaphysics, the impossible and misconceived reification of Being. Christian theologians, always quick to look for relevance, thought that this philosophical challenge applied to them too, and they responded with an even stronger purge of their own tradition. Also, there was a revolt, particularly within Protestantism, against "natural theology," that is, against the attempt to find Christian faith in anything other than the movement of God's grace in Christ. It was virtually an ongoing project among many theologians to separate philosophy and philosophical ethics from Christianity. All this was linked to widespread distrust of mysticism. For example, Plato, as Anders Nygren argued in the 1930s, like Hippolytus of Rome many centuries before, was the chief culprit in allowing us to think that there could be such a thing as natural love of God and that *eros*, the desire for God, was anything other than an egocentric love. He had infected even great Christian thinkers such as Augustine, and it was contemporary theology's duty to rid itself of foreign elements. (No matter that Nygren's ethical thesis was actually hyper-Kantianism.) Reinhold Niebuhr, for his part, asserted of mystical religion that in its passion for unity and coherence and in its search for an Absolute "beyond existence," it, "seeking after the final source of life's meaning and its organizing center, ends by destroying the meaning of life. . . . Even in the Western World, noticeably in Christian mysticism, the robust but romantic optimism of monistic philosophy is easily transmuted into a pessimistic other-worldliness. The road from Plato to Plotinus and Neo-Platonism marks this path."[1]

Not everybody tried to avoid Platonism, Christian or otherwise. Simone Weil (1909–43), one of the most original and profound thinkers of the century, certainly did not. Her social and religious thought is thoroughly infused both with references to Plato and with a Platonic spirit; she wrote numerous essays on Plato and the ancient Greeks—because she thought they were important for the present. But it is also when she is at her most Platonic that she has come under criticism for being world-denying and dualistic by the theologically minded and passed by in embarrassed silence by philosophers. Even Peter Winch, who did as much as anybody to show that Weil is a first-class philosopher, worried that she was being a bit *de trop* when most under Plato's influence.

Yet in recent years the nature of Platonism, and Greek thought in general, has been reconsidered. It is now viewed much more favorably, and a much wiser balance is being struck. When philosophizing, Plato and the Greeks were not chasing after speculative reconstructions of the world, idols of the mind as it were. As Pierre Hadot has argued, they were actually much more interested in philosophy as a way of life, grounded in a sense of the primacy of the Good and its very concrete demands on human life and conduct.[2] Hadot's point has been reiterated in any number of works in ancient philosophy. With respect to Plato himself, Julia Annas, reading him through the eyes of his near contemporaries and not ours, has argued that for Plato our final end really is "being virtuous and 'becoming like God.'"[3] So now, as many philosophers such as Lévinas have declared the priority of the ethical in philosophical thinking and as it seems that really was Plato's project, it may well be that he needs to be reread in that light and that he may have a great deal that is still important to hear.

There also have been changes within the theological world. At this point Greek thought is not seen necessarily as a competitor to Christianity—a form of anti-Christianity—but, in important ways, as similar to Christianity and helpful in its self-articulation. Even Paul, who was so crucial to Nygren's case seventy years ago, is now seen as having important similarities to the Stoics. Niebuhr's project has shown itself less the authentic prophetic Christianity he claimed and more a religious form of liberalism. It has also been found notoriously unable to tap the springs of spiritual vitality. As a result of all these things, within Christianity interest in spiritual practices and in the study of spirituality and mysticism has markedly increased. In this climate there has been renewed interest in Plato and particularly Christian Platonism. There is little doubt about the role of Christian Platonism in the history of Christian spirituality and mysticism, and of late scholars have been concerned to recover it. Important recent works have deliberately attempted Platonic theories of the Good in Christian ethics.[4] Finally, Christian Platonism's development of a tradition of "negative theology" may well be a crucial locus for challenging the current nihilism and relativism of certain aspects of postmodernism.

If Platonism and Christian Platonism have something to say in philosophical and theological moral thinking now, then it is important also to look at Weil's Christian Platonism. Simply put, to engage the pertinent issues of this tradition and its challenges in our own time, we need to engage Weil, for if anything can be made of this tradition in the present, Weil is the one who does it. This is the overriding concern of the contributions in this volume toward an understanding of the Christian Platonism of Simone Weil. It is not our intent to undertake investigations into a topic that is merely internal to Weil's thinking, and a *recherché* one at that, but rather to examine the broader moral, religious, and philosophical contributions of Christian Platonism as seen through Weil's efforts and to examine what Christian Platonism can be in the contemporary world.

However, to do that it is also necessary to take on Platonism and Christian Platonism as issues in Weil's thinking. Her deep intellectual indebtedness to Plato, that is, her Platonism, especially her Christian Platonism, has been well argued and long established.[5] Yet it has also been somewhat underdeveloped, which is unfortunate since it is so central to her thought as a whole. As the discussions of the contributors to this volume unfolded, they soon engaged broader and more contemporary areas of Weil's thought, such as her politics and moral philosophy, her views on science and metaphysics, and her most basic driving motivation — the desire to know and love things as they are. It became clear to all of us that within Weil's Christian Platonism lay the heart that gave life to so much else of what she did. So to understand in what senses she was a Platonist, even a Christian Platonist, and where she also moved the tradition is to advance an understanding of her thought in general, of its direction, to understand how she is able to move from thought to thought, and of its significance and challenges.

Louis Dupré shows in the opening essay exactly what some of the broad challenges are, both within Weil's own thought and to the larger theological world. He discusses Platonic and Gnostic elements of her thought with respect to her negative theology and the Christian Platonism of her positive theology as found in her reflections on beauty and the Good.

There is also the crucial question of what actually constitutes Weil's Platonism. In several of the essays in this collection, this question receives close examination. Michel Narcy, through a close historical reading of Weil, shows the degree to which her Platonism was determined by her teacher Alain and the sorts of problems he was working on, for example, problems of perception. But Weil not only learned from him, she also had a distinctive reading of Plato. As Narcy shows, what counts most often as "Platonism" — that is, the Theory of Ideas as Cornford had claimed — is not at all what Weil was most interested in. Rather, for her, Plato was a mystic and the prime *example* of a much larger tradition. As she freely admits, however, our knowledge of this tradition mainly depends on Plato. Furthermore, Weil thought that his most important thinking was enshrined in the myths. Michael Ross continues many of these themes in his contribution, showing that Weil's interest in Plato is in "ethical Platonism," the Platonism that concerns itself with knowing the Good. Ross also shows the degree to which Weil, despite a characteristic uncharitableness to Aristotle, found agreement with him on several points in ethical thinking. In this, of course, Weil was not unlike many ancient Platonists who also absorbed Aristotelian and Stoic arguments and conceptions into their own Platonism. In the essays by Robert Chenavier and by Patrick Patterson and Lawrence Schmidt, the importance of matter to Weil comes to the fore. However, this is not a materialism at odds with her Platonism; indeed, as Chenavier shows, it completes and makes it fully consistent. Both essays insist quite correctly that for Weil, to love what is is to love *within* the world God has created and to love fully *what* God has created. As Patterson and Schmidt suggest, there is a sacramentality (which was also original in early Christianity's adaptation of Platonic mediation) at the center of Weil's materialism. Moreover, as these authors suggest, here in the connection of Weil's Platonism and materialism is a key to understanding her political thought—and much of the contemporary relevance and challenge of her Christian Platonism. Here is where Weil points beyond Platonism, at least as it is commonly understood.

Chapters 6 through 9 address more classically metaphysical themes in Weil's thought, although clearly, given the previous discussion, the reader should be prepared to understand Weil's Platonic "metaphysics" with an open mind. Vance G. Morgan examines Weil's use of Greek mathematics. It has been easy in our world that tried to marry mathematics and philosophy in a technological way to see Platonism as the hoary father of this mistake, even as we try to perpetuate it ourselves. But for Weil and for Weil's Plato and the tradition he represents, this marriage was undertaken not for technological mastery but as a spiritual exercise, which she saw continued in Christianity and which in its concern with beauty is salutary for many of the crises that current culture faces with respect to science and technology. Morgan's examination of the place of mathematics in Weil's thought is therefore particularly helpful for understanding many of Weil's larger concerns and the way she approached them. Next, Florence de Lussy examines Weil's reflections on Being in the last notebooks from Marseilles. As de Lussy shows, one can find in these profound reflections the very heart of Weil's thought, particularly the nature of its "Platonism": the desire to awake from illusory dreams, to touch reality, to give oneself to the mystery and harmony of the universe. Emmanuel Gabellieri's essay demonstrates that "metaxology," that is, the mediation and relatedness of Being in her thought, is an explicit and conscious theme for Weil. Here certainly is the summit of Weil's speculative thought and where it can be connected to other twentieth-century thinkers such as Blondel and Heidegger. It is where her Christianity, her Platonism, and her political thinking come together. Then, in a comparison of Weil with Boethius's *Consolation of Philosophy* on the issue of freedom, Martin Andic underlines the importance of Weil's notion of attention.

He provides an effective bridge between this middle group of essays and the next group, for it is in attention that Weil's speculative and spiritual and moral thought come together and find unity.

Chapters 10 through 12 draw attention to Weil's contemporary relevance to spirituality and moral theology and deal explicitly with her *Christian* Platonism. Cyril O'Regan examines Weil's thinking on violence and evil and finds that for her, Christ is the countermimetic figure that sums up all who resist violence and seek to undo it. Certainly this is Christianity. But, as O'Regan also argues, Plato's—and Platonism's—definition of evil as "non-being" is central to Weil's thinking, and he seeks to trace it back to the ethical bedrock of non-harm. Eric O. Springsted turns to the conceptual links between Weil and Augustine— the West's Christian Plato—and how Augustine's "inner turn" and Weil's "attention" accurately interpret the spiritual heart of Plato's mysticism and are clear alternatives to the way theology and philosophy are currently done. In the concluding essay, David Tracy cites Weil as the foremost predecessor of recent attempts "to reunite the mystical and prophetic," which is certainly key to Weil's attractiveness. How she unites them, however, often takes her beyond orthodox Christianity and traditional Platonism to include tragedy. Here again one finds oneself at the core of her thought, for it is to tragedy as the deep sense of pain, misery, and separation in human life that Christ's self-emptying on the Cross responds. It is in making this connection between the Cross and tragedy that Weil is able to use numerous spiritual ways to illumine the human path.

It is perhaps worth pointing out at the beginning what should be clear at the end: this volume does not intend to present a complete and seamless interpretive framework of Weil or Christian Platonism. Still, it seems not only possible but also desirable to say something briefly about the overall nature of Weil's Christian Platonism as we have discussed it. Weil's reading of Plato is chiefly drawn from what one might call "ethical Platonism." Issues of justice, the Good, and how the Good enters human life are paramount for her. The myths and the larger tradition in which she sees Plato participating are also crucial to her interpretation, in good part because she, particularly at the end of her life, began to realize the deep importance of historical traditions to individual spiritual formation. But at the same time she is hardly devoid of numerous seemingly non-Platonic influences and tendencies, not the least of which is her strong and original reading of the kenotic character of Christ's Incarnation and Passion, which she uses to describe Creation and then reads back onto Plato.[6] Also linked to this reading is her materialism, which is really the Christian sacramental sense. To understand her Platonism, then, one needs to understand that it has certain limits, at least as Platonism is conventionally understood. One also has to understand what drives Weil's thought if her Platonism, even her Christian Platonism, does not entirely belong to a recognized school yet has much in common with other thinkers within the tradition. Weil's motivation certainly is a desire to love things as they are, both for their own sake and for the sake of the One who made them and ordered them. It is also, as is so important within the Christian Platonic tradition of Augustine, the Areopagite, Bonaventure, St. John of the Cross, and others, an understanding that the Good is, as Plato declared at the start of this tradition, "beyond Being, exceeding it in power and dignity." But connected to this are Weil's activism and political and social concerns and lessons learned from Marx. In the end, that Weil is a Platonist is not to be doubted, but she is a free and an original Platonist. That is perhaps her greatest importance. In a time when so many comfortable and familiar frameworks of thought have become unusable—or, we only now realize, should not have been used at all—we find ourselves casting about for ones that are, as Plato also said of the Good, "complete, adequate and desirable." We can try to invent these, or we can try to rediscover them in our spiritual tradition. Weil thought that the latter was the only way possible. That sort of recovering of a tradition requires originality, though. For this reason, the Christian Platonism of Simone Weil is interesting not only as an example of Christian Platonism but also, because of Weil's originality in dealing with Plato and his descendants, as an example of just what it might mean to recover a usable spiritual tradition. *What* she says about this tradition, and about Plato, is certainly important, but perhaps even more important is the *way* she says it. At the point when one takes that seriously, one may also well understand what Weil means when she says that Plato does not have a doctrine but is a mystic. For that kind of mind may well be the true heart of Christian Platonism, past and future.

Notes

1. Reinhold Niebuhr, *An Interpretation of Christian Ethics* (1935; rpt. New York: Seabury Press, 1979), 14, 15.

2. Pierre Hadot, *Philosophy as a Way of Life*, ed. Arnold I. Davidson, trans. Michael Chase (Oxford: Blackwell, 1995).

3. Julia Annas, *Platonic Ethics, Old and New* (Ithaca: Cornell University Press, 1999), 6.

4. E.g., Robert Adams, *Finite and Infinite Goods* (Oxford: Oxford University Press, 1999).

5. E.g., Michel Narcy, *Simone Weil: Malheur et beauté du monde* (Paris: Ed. du Centurion, 1967), and several articles since; Miklos Vëto, *La Métaphysique religieuse de Simone Weil* (Paris: J.Vrin, 1971); Eric O. Springsted, *Christus Mediator: Platonic Mediation in the Thought of Simone Weil* (Chico, Calif.: Scholars Press, 1983).

6. In a presentation that regrettably does not appear here, Lissa McCullough underlined this aspect of Weil's thinking on the Good as uniquely Christian, even as counter-Platonic.

CHAPTER 1

Simone Weil and Platonism

An Introductory Reading

LOUIS DUPRÉ

That Plato heavily influenced Simone Weil's thought is generally known. Questions remain, however, concerning the nature of her Platonism. Despite the constant references to Plato, was it not a *Neoplatonic* reading, which expanded the philosopher's thought in a direction he had not intended, though he might not have disowned it? More important, do the Gnostic tendencies of Weil's thought, which she also covers with Plato's mantle, in the end, not conflict with both Plato and Neoplatonism, though they had undoubted roots in Plato? In this introductory reading I shall leave the genetic questions concerning Weil's Platonism—in particular, the part of her master Alain's antidualistic interpretation—to others. I shall merely consider Plato's *general* influence in three central theses of Weil's work: the Platonic sources of Weil's negative theology; the Platonic-Gnostic interpretation of creation as an act of divine self-emptying and the establishment of an extra-divine realm of necessity; and the Christian Platonism of the theory of beauty as reflection of God.

Plato as a Source for Negative Theology

I am not sure that reading Weil's biography provides the most appropriate introduction to an understanding of her spiritual theory, least of all her Platonism. Much of her short life was devoted to social and political thought and to work with the syndicalist movement in France. Of course, she was also a scholar and a teacher at various lycées—the latter with a conspicuous lack of success in preparing her students for the state baccalaureate exam (which in part accounts for the many transfers from one lycée to another), the former in a way that earned her the reputation of being one of the sharpest and most comprehensive minds of her time. How she combined these tasks has never been fully clarified. Without highly specialized training, she acquired an advanced knowledge of mathematics and became a classical scholar capable of reading even arcane ancient texts in the original language.

Nor is Weil's particular mixture of utter consistency and inconsistency less enigmatic. Anyone who has read the detailed biography, lovingly but honestly written by her close friend Simone Pétrement, somehow senses the truth of Chesterton's saying that total consistency may come close to insanity.[1] It certainly made living with the unbendingly consistent Simone Weil exceedingly difficult to friends and relatives. At the lycée, Weil, having found her answers in Alain's philosophy, openly showed her contempt for other teachers, even such luminaries as Brunschvicg and Seignobos. At the École normale, her intellectual attitude, rigidified by communist ideology, became even more intolerant. Most of her fellow students avoided her. Teachers, with the exception of Alain, disliked her in various degrees. Yet this same young woman was passionately loved and admired by the few students capable of keeping up with her teaching, as well as by syndicalists and close friends. They discerned in her one of the most penetrating minds of their time as well as a person of the utmost moral integrity.

Her uncompromising sense of justice and social equality instigated her to actions and attitudes that hurt others more than they helped. It led her to cruel gestures of independence. She used to leave payment on the table when she ate at her parents' home and had the habit of moving to another, less comfortable hotel when vacationing with the family. In the syndicalist movement, she assumed the humbler assignments and the higher risks. She lived like a pauper, surrendering most of her salary to the union and working in factories to share the lives of the modern slaves. Her total devotion to the workers' causes led her to eschew political compromises. That was the main reason for her aversion to communism, which time and time again sacrificed the cause to the Party. She rejected any revolutionary action that was grounded in Marx's utopian belief that a social revolution will automatically introduce social liberation. She correctly foresaw Hitler's political designs on Europe, yet nonetheless supported Chamberlain's appeasement policy as long as it left any hope of preventing the horror of a world war.

Unfortunately, in applying her high moral principles, she displays a conspicuous lack of common sense and even consistency. Thus the belligerently anticommunist and pacifist Simone joined a French legion to fight on the side of the communists in the Spanish Civil War. Being very near-sighted and impractical, she was of little use to her companions. Her long-suffering parents, at serious risk to their own safety, traveled to Spain to recover their wayward daughter. When they finally discovered her, with a leg badly burned by cooking oil and infected, she reluctantly accompanied them to France for treatment. Back home she immediately resumed preaching anticommunism, radical pacifism, and supporting Léon Blum's policy of nonintervention in Spain. That is, until one day, learning that the communists had lost an important bridgehead, she and some companions attempted to steal weapons from the local armory and send them to Spain—a scheme unworthy of France's most promising young intellectual.

Eventually Plato's philosophy, which until then had played mainly a theoretical part in her intellectual life, began, together with the discovery of Christianity, to integrate her great but unfocused qualities. Several factors played a role in this "conversion." She knew Plato intimately, loved Homer and the Greek tragedians, and became deeply interested in music and poetry. But perhaps the most decisive event for the fundamental change in her attitude was her first visit to Italy in April 1937 when she became acquainted with Tuscany, Umbria, and the art of Giotto. In Assisi, she discovered St. Francis and became irresistibly attracted to Christianity. Those new impressions were given time to germinate during her Easter retreat in 1938 at the abbey of Solesmes. She attended all the offices. Afterward she withdrew from active participation in trade unions (though not from writing on social problems), gave up teaching, and entered into a period of intense reflection.

Henceforth, Plato occupies a central place in both her intellectual development and her growth toward Christianity. She reads him as a mystic, heir to a mystical tradition. In him the spiritual meaning of the entire early Greek literature culminates. "All Greek civilization," she writes in a text posthumously published in *La Source grecque*, "is a search for bridges that relate human misery to divine perfection. Their art, which is incomparable, their poetry, their philosophy, the science which they invented . . . are nothing but bridges. They invented the idea of mediation" (*IC* 75). For Weil, Plato mediated his own mediating thought with the future message of Christ. In his concept of *anamnesis*, which Weil traces to the mythic spring that flows from the lake of memory described in a Homeric hymn of Orphic inspiration, Plato recapitulates the earlier Greek tradition of truth as inwardness. Plato's doctrine, in Weil's mind, contains a pre-Christian message of justice and love. In the *Theatetus* (176a) and the *Republic* (bk. II) she detects a call for a justice that differs from the "natural," political justice that produces good mixed with evil. Rather than be defined by society, that purer justice ought to define our attitude toward society.

Plato's perfect justice is itself a fruit of *love*. "Justice," Weil writes in a beautiful essay on the Pythagorean doctrine, "is a supernatural friendship that results from harmony. Harmony is the unity of contraries" (*IC* 174). Such a reconciliation of contraries occurs only in love. In love God created the world. Weil finds this idea articulated in Plato's *Timaeus:*

> The essential idea of the *Timaeus* (28c) is that the foundation, the substance of this universe wherein we live, is love. It has been created by love and its beauty is the reflection and the irrefutable sign of this divine love. . . . When one sees a truly beautiful human being, which is very rare, or when one hears the song of a truly beautiful voice, one cannot deny the belief that behind that beauty which speaks to the senses there is a soul made of the purest love. Very often this is false. But for the universe it is true. (*IC* 102)

God communicates with us through what Plato calls his "only Son," that is, the World Soul. The beauty of God's Image in the world attracts us to love God in return. For Weil, love constitutes the central link between Plato and Christianity. A second idea that appears in the *Timaeus* (37d) is hardly less Christian, namely, that God's love is not merely expressed but also *mirrored* in creation and hence becomes the model of our love for God. "For we also have originally been, and must become again images of God. We can only do so by the imitation of the perfect Image which is the only Son of God" (*IC* 103).

In light of these passages taken from the *Timaeus* and amplified by the descriptions of the nature of love in the *Symposium*, Weil reinterprets ancient Greek myths and dramas. Among the former, the beautiful stories of Persephone and of Actaeon occupy a place of honor. Persephone, the daughter of Demeter, the Earth Mother, falls into the snare planted by Hades when she picks the beautiful Narcissus flower. The god of the underworld carries her away to his dark kingdom. When her mother's prayers to Zeus obtain her return to earth, Hades, before letting her go, gives her a pomegranate seed that, like a love potion, induces her to return to him each winter season. As Weil reads the myth, the beauty of the earth, condensed in the Narcissus flower, entraps the soul by the irresistible love of God. The pomegranate seed urges her time and again to return to God. Weil merely alludes to the story of Actaeon, the mythical hunter who surprised the chaste Artemis while she was bathing in a secret pond. The goddess punished his indiscretion by transforming him into a stag—and so he fell prey to his own dogs. Pursuing the divine quarry, Actaeon the hunter became the hunted. "E l'gran cacciator dovenne caccia," as Giordano Bruno puts it in his memorable sonnet. The soul that actively seeks God ends up being a captive of God and absorbed within God.

Creation as Divine Self-Emptying

Yet another element that was to play a significant role in Platonic and in Christian mystical theology, the hiddenness of God, Weil finds in the movement of *recognition*, the *anagnorisis*, in Greek drama. She illustrates this by an exegesis of a moving passage in Sophocles' *Electra*. Electra, living as a slave in her parental home after her mother murdered her father, Agamemnon, and married the unworthy suitor, Aegisthus, mourns her lost brother, Orestes, who would have freed her and avenged her father. Suddenly she sees a man approaching with a small urn in his hand. From his ambiguous words she gathers that this messenger brings the ashes of her brother Orestes, and she exclaims:

> O vestige of him who was for me the best beloved of humans . . .
> Now I weigh you in my hands and you are nothing,
> But as a child from this house I sent you forth in splendor.
> If only you had been able to quit this life earlier
> before I sent you into a strange land,
> these hands that stole you away to save you from murder.
> . . . .
> I was not able with tender hands, I, grief stricken,

> to wash and prepare you and upon a blazing fire
> to carry you as one ought to carry such a precious burden.
>
> (Vss. 1126–40; *IC* 13)

But then brother and sister recognize each other, as Mary Magdalene recognized the risen Christ in the gardener. For Weil, Electra represents the human soul exiled from her celestial kingdom and fallen into affliction: "Just when the soul . . . has ceased to wait for God, when the external affliction or the interior aridity forces it to believe *that God is not a reality*, if then, nevertheless, the soul still loves; and holds in horror those worldly riches which would take his place, *then* God comes to the soul, reveals Himself, speaks to it, touches it" (*IC* 8).

This Christian interpretation harkens back to a central theme of Neoplatonic philosophy: God is unknowable, yet to some he reveals his presence. On the basis of a passage in Plato, Weil takes the theme of negative theology to an unprecedented extreme. In book VI of the *Republic* Plato cryptically asserts that the *Good* is beyond *Being*. Neoplatonic theologians and Christian mystics have understood this to mean that God remains entirely beyond comprehension. Yet Weil gives it an even more radical meaning. For her, "beyond Being" means that God is a "nothing" (*un néant*), as she writes in her *Notebooks* (C III 120). In the order of Being in this world—the only one we know—God occupies no place whatever; he forms no particular determination. Rowan Williams reinterprets this to mean that the idea of God consists in that *relation to the world toward to which* a person aspires who has a radical hunger for the Good as such.[2] His reading may be too strong to be generalized. But, I think, it is the only coherent one of the well-known entry in the *Notebooks*: "I am absolutely certain that there is a God, in the sense that I am absolutely certain that my love is not illusory. I am absolutely certain that there is nothing real which bears a resemblance to what I am able to conceive when I pronounce that name, since I am unable to conceive God" (*NB* 127). Weil qualifies this by another entry in which she reduces her assertion to the human awareness of God's existence. "We have to believe in a God who is like the true God in everything, except He does not exist, for *we have not reached the point where God exists*" (*NB* 151). Though Weil rejects any "ontology" of God, any interpretation in terms of Being, she nevertheless clearly assumes the existence of a divine realm that differs from this world. That this realm is not a mere absence appears obvious from the primary role God plays in our love for the world. "We must love what is *not* the world before we can rightly love the world," is a direct echo of St. John of the Cross's well-known verses in *The Ascent of Mount Carmel* (bk. I, 13). Our very aspiration to love and to love rightly is the only way to avoid an ontological description of God as a divine "object."

I recognize in those radical statements the need to love perfectly and, in doing so, to move *beyond* faith and hope. Weil understands the full implication of perfect love (*l'amour pur*) as Madame Guyon and probably also Bishop Fénelon had conceived it. We must so love as to be ready to dispense with the *experience* of faith and hope. While in earlier times faith, even if not "experienced," still appeared supported by reason, in our time that rational support has dwindled and completely disappeared in the masses. Weil who wanted to share the suffering inherent in that unbelief, argued that love sufficed, since God is the heart of love. Love alone plumbs the depth of faith—whether or not we experience that faith. Hence she writes: "God is absent from the world, except through the existence of those in the world in whom his love lives" (*FLN* 103).

Her negative theology has profoundly practical implications. If the Good lies beyond Being, it is only by non-being that we can pursue it. Nothing but some form of annihilation enables us to partake of the good. Here lies the origin of her theory of *decreation*, the seeds of which may be found in such mystical writers as St. John of the Cross and Fénelon. Those who truly want to love God must create an empty space for him, or, as Eckhart more radically puts it, they must allow God himself to create that empty space in them. Weil bases her idea of self-emptying on a particular idea of God. We must imitate God as God empties himself in creating the world, and *decreate* ourselves. This requires an uprooting of one's very selfhood, a total submission to the suffering caused by a world abandoned by God.

Obviously Weil's theory of creation differs from standard Christian doctrine and, indeed, no less from Plato's theory, though it is linked to both. It has both Jewish and Christian theosophical precedents. In the sixteenth century the Jewish mystic Isaac Luria had, on the basis of Gnostic traditions, presented creation as a "contraction" of God, or, more specifically, a withdrawal *within* God. In an infinite God no spiritual space remains for the finite until God makes room for it *within* himself (*CS* 67). God must therefore in some way withdraw from his own infinity. Miklos Vető, in his excellent study of Weil's metaphysics,[3] refers to Luria's concept of *Tzimtzum* (concentration or withdrawal) and, even more appropriately, to the theology of Chaim Vital, Luria's disciple who shows how God's self-emptying is induced by love for the creature. Maurice Blondel reformulated the same thought in Christian terms when he applied to God's act of creation the words Paul writes in *Philippians* (2.7) about Christ: *Exinanivit semetipsum.*[4] Weil and her friend Simone Pétrement appear to have adopted this position and thought it through to its ultimate consequences. According to them, creation operates a split between God's absoluteness (presented by the Father) and God's goodness. It requires an act of redemption to reunite the two attributes. Weil refers to it as the primeval need for a reconciliation *within* God, an idea previously expressed by the Christian theosophist Jacob Boehme. "It is the involvement with space and time which constitutes this cleavage which is already a sort of Passion. The *Apocalypse* (13.8) also refers to the Lamb slain from the foundation of the world" (*IC* 73). This dualism within God, as well as the opposition between creation and redemption, has of course been a common theme in various forms of Gnosticism. It was the reason Simone Weil had serious problems with the historical books of the Old Testament; in her opinion, they one-sidedly and uncritically praised divine power while neglecting divine love. It also explains her sympathy for the Manichaean sect of the Cathari who rejected the Old Testament as the work of an evil god. Later she qualified her position by extending her sympathy to those Christians of southern France who stood between the ordinary members of the Church and the Cathari proper. She considered them victims of an ecclesiastical government driven by power.

The need for redemption exists not merely within the godhead but also in creation. Once expelled from God's "essence," all creatures become subject to an order of necessity over which God exercises no further direct control. The limits that order imposes on finite (and potentially conflicting) beings requires the existence of laws that God himself wills unchangeably, however much pain they inflict on his creatures. As material beings, we are permanently subject to the unchangeable necessity of the physical laws that rule a cosmos of which we form an integral part. Weil experienced this in her own body, which was racked by constant headaches. She saw the tragic alienation of the cosmos prefigured in the enigmatic passage of the *Timaeus* (36b) where the Demiurge splits the World Soul, "the happy god," into two parts and crosses them in the form of an X that wraps the world and gives it life. The cross suggests the separation within God, so prominent in Boehme's theory and, in one form or another, in all Gnostic dualism. The sphere of light becomes definitively separated from the realm of darkness. But the cross also presages the suffering and death of God's Son for the sake of reuniting the power of God with God's goodness. That Weil's theosophical interpretation of the *Timaeus* is highly arbitrary matters less than her belief that those Christian mysteries possess universal meaning and were anticipated by Plato.

That the cosmos includes autonomous beings, creatures endowed with free will who are naturally inclined to assert their independence, appears to contradict the rule of Necessity but actually confirms it. For a free being to be created entails the need to assert its independence. Weil concludes: "What is creation from God's point of view is sin from the creature's point of view" (CS 168). The person's autonomy seems to interrupt the continuity of the necessary order decreed by God. His self-asserted otherness lies at the root of all evil. Yet in a profounder sense that self-assertion constitutes a *necessary* part of human nature: it is nature's inescapable drive toward being, what Spinoza called its *conatus essendi*. That drive, not self-assertion, moves the person toward the suppression of others. As long as the mind is determined by the imagination rather than by the intellect enlightened by love, it recognizes only its own right to exist and inevitably conflicts with that of others. Hence the constant threat of war.

Weil splendidly develops this idea in "The *Iliad*, Poem of Might" (SG 9–43; IC 24–55). Whenever the person claims an exclusive ownership in the world, the *other* becomes an enemy. Homer's poem symbolizes the inevitability of a destructive competition in the sovereign, unchangeable will of the gods. "The arm of Achilles had felled him [Hector] because of the green-eyed Athena" (IC 25). A geometric system of retribution moves the epic, even as it moves the Greek tragedy, Pythagorean doctrine, and even, Weil claims, parts of Plato's philosophy. It causes a self-perpetuating cycle of violence. In attempting to destroy the enemy, the person submits to a necessity that destroys not only the victim but the attacker as well. War transforms what may have begun as a noble act of self-defense into a chain of destruction in which the victor suffers no less than the vanquished. "The bitterness of [the *Iliad*] is spent upon the only true causes of bitterness: the subordination of the human soul to might; which is, be it finally said, to matter" (IC 51). Cyril O'Regan excellently describes the dialectic of violence in chapter 10 of this volume.

In this, then, consists the tragic paradox of war, that the greatest act of self-assertion reduces the person to the basest necessity. Only those who voluntarily *submit* to the order of necessity are truly free. That submission may even require participation in war, as the god Krishna reminds the warrior Arjuna whose "limbs give way, [whose] mouth draws up, and [whose] hairs stand up in dread" when he confronts his brothers, sons, fathers, and teachers on the other side of the battle.[5] Krishna exhorts him to do his duty and to fight, not to count the fruit but only the work one is called to do, and to submit to the law of necessity. How do we attain this total obedience to necessity? It begins with a perspectiveless understanding of the human condition (a rule reminiscent of Buddha's Four Noble Truths). Objective understanding removes the ego from the central position that self-assertion claims. The objective attitude required by science brackets the self. But because the body remains subject to the necessary conditions of nature, the mind is incapable of maintaining this detachment. Love alone enables us to partake in God's consistently nonperspectival attitude. This, according to Weil, is the true meaning of Plato's myth of the cave in the *Republic*. "One would make a complete mistake in believing that the metaphor of the cave relates to knowledge and that sight signifies the intelligence. The sun is the good. Sight is then the faculty which is in relationship with the good. Plato in his *Symposium*, says as definitely as possible that this faculty is love. By the eyes, by sight, Plato means love" (*IC* 134). Love alone is able to convert the realm of necessity into one of love, and thereby to overcome the three-fold division: between the absolute and the creating God, between creature and God, and between person and person. Christ initiated the process of reconciliation. To complete it we must adopt Christ's attitude and embrace the realm of necessity with its suffering and self-denial. "Necessity is an enemy only as long as we think in the first person" (*IC* 180).

The only adequate attitude with respect to creation, then, consists in emulating the total obedience that the universe unconsciously assumes. To the divine renunciation, whereby God allows part of himself to become other than God, we must respond by renouncing that part of ourselves which is the self-will. Human obedience can only be given voluntarily. Those who refuse to grant it still form part of the eternal order of this world, but they remain restricted to the order of necessity. Those who obey also remain subject to mechanical necessity, and hence to suffering; yet, freely accepting this necessity, they move beyond that realm and give it a new meaning.

> [T]hey are like shipwrecked persons clinging to logs upon the sea and tossed in an entirely passive manner by every movement of the waves. From the height of heaven God throws each one a rope. He who seizes the rope and does not let go, despite the pain and fear, remains as much as the other subject to the buffeting of the waves; only for him these buffets combine with the tension of the cord to form a different mechanical whole. (*IC* 194)

Loving God, then, consists in consenting to necessity. But that consent is also the supreme love of the world as expression of God.

> The universe is a memento for us, the reminder of some beloved being. The universe is a work of art; what artist is the author of it? We have no answers to these questions. But when love, from which the consent to necessity proceeds, exists in us, we possess experimental proof that there is an answer. (*IC* 183)

Beauty as a Reflection of God

The first two parts of this chapter imply that Weil's extreme version of a negative theology of (Neo)platonic origin was prevented from lapsing into atheism by a dualism of Gnostic-Platonic lineage that unambiguously recognizes a spiritual realm independent of that finite necessity. The two are reunited by the mutual link of love. Here I briefly consider an aspect of her work that though related to both of these realms is nevertheless essentially *Christian*-Platonic, namely, the beauty of creation. To Weil, the world appears most beautiful precisely in its necessity. She regards mathematics as constituting the very structure of necessity and, at the same time, its supreme, formal beauty.[6] The world may indeed be cruel to its sensitive inhabitants, but it is not an evil place created by a cruel God. God created the world out of love, Plato claims in the *Timaeus*, and Weil echoes that: "The foundation, the substance of this universe wherein we live is love. It has been created by love and its beauty is the reflection and sign of this divine love" (*IC* 102). The universe mirrors God so perfectly that the cosmos becomes a model to imitate. In the *Timaeus* Plato declares God's only Son, the soul of the cosmos, to be the divine model that, "having eternal life, has tried to give as much as possible of that life to the universe" (37d; *IC* 103). This is obviously a Platonic-Christian rather than a Gnostic interpretation. Indeed, as J. P. Little has observed, it was particularly beauty's function in the process of *decreation*, the doctrine that comes closest to a Gnostic version of Christianity and of Platonism, which Weil most strongly emphasized in her theory of beauty.[7] She did so for the same reason that she had recommended science as a form of spiritual asceticism: contemplation frees the mind of personal projections and desires.

With Kant, Weil considers the aesthetic experience a mode of *disinterested* interestedness. This description, though it owes more to Kant's subjective *Critique of Judgment* than to Plato's *Phaedrus*, nonetheless serves a clearly Platonic goal—to extricate the soul from terrestrial involvement and to lead it to celestial contemplation. In "Forms of the Implicit Love of God" in *Waiting for God*, Weil writes that beauty is the only true end *within* this world. A thing of beauty contains no good other than itself: it never serves as means for an ulterior end. She thereby refers to Kant's aesthetic "purposeless purposiveness." Beauty offers no good other than itself. Yet somehow it contains a promise of all good. Not an attribute of matter itself, it consists in a relation of the world to human sensitivity.[8] Yet, unlike for Kant, for Simone Weil as for Plato, beauty possesses that inherent purposiveness only because in it appears the *good* itself, the ultimate end of all. It enables us to love the order of necessity as an expression of the supreme good. Without the shine of beauty God would fail to attract us in the only form in which he is accessible to us—the world. Beauty also inspires us to love other humans. Only humans are capable of responding to our admiration of their beauty. All other parts of creation are silent. "The love we feel for the splendor of the heavens, the plains, the sea, and the mountains, . . . is an incomplete, painful love, because it is felt for things incapable of responding, that is to say to matter" (WG 171). In the end, then, all beauty expresses the desire for incarnation: on the primary level, the incarnation of responding creatures; on the highest level, the incarnation of that supreme goodness which allures the mind in its earthly reflection. Weil's theory of beauty is Platonic in a Christian, not a Gnostic, sense.

Attempting, then, to assess the respective import of the Christian, the Platonic, and the Gnostic elements in Weil's theory, I consider her primarily *Christian* in her view of creation as an expression of divine love, *Platonic* in her sharp distinction between the realm of light and necessity, Gnostic to the extent that these two realms are *separate* and their reconciliation questionable. Yet each of these elements appears in a Platonic light, the Gnostic one as well as the Christian. Does the Christian-Platonic element prevail over the Gnostic-Platonic, or is the opposite the case? Weil's emphasis on the unredeemable harshness of life on earth and on the necessity of suffering, not only resignedly undergone, but actively sought out in solidarity with a suffering creation, seems to favor the Gnostic supposition. Susan Taubes, in a critical though deeply empathetic essay, considers Weil's theology of affliction one of death without resurrection: "Her mysticism bears some resemblance to St. John of the Cross's dark night. But, while the Spanish mystic describes the soul's death *before* its rebirth in God, for Simone Weil the dark night of God's absence is itself the soul's contact with God."[9] To be able to endure the void, to suffer evil is sufficient. No further redemption need be expected.

Weil's Gnostic leanings can hardly be doubted and may in fact have been even more radical than ancient Christian Gnosticism was. Contrary to that ancient Gnosticism, hers was shorn of any final triumph of good over evil. "For her," Taubes claims in a memorable page,

> the figure of the crucified Jesus abandoned by God and dying without hope of resurrection, does not, however, yield the image of man's tragic complaint against a deaf sky. . . . Its image is not the hero fighting against great odds and defeated in the end, but the masses of helpless victims subjected to meaningless waste and torture, defeated from the beginning. . . . It was surely a profound experience of the pits of unredeemed humanity suffering in the contemporary world, combined with a pitiless realism regarding the effects of affliction on men's souls that led Simone Weil to realize that any attempt to resurrect the dead God is doomed to remain romantic rhetoric. . . . A God who does not exist, who emptied himself into the world, transformed his substance in the blind mechanism of the world, a God who dies in the inconsolable pits of human affliction.[10]

Taubes supports this gloomy picture by using Weil's own words: "If the Gospel omitted all mention of Christ's resurrection, faith would be easier for me. The Cross by itself is enough."[11] In a learned study, Pétrement considers Gnosticism the most ancient and the most authentic interpretation of Christianity.[12] She discussed this project with Weil, and the two undoubtedly influenced each other.

Still, this interpretation may have to be qualified. Emmanuel Gabellieri, in his insightful contribution to this volume, shows the overridingly Christian structure and sources of Weil's thought. Even her "Platonism" requires some qualification. At least for a long time it remained heavily influenced by her teacher Alain's antidualism. Michel Narcy is right (chap. 2): Weil remained in some respects faithful to some form of antidualism, albeit no longer Alain's. This also caused her reading of Plato to be more Christian than the text warrants. I must leave these questions open, hoping that further study of Weil's remarkable work may help us not only to answer them but also, more important, to find our own way in the Christian, Jewish, and Platonic heritages.

Notes

1. Specifically, "a mad man has lost everything *but* his reason." —*Ed.*

2. Rowan Williams, "The Necessary Non-Existence of God," in *Simone Weil's Philosophy of Culture*, ed. Richard H. Bell (Cambridge: Cambridge University Press, 1993), 55.

3. Miklos Vetö, *La Métaphysique religieuse de Simone Weil* (Paris: J. Vrin, 1971). Translated by Joan Dargan as *The Religious Metaphysics of Simone Weil* (Albany: SUNY Press, 1994).

4. See Maurice Blondel, *L'Être et les êtres* (Paris: Alcan, 1935). Also see Emmanuel Gabellieri's development of this parallel in chapter 8 of this volume.

5. Bhagavad Gita I.29.

6. The transcendent quality of mathematical beauty is beautifully argued by Vance Morgan in chapter 6 in this volume.

7. "Simone Weil's Concept of Decreation," in Bell, *Simone Weil's Philosophy of Culture.*

8. "The beauty of the world is not an attribute of matter in itself. It is a relationship of the world to our sensibility, the sensibility that depends upon the structure of our body and our soul" (WG 164).

9. Susan Taubes, "The Absent God," *Journal of Religion* (January 1955), reprinted in *Toward a New Christianity*, ed. Thomas J. J. Altizer (New York: Harcourt, Brace and World, 1964), 111.

10. Taubes, "The Absent God," 115–16.

11. Quoted in ibid., 115.

12. *Le Dualisme chez Platon, les gnostiques et les manichéens* (Paris: Presses Universitaires de France, 1947).

CHAPTER 2

The Limits and Significance of Simone Weil's Platonism

MICHEL NARCY

I draw the terms within which I frame my remarks from a work that clearly offers many lessons for any discussion of Christian Platonism. The historian's task, writes Endre von Ivanka in a footnote to his *Plato Christianus*, "is not to pass judgment on the potential uses . . . of the ideas which he examines . . . , but simply to examine the coherence of a thought and the field of ideas which gave rise to it, with respect to their basic meanings"; to this end, the historian must "be familiar with the mental constructs and the vocabulary of the period and the milieu in which it (i.e., this basic meaning) was formulated."[1] The questions I propose to examine and to which I believe I can offer at least a rudimentary answer are those of locating the "field of ideas" within which Simone Weil formed her notions of Platonism, and the "mental constructs and the vocabulary" through which Platonism acquired meaning for her. They also involve identifying—based on what constituted Platonism for the time and place in which she studied—the extent to which she could consider herself a Platonist, as well as the significance of her interest in Plato.

The allusions to Plato in Weil's writings are innumerable. Indeed, they cannot be counted, because quite often, even in the majority of instances,

Plato is not cited. One must thus be familiar with both Plato and Weil herself to recognize—in an expression used by the latter—a quotation from, a paraphrase of, an allusion to, or an echo of Plato. Let us take as an example the injunction we read in "The Person and the Sacred" that one should place in the mouths of the unfortunate "only those words whose proper place is in Heaven, above Heaven, in the other world" (*EL* 30). Who among Weil's colleagues in London was able to recognize in this phrase an allusion to the myth of the celestial procession of souls in the *Phaedrus?* It is in this myth that the soul, portrayed as a chariot team composed of a docile horse and a restive horse and their driver, following the procession of gods to the height of the celestial vault, seizes the moment to "lift the head of the charioteer into the outer world,"[2] to glimpse justice, wisdom, and knowledge.[3] We know from other passages where Weil is more precise[4] that this is the myth she alludes to each time she discusses realities—here curiously termed "words"—that are located beyond heaven. Thus we see an image, whose place in the Platonic corpus is at once precise, unique, and irrefutable, becoming for Weil a sort of idiomatic expression.

We could multiply effortlessly the signs of a genuine permeation of Weil's prose by Platonic images. We need only think of those of the cave and the great beast, which recur constantly after their first appearance in the *cahiers*.[5] Although these images appear only once in the entire Platonic corpus and thus require detailed exegesis, Weil usually uses them without commentary, as if their meaning were as obvious as any other commonplace allusion. In other words, what in Plato is myth, allegory, or image, and is explained as such, becomes part of Weil's personal lexicon for everyday usage.

It is difficult, in view of this permeation of Weil's prose by her reading of Plato, not to see her as a Platonist. It is this obvious fact that I would like to refute here by setting the boundaries within which we can talk about Weil's Platonism. Only with these boundaries in place will it be possible to specify Plato's place in Weil's thought, or, more precisely, to identify those motifs in her reflections that come from Plato.

The Boundaries of Simone Weil's Platonism

The boundaries of Weil's Platonism are first of all chronological: despite what one reads too often in studies on Weil, she did not always draw from Plato. As I have pointed out elsewhere,[6] in the three volumes of *Écrits historiques et poli-*

tiques that constitute volume 2 of the *Oeuvres complètes*, we find Plato's name mentioned only five times, in addition to a rough quotation. We can scarcely see in this quote—"wonder is the father of wisdom" (OC II.2 130; *Theaetetus* 155d2–4)—a sign of any particular allegiance to Plato, for it belongs to the baggage of any lycée graduate.

It is nonetheless true that the Simone Weil's first philosophical essay, collected in the *Oeuvres complètes*, opens with a reference to Plato: "Among Plato's finest thoughts are those which came to him by meditating on the myths" (OC I 57 = Oe 803). Alain's young pupil claims to be inspired by this example to "draw" ideas, in turn, from one of the Brothers Grimm tales. And the Index of Proper Names in the *Premiers écrits philosophiques*, which abandoned efforts to list them all, bears no fewer than twenty-eight occurrences of the name of Plato. And so a long digression, begun when she left Alain's class, ended in spring 1940, when, as we know from her correspondence with her brother at this time, she returned to the study of Plato.[7]

In Weil's correspondence we note something quite striking: the arguments that she makes about Plato, and about Greek thought in general, are already those to which she will return again and again in the *Notebooks* or in her writings from the same period, which have been collected under the title *Intimations of Christianity in the Ancient Greeks*. In particular, the opening assertion of the essay "God in Plato" that Plato "is a *mystic* who inherits a mystical tradition in which all of Greece was immersed" (SG 77) already appears explicitly, with its two component elements worked out in detail moreover, in her letters to André Weil published in *Sur la science:* "If one may call mysticism the achievement of states of ecstasy, the fact of attaching great value to them, if not directly triggering them, at least puts oneself in such a frame of mind that they become possible— then Plato is *first and foremost* a mystic" (SS 242).[8] She evokes, in support of this interpretation, the praise of the divinely inspired *mania* in the *Phaedrus*.[9]

Just as in "God in Plato," where she also wrote that the first thing to know about Plato is that "he is not a man who invented a philosophical doctrine," that "he constantly repeats that he invented nothing, that he has only followed a tradition" (SG 79), in 1940, in another letter to her brother, she claims: "Plato is a traditionalist to the extreme, and often says: 'The ancients who were much nearer to the light than we are'" (SS 218).[10]

Plato as mystic and traditionalist: neither of these assertions is Weil's own. The first had been well recognized since the writings of Mgr. Auguste Diès and Fr. Festugière on Plato, which appeared in 1926 and 1936, respectively.[11] The second assertion can be traced to Aristotle's judgment that Platonic participation is just another name for the Pythagorean imitation of numbers.[12] Weil, usually so critical of Aristotle and always quick to denigrate him in relation to Plato, relies precisely on this judgment to make her argument. She invokes Aristotle in order to refute the notion that the discovery of the incommensurables destroyed Pythagoreanism more than it did Platonism: "Aristotle says of Plato that his doctrine is purely and simply that of the Pythagoreans, of which he has changed but a single word, saying 'ideas' instead of 'numbers'" (SS 224). She expressed herself with this much circumspection only in her first draft; in the final version, she is even more peremptory: "Platonism and Pythagoreanism . . . are practically equivalent" (SS 218).

Once again, the assertions that Plato is a mystic and a Pythagorean are part of a whole. So if Aristotle is useful to Weil in this instance, it is because he allows her to find in Plato the same "link between mathematical concerns on the one hand and philosophic-religious concerns on the other" as are found among the Pythagoreans, for whom the existence of this connection "is historically recognized" (SS 218).[13] Thus Simone Weil's fundamental thesis about Plato appears to have been definitively formulated by 1940, before her major undertaking of the cahiers and her lectures to the Dominicans in Marseille.

The first question to ask is, Is it possible to trace this Plato, who seems to close a digression begun on leaving Alain's classroom, back to Alain's teaching itself? Yes, but only to a limited extent, and this limit coincides exactly with those of Simone Weil's Platonism. To begin with, let us read Alain's commentary on the allegory of the cave and on its conclusion, that is, the return to the cave imposed on the philosopher:

> Let us understand that life in this cave, for these captives, chained by the neck, is real life, and there is no other. . . .
>   Because we must recognize that there is no longer any falsehood in the shadows, once we perceive the ideas behind them; it is this world which is the truest and most beautiful, and what's more, the only one.[14]

Alain's reading of Plato, which recognizes in the latter "only one" world, and Weil's, which retains the image of the celestial vault separating this world from "the other world," appear to be diametrically opposed: the Plato with whom Weil renewed acquaintance after her years of teaching and of militant (even military, in Spain) activism seems poles apart from the one she knew in Alain's class.

Of course, it is not because Weil, after using Alain's *Plato* as a textbook,[15] came to understand Plato differently than her teacher did that we must speak of a limit to her Platonism. We would still have to prove that she was less of a Platonist than her teacher, which is not at all certain. To the contrary, what I would like to demonstrate is that the limits of Weil's Platonism are found precisely in her loyalty to Alain's philosophy.

If we maintain, as Alain did, that for Plato there is no other life, and above all no other world, than that of the cave, how do we understand the ideas? For not only does the allegory tell us that that they do exist outside of the cave, but their *chorismos*, their separation from perceivable objects, from experience, has always been considered by Platonists themselves as one of the principal Platonic dogmas, if not the principal one. Alain is naturally aware of this. He writes: "Through Platonic analyses, . . . it is clear that idea is separate. . . . The notion of five is not inherent in its manifestation as knuckle bones."[16] Not only is the idea separate, he continues, but "it forms with all other ideas another world of existence"—"which must be called imaginary," he immediately adds.[17] But by what authority do we declare Platonic ideas imaginary? By Aristotle's, of course, for whom "saying that the ideas are models and that other things participate in them, is . . . to use poetic metaphors."[18] This is a harsh judgment, which paradoxically rescues Plato in Alain's eyes:

> [T]hese ideas detach themselves and even fly away; they are somewhere up there; they are transcendent. Be careful here. Metaphor is almost everywhere in Plato; it carries away, lifts up the reader. . . . But . . . metaphor is always such that it can never deceive us. . . . I am assured that Plato overcame these ideas that are objects, and that he at least glimpsed, and that is saying too little, these other ideas which are the ideas, and that the imagination cannot grasp."[19]

The Platonic idea, in other words, is a metaphor for the Cartesian idea, or better yet, for the concept, which preserves it from being a thing. This also allows us to attribute to Plato the idea of an immanent intelligibility in the fabric of experience:

> The shadows of the cave are projections against the wall of our senses. . . . The objects in the real world are intelligible connections which give meaning to appearances. . . . This journey of the freed captive is the mathematical

detour . . . to these disembodied relations which discourse alone can grasp, to these simple, bare and empty functions which are the secret of so many appearances.[20]

Natorp exonerated Plato of the realist's belief in the existence of ideas, called Platonic realism;[21] the difference between the perceivable and the intelligible understood as the ontological primacy of function over substance, suggests Cassirer.[22] Erroneously, of course, for we know, having read a few pages earlier, at the beginning of the chapter on the cave, that Alain's reading of Plato derives from Lagneau's cube—"this cube that no eye has seen nor will ever see as it is, but by whom only the eye can see a cube."[23] This can only be the reading of a Kantian, even were he Lagneau rather than Natorp. Alain's Plato is a Plato read through Kant, a neo-Kantian Plato.

This says a lot about Alain's philosophy. It is not for nothing that at the beginning of chapter 5 of his *Plato*, titled "The Cave" (the source of the preceding quotes), Alain prefaces his paraphrase of the allegory with "preliminary remarks," which, he acknowledges, "are found nowhere in Plato."[24] Before recounting in Plato's way the movement from appearances—shadows—to reality, and to prevent the imagination from being sidetracked by this tale, as can happen, one must teach what appearance and reality truly are and not just in Plato. Appearance is "a balloon which rises in the air . . . , a cork which rises in the water . . . , a stone which falls . . . , the stone which rises and the stone which falls"; reality, in all these phenomena, is "the same accelerated movement which is self-perpetuating," in other words, gravity. "These examples were not well-known by the ancients," Alain continues, "nor most likely by Plato." "Not well known" is a euphemism; it is perfectly clear from these examples that Alain's "preliminaries" to Plato are Galilean physics.

At the same time, they constitute, if not Alain's whole philosophy, at least his metaphysics or his ontology. The thesis of *Entretiens au bord de la mer*, published only three years after his *Onze chapitres sur Platon*,[25] that the world of changing appearances, which fires the painter's imagination, and the network of functions revealed by physical mathematics are one and the same world, is contained in its entirety in Alain's "preliminaries" to the cave.

There is no doubt that Simone Weil made these preliminaries her own. Though she later encountered the image of gravity in the myth of the *Phaedrus*,[26] it is in physics textbooks—or in Alain—where she learned that "gravity is the supreme force"(*OC* VI.1 352). The passages quoted above from Alain allow us to hypothesize that he is the source both of Weil's conviction that the Greeks of Plato's time possessed the notion of function and the value she ascribes to that notion, such that she returns to it each time she speaks of Greek science, from the correspondence with her brother in 1940 to the "Sketches of a History of Greek Science" that she drafted in Marseilles.[27]

Generally though she pursues them to conclusions that Alain would perhaps not have imagined, she is merely adopting as her own the theses of *Entretiens au bord de la mer* when she writes that only "necessity is a solid reality" (*OC* VI.3 95), that this necessity is "the very object of mathematics," so that "mathematics is the supreme, indeed the only, science of nature" (*IPC* 146). We see the cube, which served as a preliminary to Alain's explanation of the cave, reappear, finally, labeled with its inventor's name, Lagneau, as an essential component of the talk on Pythagoreanism that Weil sent to Fr. Perrin from Casablanca.[28] Essential because she appeals to Lagneau's famous analysis[29] in order to strip of its strangeness the phrase attributed to Philolaos, "It is number which gives things a body," and to show that the statement is "literally true" (*IPC* 141–42)[30]—even if, as Weil acknowledges, Lagneau "was probably unfamiliar with Philolaos' formulation of it" (*IPC* 143).

In other words, Lagneau's position, which cannot be historically linked to Pythagoreanism, is necessary to accommodate this doctrine, which would otherwise be unusual. Lagneau represents a mode of thought that rejects the separation of the intelligible from the perceivable, and for which, quite the opposite, the inherence of the intelligible in the perceivable is at once the lesson taken from and the key to perception.

"[M]athematics . . . ," writes Weil in "The Pythagorean Doctrine," "constitutes . . . the only knowledge of the material universe in which we live" (*IPC* 160). There is no need to emphasize that this assertion derives more from Alain than from the place assigned to mathematics in the famous line from book VI of the *Republic*. "The perception of tangible objects," continues Weil, "in even the least developed human beings implicitly contains a great quantity of mathematical relationships which are its condition" (*IPC* 160–61). Thus it falls to a theory of perception deriving directly from Lagneau and Alain to transmit the truth of Pythagoreanism; Pythagoreanism and Platonism are, as we know, one and the same for Weil. She would probably not have agreed to raise, with respect to Plato (as Kant did), the possibility of understanding an author better than the author did himself.[31] It is nonetheless significant that by linking Pythagoreanism to Lagneau's theory of perception, she remains true to the thought of her teacher Alain, for whom modern Platonism is coterminous with Kantianism.[32] As a theoretician of knowledge and a metaphysician, her Plato is a Plato in waiting, not only for Kant, but also for post- or neo-Kantians such as Lagneau and Alain in France and Natorp and Cassirer in Germany. As a philosopher in his own right, Plato (as Weil wrote in 1934) "is only a *precursor*" (OC VI.1 87).

Platonism, Paganism, and Christianity

Here the opening sentence of Simone Weil's first essay for Alain's class, which has become the first sentence of the published collection of her philosophical works, takes on its full impact: "Among Plato's finest thoughts are those which came to him by meditating on the myths" (OC I 57 = Oe 803). Thus she apparently learned early in Alain's class that Plato's finest thoughts were not contained in any theory, especially in the Theory of Ideas, but in the myths. This leads us to believe that Weil was not being unfaithful to Alain when she wrote, some sixteen years after her first essay: "The wisdom of Plato is not a philosophy, a search for God through human reason" (SG 89). But she likely departs from her teacher when she continues: "Plato's wisdom is nothing short of the turning of the soul toward grace" (SG 89).

Between these two sentences we find what appears to be praise of Aristotle ("Such a search [i.e., a search for God through human reason] Aristotle did as well as one can"). This is actually a damning claim, since we know that for Weil, it is not we who to seek God but God who seeks us (IPC 9). Philosophy is thus vain, in the dual sense of being both empty and fatuous. Plato's wisdom, considered mystical for his "putting himself in such a frame of mind that [states of ecstasy] become possible" (SS 242), appears to be another way, perhaps better adapted for her reader, to say "turn the soul toward grace."

Considering this antithesis between wisdom and philosophy, it is certainly not going too far to demonstrate, as I have, how little Simone Weil is a Platonist in a strictly philosophical sense. The next step is to seek the meaning she gives to Plato in the area of what she had learned to call "[his] finest thoughts," the myths.

Rather than get lost by inventorying the passages from Plato that she recopies, translates, comments on, or evokes in the *Notebooks* and other texts of Marseilles, I seek the decisive indications in the correspondence with André

Weil in 1940, and more precisely in Simone Weil's answer, reworked to the extent that three versions of it exist, to the letter her brother wrote her on March 28, 1940.[33] In response to her brother's barely concealed reproach that she did not like Nietzsche, Weil made acerbic remarks about the latter, declaring that he inspired in her "an overwhelming, almost physical revulsion" (SS 231 = Oe 571).[34]

> He [i.e., Nietzsche] is completely mistaken about Dionysos—to say nothing of the opposition with Apollo, which is pure fantasy, because the Greeks confused them in the myths and sometimes seem to assimilate one to the other. Why didn't he take into account what Herodotus said—and Herodotus knew what he was talking about—that Dionysos is Osiris? Consequently, he is the God whom man must imitate in order to achieve salvation, who joined man in suffering and death, and whom man can and must join in perfection and happiness. Exactly like Christ. (SS 232 = Oe 571)[35]

In one sense, everything is said; once again, this draft of a letter confronts us with the proof that at this point, Simone Weil is in possession, at least in their main tenets, of all her theses concerning the affinity of Greek thought with Christianity. Yet where, one may ask, do we find Plato in these lines? The answer is in the assertion that if Dionysos is the same as Osiris, then "consequently he is the God whom man must imitate in order to achieve salvation." Every student of Plato suspects that these words are an allusion to the need to identify with God, prescribed in the *Theaetetus*, as the only means to flee the ills with which mortals are perforce afflicted.[36] The first draft of her letter of March 28, 1940, proves this: "Both of them [i.e., Dionysos and Osiris] thus represent the God whom one must 'imitate' (as Plato says) in order for the soul to be saved; exactly like Christ" (SS 247–48).

As explicit as Weil is about Plato, she is also, in this early statement, highly incisive. As revealing as the idea, added later, of a mutual assimilation or a permutation of the human and divine condition may be, Weil appears to stick to essentials here, that is, the identity of the three terms Dionysos-Osiris, the god offered as a model for imitation in the *Theaetetus*, and Christ. The last two terms obviously give us the formula, or at least one of the formulas (there are many others) for Weil's Christian Platonism; the first term, Dionysos-Osiris, indicates that if this is indeed Platonism, it is a Platonism that extends to Greek religion and even beyond or before it, granting the authority of Herodotus, to Egyptian religion.

One may object that this reads a great deal into a single sentence; in fact, Weil refrains from pursuing the matter by saying: "But it would be too long to elaborate on this." This is an intriguing concluding remark considering the number of pages in the *Notebooks* in which Weil delves into the study of Greek mythology. We find a tireless rereading of Hesiod's *Theogony*, the Homeric hymn to Demeter, Greek tragedy, Plutarch's *Isis and Osiris*, Nonnos of Panopolis's *Dionysiacs*, an establishing of or a searching for connections, following in the footsteps of Herodotus or Plutarch, not only between the Greek and Egyptian religions but also with the pre-Hellenic Cretan and Phoenician cults as revealed by current archaeology,[37] and the most diverse mythological data imaginable — even beyond the Mediterranean basin[38] when possible — amassing in the process an erudition that is dizzying.

We must immerse ourselves in these pages. Weil's reconstructions often seem arbitrary, and certainly are in the eyes of historians of religion. She was aware of this, as she wrote at the bottom of a page in one of her notebooks: "We must present these interpretations of myth as myth, and not as scientific work. Otherwise, everyone will reject them" (*OC* VI.3 237). They are far from arbitrary, though, at least in their guiding principle, when seen from the point of view of the internal logic of Weil's thought. First, it is her reconstructions that lend full weight to the assertion appearing as an epigraph to "God in Plato," which we tend to gloss over rather quickly but according to which Plato — the same Plato who is declared farther on as "the father of Western mysticism" (*SG* 80) — is nonetheless "heir to a mystical tradition in which all of Greece was immersed" (*SG* 77).[39] And it is not without reason that "God in Plato," like Alain's chapter on the cave, contains preliminaries. Very different preliminaries from Alain's, of course — above all because they are not about philosophy. After the initial statement that I quoted above are, in telegraphic style, the same enumerations of vocations of the different ancient peoples as in "In What Consists the Occitanian Inspiration?"[40] an enumeration that ends with the vocation peculiar to Greece: "misery of mankind, distance, transcendence of God." This article, which first appeared in the wartime *Cahiers du Sud* says, more explicitly: "revelation of human misery, of the transcendence of God, of the infinite distance between God and man" (*EHP* 77).

Thus Greece does not appear in Weil's remarks except as buttressed by a world whose expanse exceeds even that which Polybus and the imperial world called the *oikoumene*, since it extends to China and India and includes, significantly, Israel. And the Plato of "God in Plato" also appears subsequently buttressed in turn by "all of Greek civilization." After an interlude on the *Iliad*'s portrayal of human misery, the text continues, like that in the *Cahiers du Sud* article, with the assertion that "all of Greek civilization is a search for bridges to span the gulf between human misery and divine perfection" (*IC* 50), in other words, a search for mediation. But instead of being led directly to Plato, as might we expect, we are introduced to yet more "fragments" of Greek spirituality prior to Plato—those of which, the epigraph tells us, he is the heir—inserted between her opining that the Greeks "invented (?) the idea of mediation" and the exposition of Plato's thought on God, or more precisely, on the ascent of man toward God.

Of these fragments, only the text of an Orphic fragment is given, or at least a fragment presented as such in Diels's collection. This text, found on a tablet in a tomb in southern Italy, promises salvation to the dead person's soul if it drinks "the chilled water which springs from the Lake of Memory." This text is familiar to readers of the *Notebooks*, for it appears, whether in whole or in part, in French or in Greek, on both the front and back covers of at least two of them, and the line just quoted recurs several times.[41] Weil makes mention, moreover, but without further details, of fragments of the Pythagoreans, of Heraclitus, of Cleanthus—of course, of the passage from the *Hymn to Zeus* translated in notebook 7[42]—and finally of Euripides' *Hippolytus*. These are texts on which Weil intended to comment for her audience, but we know nothing about her commentary. We can read her commentary on the Orphic tablet, however, which is not without consequence for her intended interpretation of Plato:

> This Memory is the same as the principle of Platonic reminiscence and as Aeschylus' "painful memory.[43]

> This text already contains something of Greek spirituality such as is found in Plato. (*SG* 79)

There is no break for Weil between the authors whom Diels grouped under the label "pre-Socratic" and Plato. To put it another way, for her Plato is not original: "He constantly repeats that he invented nothing. . . . We must take him at his word" (*SG* 79).

It is best to acknowledge immediately that from Weil's position on Plato there ensues a consequence of prime importance with respect to our attribution to Weil of Christian Platonism. Those Christian apologists of the first centuries who found in Platonic doctrine a favorable ground for Christianity were required to prove their position by bringing out everything in Plato's doctrine that sharply contrasted with the paganism of his contemporaries and even of his successors. Some even forged the legend of a Mosaic influence on Plato;[44] to Christianize Plato, they had to remove him, uproot him, exclude him from Greek tradition. Weil argues the opposite position: between Orphism and Pythagoreanism, the mystery religions on the one hand and Plato on the other, there is no difference. While the Fathers who used Plato for apologetic ends tirelessly demonstrated that Plato was superior to Greece, Weil writes that "we do not know if Plato represents the best of Greek spirituality; nothing else is left to us" (SG 80).

It would be a mistake, in other words, to conclude, based on the fortunes of Plato's writings, that his doctrine is superior. If Plato lays the groundwork for Christianity, we must accept—and this is Weil's position—that the doctrines that inspired him do as much as his. A single example of this is Weil's attempt, toward the end of notebook 9, to fit the cosmogony of *Timaeus* to that bible of Greek polytheism, the *Theogony* of Hesiod: "(Conjecture!) Hesiod's *Theogony*. First Chaos. Then Love uniting the Same and the Other (the Earth and the Sky)" (OC VI.3 233).

The Same and the Other, terms patently absent from Hesiod, unquestionably come from the *Timaeus* where, after participating in the creation of the World Soul, they are the respective properties of the circles into which the World Soul is divided: the equator and the ecliptic.[45] A little farther on, however, Weil reconsiders her conjecture but without abandoning the idea of a superimposed reading of the *Timaeus* and the *Theogony*:

> The Sky and the Earth are not the Same and the Other. They are God and Matter, the Foster-Mother, the Imprint Bearer, the Mother of the *Timaeus*. In the beginning there was nothing. Then Earth and Love appeared. Love and Earth certainly produced the Sky, with whom Earth was subsequently united in love in order to beget Zeus (in the process bypassing Cronos and Rheia). Love, Sky, Zeus constitute three Gods, a Trinity; the Earth is their spouse and mother. Plato often calls Sky the World Soul. Love would then be the Spirit. (OC VI.3 235)

I will not judge whether this second attempt is more successful than the first. I only wish to emphasize that it is more significant for the question that concerns us. What makes this conjecture superior in Weil's eyes is that it allows her to show in the opening passages of the *Theogony*, as in the *Timaeus*, an account of the creation of the world,[46] that is, a Greek counterpart to Genesis, but a Genesis that differs from the biblical account by its introduction of the Trinity in the figures of three divine beings. That there is a Trinity in the *Timaeus* is a point on which Weil's religion, as it were, is already firm: in notebook 6 she links the Demiurge, the World Soul, and the Model imitated by the Demiurge in *Timaeus* to the Father, Son, and Holy Spirit, respectively.[47] Exactly as in notebook 6, and as a parallel to her exposé on the Platonic Trinity she had spoken of a Hindu Trinity,[48] her search is now for a Hesiodic Trinity. Actually, she is constrained by her concept of Plato as heir, traditionalist, and innovator in nothing. If large portions of the Greek tradition are lost to us, so that Plato is our only witness to it, conversely everything found in Plato must be witnessed to by the earlier surviving tradition. If the Christian notion of God must exist in Plato, it must also be present in earlier notions of the divine, thus in Hesiod.

But it is not just the logic of her interpretation of Plato that is at stake. Her need to extend this interpretation of Plato to the whole of Greek thought in all its forms, from Pythagorean mathematics to the most primitive mythology—including myths that, if we believe the dialogues, Plato found most repugnant[49]—derives from one of the most basic principles of her thought: the rejection of the idea of progress. Let us recall that for Weil, there is no historical progress, just as there is no history of truth, and no history of salvation. Her negation of the idea of progress, whether in secularized form or in the religious form for which she reproaches Christianity, governs her rejection of both Marxism and a good portion of the Bible. If one is to believe her "spiritual autobiography," it appears that this refusal of the idea of progress is deeply rooted in her and goes back to her conviction, formed in adolescence, that "every human being, even if his natural faculties are almost nil, enters this realm of truth reserved for genius, if only he desires truth and strives perpetually to reach it" (AD 72 = Oe 769).

For it follows from this that truth is the privilege of no one person, and consequently of no one people, no one period, and no one religion. If the desire for truth is sufficient to attain it, truth can never have been refused to anyone: in questions of truth, indeed of revelation—since Weil does not hesitate to use this term—neither Christianity nor Plato enjoys privileged status, and truth or Christian revelation was necessarily present not only in Platonism but at every moment in human history.

In her spiritual autobiography, Weil purports to have acquired this conviction by age fourteen. At that time she had not yet met Alain or taken her year of philosophy before the *baccalauréat*; we can hypothesize that she had not yet begun reading the philosophers. For this reason, the history of philosophy and the search for sources no longer apply here. Simone Weil, who in explaining her own crisis readily compares her brother to Pascal (AD 72 = Oe 769), can perhaps be compared to Descartes in this regard. Exactly as Descartes, in his *Discourse on Method*, explains the discovery of the *cogito* as the fruit of a solitary meditation[50] that appears to owe nothing to the nonetheless considerable history of philosophy (not even to the history of skepticism), Weil, in her letter to Father Perrin, traces her first certitude back to an experience too early to bear the mark of any outside influence.[51] Thus, in the same way that she later came across in Plato (or believed she had come across) the idea of the real that was hers at age twenty,[52] it is plausible that in Le Senne's or in Alain's class, Weil was able to recognize in the first sentence of the *Discourse on Method* ("Common sense is the thing in the world which is most widely shared")[53] her own conviction that truth is given to all who desire it.

But if her universalism explains the way in which Simone Weil read Plato, how do we account for the privileged place that Plato holds in everything she wrote after 1940? One need only consult the *Notebooks* to realize that the only philosopher she was still reading at that time, besides those whose fragments were collected in Diels's anthology, which she also examined, was Plato. With the exception of a few contemporaries such as Alain, whose *Entretiens au bord de la mer* she reread,[54] or Gaston Berger, whom she frequently saw in Marseilles, her allusions to modern philosophers, Descartes included, seem little more than the echo of what she learned as a student. She read Plato in this period, with pen in hand, when she was not translating him or simply transcribing him. So if the key to Weil's reading of Plato is what the latter shares not only with the entire preceding Greek tradition but also with anyone who "desires truth and strives perpetually to reach it," why could this key not be used to read other philosophers?

The answer most likely lies in the words that follow the statement that Plato "is not a man who invented a philosophical doctrine": "Contrary to *all* other philosophers (*without exception, I believe*), he constantly repeats that he invented nothing" (SG 79; my emphasis). As "a traditionalist to the extreme," as Weil wrote to her brother, Plato is an exception among philosophers. If his traditionalism allows us to find universal truths in him, then we must conclude that, to the contrary, all discovery in philosophy, as perhaps elsewhere,[55] encloses its author in his distinctiveness and cuts him off ipso facto from the universality of truth. Opposing philosophy to "the wisdom of Plato," Weil has defined the former as "the search for God through human reason" (SG 89). Between this trust in reason that appears to be the distinguishing mark of every philosophy and the imputation to all philosophers—with the exception of Plato, as far as he is one—of starting with a tabula rasa, there is certainly a connection.

The exception thus made for Plato is the opposite of what Alain taught; for Alain, "all [philosophers] say the same thing."[56] If we, like Descartes, must begin by making a clean slate of the opinions we had initially adopted unquestioningly,[57] it is only to free our will so as to make proper judgments. For it is by this will that each individual realizes that he or she is a mind, and capable of truth. It is by the yardstick of this concept of truth and of that correlative of philosophy and its history, that we must measure the genuine closeness of Simone Weil and her teacher, and at the same time the distance from him created by her reading of Plato.

Translated by Chris Callahan

Notes

All quotations whether from Simone Weil or other philosophers are mine unless otherwise indicated.—*Trans.*

1. Endre von Ivanka, *Plato Christianus: La réception critique du platonisme chez les Pères de l'Église* [1964], trans. E. Kessler (Paris: Presses Universitaires de France, 1990), 94 n. 1.
2. Plato, *Phaedrus*, 248a2–3 (trans. B. Jowett).
3. Ibid., 247d6–7 (trans. B. Jowett).
4. For example, in her "Reflections on Quantum Theory" (SS 187–209 = Oe 579–92): "Men of flesh and blood, here on earth, most likely cannot have an image of truth which is not defective, but they must have one—an imperfect image of the nonrepresentable truth that we have glimpsed, as Plato says, beyond heaven" (SS 205 = Oe 590). "Men of flesh and blood, here on earth," clearly alludes to what we read earlier in *Phaedrus* on the makeup of mortals (*Phaedrus*, 246c1–6).
5. It is in *cahier* 3 (OC VI.1 311) and 6 (OC VI.2 289 = Oe 816) that the allegory of the cave (*Rep.* VII 514 sqq) and the image of the great beast (*Rep.* VI 493a–d) are found.
6. Michel Narcy, "Simone Weil et la cité platonicienne," *Recherches sur la Philosophie et le Langage* 13 (1991): 237; "Les Grecs, la science et la vision du monde de Simone Weil," Avant-propos 1 to OC VI.2 22 and fn. 6.

7. SS 213–52. The drafts of her letters to André Weil mix textual quotations (thus the passage from *Philebus* [16c5–e1] translated on 250–51, then retranscribed more briefly [16c5–10] on 243 and 234) with simple reminiscences: the expression "intelligible heaven" (244, 229) is absent from the *Meno*, and the allusions to the *Theaetetus* (230) or *Gorgias* (236) are not necessarily based on a recent reading. The allusion to the *Phaedrus* (233), on the other hand, probably is (see n. 10). The last of the three drafts is reproduced in *Oe* 568–75: for the passage from *Philebus*, see 572; for the allusions to *Meno* and *Theaetetus*, 569, 70.

8. See 233 = *Oe* 572; my emphasis.

9. As is indicated by her mention in the same sentence of Dionysos, inspirer of "the *mania* of the mysteries," Weil is referring here not, as one might think, to the opening of Socrates' second speech in the *Phaedrus* but quite specifically to his later reference to that speech (*Phaedrus*, 265a10–b4).

10. See Plato, *Philebus*, 16c7–8, "the ancients, who were our betters and nearer the gods than we are" (trans. B. Jowett).

11. On the affinity of Weil's Plato with Diès (*Autour de Platon: Essai de critique et d'histoire*) and Festugière (*Contemplation et vie contemplative chez Platon*), see Michel Narcy, "Le Platon de Simone Weil," *Cahiers Simone Weil* 4 (December 1982): 254–57.

12. Aristotle, *Metaphysics*, A, 6, 987b10–13.

13. I must add that for Weil the "ancients" that Plato talks about cannot be the Pythagoreans, who were much too recent to be designated by him with such a term: "He must therefore be referring to pre-Hellenic inhabitants of Greece, or of a foreign country, perhaps Egypt" (SS 234).

14. Alain, *Les Passions et la sagesse*, Édition établie et présentée par G. Bénézé (Paris: Bibliothèque de Pleiade, 1960), 881–82. Cf. *Republic* VII 519c sqq.

15. This is the hypothesis authorized by the "Notes on Plato" (in reality notes on the *Republic* taken by Anne Reynaud-Guérithault in Roanne in 1933–34 (*LDP* 231–37), which turn out to be inspired directly by Alain's *Plato*.

16. Alain, *Plato*, 869.

17. Ibid., 870.

18. Aristotle, *Metaphysics*, A, 9, 991a20–22.

19. Alain, *Plato*, 870.

20. Ibid., 880.

21. Paul Natorp, *Platos Ideenlehre: Eine Einführung in den Idealismus* (Leipzig: F. Meiner, 1903).

22. Ernst Cassirer, *Substanzbegriff und Funktionsbegriff: Untersuchungen über die Grundfragen der Erkenntniskritik* (Berlin: B. Cassirer, 1910).

23. Alain, *Plato*, 877.

24. Ibid., 877, 876.

25. The first edition of *Onze chapitres sur Platon* was published in 1928; *Entretiens au bord de la mer*, in 1931.

26. See OC VI.2 446: "My image of gravity is [found] in the myth of the *Phaedrus*."

27. See SS 215, 217, 223, 264; *IPC* 123, 176.

28. "The Pythagorean Doctrine," *IPC* 108–71. A summary of this text appears in the first of the *Notebooks from America* (CS 29–37) under the title "Summary of the Paper for Fr. Perrin," which was actually begun shortly before her departure from Marseilles, after she had entrusted the eleven "Marseilles Notebooks" to Gustave Thibon. We know from the accompanying letter to Solange Beaumier (*AD*, letter V 92) and from a letter to Joë Bousquet recently discovered by Florence de Lussy (*Cahiers Simone Weil* 19.2 [June 1996]: 143) that this text was written or at least completed in Casablanca.

29. Transmitted most likely by Alain. Returning, in the last pages of notes of "The Pythagorean Doctrine," to the example of the cube, Weil writes: "No one has ever seen, no one will ever see, a cube" (*IPC*, 169). It is difficult not to hear the echo of Alain's "cube which no eye has seen and will never see as it is" (Alain, *Plato*, 877).

30. The sentence attributed to Philolaos is adapted from Diels-Kranz's fragment 11 of Philolaos (*Die Fragmente des Vorsokratiker*, 6th ed.) I, 411, 18–412, 1.

31. See Kant, *Critique of Pure Reason*, Transcendental Dialectics, bk. 1, 1st sec.

32. See Alain, *Plato*, 921, almost at the conclusion.

33. André Weil's letter was published for the first time by Florence de Lussy, *Oe* 565–67, followed by the final version of Simone Weil's answer (*Oe* 568–75 = SS 227–38).

34. The same terms appear in the second version (SS 240); in the first, Weil wrote: "I cannot stand Nietzsche; he makes me ill, even when he expresses things that I think" (SS 247).

35. Cf. SS 240, 247.

36. See Plato, *Theaetetus*, 176b1: "To fly away is to become like God" (trans. B. Jowett). It is noteworthy that Weil spells "God" with a capital G in all three versions of the letter. This can be read as a translator's choice, for in the Greek expression, *homoiosis theoi*, the absence of an article allows one to understand "like *a* god rather than "like God," depending on whether one considers Plato a poly- or a monotheist. On this point as well, we note that Weil's position is already defined by spring 1940. Not only does she translate *homoiosis theoi* as "assimilation to God" in "God in Plato" and "The Descent of God" (*SG* 80–81; *IPC* 80), but in her copy of the *Timaeus*, preserved in the Bibliothèque nationale de France, we can read this handwritten note as a reaction to A. Rivaud's translation of the words *ho theos* as "the God" (30d3): "It is dishonest to translate *ho theos* by *the* God, because the Gospels, when speaking of God, always say *ho theos*."

37. See, e.g., in notebook 7 (*OC* VI.2 455) the association between Cleanthus's *Hymn to Zeus* (v. 10: "the double-edged lightning"), the "double-edged Cretan axe," and the "sword of the Gospels." Sir Arthur Evans had only begun digging at Knossos in 1900; volume 1 of his principal work, *The Palace of Minos* (London: Macmillan), was only published in 1921, and volume 3, in which he discusses the cult of double axes, in 1930. In the meantime, Gustave Glotz's *La Civilisation égéenne* (Paris: La Renaissance du livre, coll. "L'évolution de l'humanité," 1925) and volume 1 of his *Histoire grecque* (Paris: Presses Universitaires de France, 1926), whose second chapter was devoted to pre-Hellenic Crete, had appeared. Another example is the reference to the texts of

Ras Shamra that is found in notebook 10 (*OC* VI.3 296): the dig at Ras Shamra (Ugarit) began only in 1929, and the text quoted by Weil was first published by Charles Virolleaud in 1930 ("Un poème phénicien de Ras-Shamra: La lutte de Môt, fils des dieux, et d'Aleïn, fils de Baal," *Syria* 12 [1931]: 193–224, quote on 195). Another translation of it had been made in the same year by René Dussaud ("La mythologie phénicienne d'après les tablettes de Ras-Shamra," *Revue de l'histoire des religions* 104 [1931]: 353–408, quote on 388), and Weil could also have read about this discovery in the latter's *Les Découvertes de Ras-Shamra Ugarit et l'Ancien Testament* (Paris: Librairie Orientaliste Paul Geuthner, 1937).

38. As the opening of "The Descent of God" attests, where Weil, after translating and writing a commentary on a part of the Homeric hymn to Demeter, does the same with the Scottish tale of the Duke of Norway (*IPC* 13–15).

39. This is indeed an epigraph. It appears in the manuscript in a plate and was visibly added later to the upper left corner of the first page, while the text proper begins below the title with the words "Vocation of each of the peoples of antiquity."

40. *SG* 77, cf. *EHP* 76–77.

41. Fragment 1 [66] B 17 Diels-Kranz. Cf. *OC* VI.1 288, 289, 378; *OC* VI. 2 59; *OC* VI.3 233, 237.

42. *OC* VI.2 454–55; cf. *OC* VI.3 167. See also *SG* 161.

43. See Aeschylus, *Agamemnon*, l.180 (*mnesipemon ponos*). It is noteworthy that in the present context Weil prefers this expression to the one she had made into a maxim and which figures in l.177: *to pathei mathos*, "through suffering, knowledge."

44. See chapter 5 in this volume.

45. Plato, *Timaeus*, 35a–36d.

46. See *SG* 129: "The *Timaeus* is a history of creation."

47. See *OC* VI.2 348, 370 = *Oe* 867, 887. See also *SG* 129 ("There is in the *Timaeus* a Trinity: the Worker, the Model of Creation, and the World Soul") and 131. The Model imitated by the Demiurge is by definition eternal, and it is not problematic to consider the Demiurge himself eternal. But this is not true of the World Soul, whose making, or creation, by the Demiurge is described by Plato. This difficulty does not escape Weil: in the margin of her copy of the *Timaeus*, where Plato writes "What is born must be corporeal" (31b4), she notes: "So the World *Soul* was not born" (see *OC* VI.2, n. K6, 273, 624).

48. See *OC* VI.2 328, 371 = *Oe* 849, 887.

49. See Plato, *Euthyphron*, 5d–6c, 7a–8a; *Republic* II, 377d–383c.

50. See Descartes, *Discourse on Method*, pt. 2.

51. Weil will claim the same "naïvete" to explain "the sudden hold that Christ had over [her]" during a recitation of George Herbert's poem *Love*: "I had never read the mystics, she assured Fr. Perrin" (*AD* 76 = *Oe* 771–72), at the same time that, in "God in Plato," she had already designated Plato—whom she had read and taught before 1938—as "the father of Western mysticism" (*SG* 80).

52. "The beautiful is the manifest presence of the real. It is that and nothing else that Plato says—*to on*. That is what I believed, at age twenty, when I wrote 'Éclair,' but I did not realize it" (*OC* VI.2 485; see chap. 7, this volume). For the text of "Éclair," see *P* 21.

53. Descartes, *Discourse on Method*, pt. 1.

54. We know from a letter to Gilbert Kahn dated June 30, 1941 (*Cahiers Simone Weil* 16.4 [December 1995]: 336) that she had borrowed this work from him.

55. Even outside the field of philosophy, Weil is clearly reticent to attribute any discovery to the Greeks themselves. Thus she writes with a question mark that "the Greeks invented (?) the idea of mediation" (*SG* 79); or again, "the idea of constructing lines to represent functions . . . is present in Greek geometry *from the beginning*" (*SS* 23; my emphasis); "I think that the notion of proportion, such as is found in Book V of Euclid, is much earlier than Eudoxus" (*SS* 239; cf. 230, 246–47).

56. Quoted by Hubert Grenier, "Philosophie et histoire de la philosophie chez Alain," in *Alain lecteur des philosophes de Platon à Marx*, ed. R. Bourgne (Paris: Bordas, 1987), 184.

57. See Descartes, *Discourse on Method*, pt. 2 (Adam and Tannery), 15.

CHAPTER 3

Transcendence, Immanence, and Practical Deliberation in Simone Weil's Early and Middle Years

MICHAEL ROSS

That Platonism played some role in Simone Weil's thought cannot be denied. But just what kind of Platonism was it? I begin my answer to this question by suggesting that how she used Platonism in the early and middle years of her career was decisive for her later deployment of it. This use began with one set of distinctively Platonic questions, and it was precisely these questions that came to dominate all her later thinking and writing. Weil asked herself, how can the possibility of attending to the good be understood philosophically, and how, nurtured by such a philosophy, can the good be actively attended to in the world? The aspect of Plato's philosophy with which she most agreed was that knowing *and* doing the good—not just thinking about it—is the central question for human thought and action. In her interpretation, Plato was saying that to know the good was to know *that* and *how* the phenomena of the good appeared in the world to the knower. It meant also that knowing *how to do* the apparent good was vitally important. For her, knowingly doing the good was an enactment of an intellectual understanding—a kind of instrumental thoughtfulness—of what the good called for in every practical and political situation. Finally, it meant that the human performance of this good was an achievement of human being as it struggled to project itself in the world. Given all this, I argue that Weil's Platonic thought starting with the early and middle years is best considered an ontological ethics thick with these phenomenological and existential themes.

We know that throughout her career Weil took ideas from philosophers of the first rank, altered them, and then subordinated them to her own agenda. The result of this syncretism was a project that invariably avoided entailment in themes and conclusions to which she did not wish to subscribe. This strategy applied especially to her use of Plato, which means that her project, even in its later years, cannot be credited only to him or even to Christian Platonism. From the beginning it embraced a number of other traditions. Along with a version of Plato's theory of form—which was the spine to which she attached other ideas—these traditions included Stoic ideas about the acceptance of natural necessity,[1] Enlightenment notions of methodical thoughtfulness, Kant's deontological account of obligation, and Marx's notion that productive work is a basic activity of the human condition. Here I want to add to this list by saying that when it came to figuring out *how to do the good* she made use of notions that surprisingly have a striking resemblance to Aristotle's notion of practical wisdom. I explore these resemblances later. It seems clear that Simone Weil blended these seemingly disparate traditions into a composite that modified each one while producing her own distinctive variation of them.

For her, ethics was not a freestanding discipline with its own self-description. It is clear from the earliest student essays that Weil grounded her project in an ontology.[2] We see this perspective continuing in her later focus on work or labor[3] and finally in her turn toward a Christian theo-ontology. To get at an ontological ethics, she explored, especially in the early and middle years, a style of description that focused on the phenomenality of the good that is brought forward for reflection from its fleeting displays in the world. This genre made use of her teacher Alain's discursive philosophical style along with ideas about description drawn from the French schools of perception (Maine de Biran) and reflection (Jules Lagneau).[4] These ideas also have a striking similarity to Edmund Husserl's account of phenomenological description. All three of these traditions were au courant in Weil's student days in Paris.[5] Still the similarity of Weil's account to Husserl's, especially her insistence on the notion that consciousness and its objects are inextricably linked, suggests that she absorbed something like his account of phenomenality.[6]

Attending to the Good

What did attending to the good mean to Weil? As I am applying this phrase to her work, it described the stance proper or fitting for human beings to assume in regard to human life.[7] No one of course escapes the human condition. But for Weil, when we become conscious of our place in it—that is, consciously encounter its reality for ourselves and others—it becomes fitting that we attend to its good. This is a fundamental Socratic tenet, endorsed by Plato, the Stoics, and Aristotle. It is a given of our condition for Weil that we are called to attend to our own immersion in and share of the limitations and potentialities of our condition and to attend to the share all others have in its limits and benefits. To adopt any other stance is to allow or even support the use of force and violence against oneself or one's own kind. Force was for Weil the constantly competing but unacceptable alternative. A proper stance toward the good did not exclude one's obligations to oneself, but neither could it exclude attending to the good of other individuals and of communities.

Though Weil did not employ explicitly the phrase "attending to the good," she used a cluster of other related terms. When she used the words *attendre, attente, attention,* and *attentive*—words that most interpreters agree played a central role in both her early and later periods—it was in what I believe was a phenomenological description of our relationship to other things and persons. This is a relationship of manifestation that obtains between the being who receives the display of another and this other who is *still related* to the one who receives.[8] *Attendre* and *attente* refer to the arrival of the other to the one who *waits*, whereas *attention* and *attentive* have to do with the way the other is *presented* in a correlation to the one who *receives* this presentation. It is critical to note that this phenomenology of presentation and reception as described in these words also has to do with specific practices of care (*soin*), concern, and considerateness. As Weil used them, they unmistakably and deliberately convey the sense that when we wait on another's arrival, or pay attention to the appearance of another, we are attending in concrete ways to their good.

That attending for Weil always entailed a relationship between the one who attends and the one whose good is attended to is a critical move in her thought. It is always for the good *of* the other, not simply the good done *to* the other or the good done for one's own sake. Weil eschewed all forms of egoism in which the I or the other possesses his or her own good. The good occurs in the *relationship* of the two sides. It does not belong to either and thus is not available as something that either can assert for themselves. Also, this relationship is not a static one. Weil's imagery is that of a dyad; attender and attendee meet in a field of interaction where the good itself is located and is displayed in such a way that the action of each affects the other. From the way she speaks in the early essays about perception, it is clear that this kind of relationality is an interdependence, a *correlation*.[9] The mutual impact experienced through the good, which makes the action of each a function of the impact of the other's activity, also displays a dynamic *movement* across the field of the good that joins the two. These two categories are critical factors both in the encounter of consciousness with its object-as-other and in the attending relationship between the I and these others-as-persons.

Why does Weil privilege metaphysical categories if her major concern is with the good? No doubt, the Platonic tradition is influential here. In Plato, the ethical dimension of the good is linked to an ontology that distinguished between the appearance of things and the appearance of things in their full intelligibility. It is also linked to an account that designates sharply defined levels ranging from mere opinion to pure knowledge. Weil rejected this divided line account of knowing and doing. But she did think that knowing things was the basis for knowing the good. Instead of the divided line, she turned to correlation and movement to describe the way things, their forms, and the form of the good present themselves to the mind.[10]

In the early essay *Le Beau et le bien* (1926), Weil defined the good in these terms: (a) it is expressed in the intention that motivates action, (b) it conforms to precepts of the good that are capable of being universalized, (c) it occurs and can only be achieved in a world of natural necessity, (d) it is a calling of human being, (e) it is rationally knowable and uniquely present to consciousness, (f) it must be constantly attended to, and (g) it is known with a special kind of adherence to the one who constantly attends to it.[11] The good also inheres as a reality of the correlation between consciousness and the order of things. The natural home of the good, literally the place in this world where it is found, is the place where the action that displays it occurs, that is, the space between pairs of others who must live out their being in the order of things. This space is the locus of the good because, though it can be displayed in actions, it does not belong to any one actor. Rather, it resides in the morally relational space in which any two or more actors are joined.

One implication of the idea of attending to the good is that the being toward which one stretches or extends has a *value* that the waiting or receiving person wants to affirm — that he or she wants enough to wait for while this value presents itself. For Weil, every actor in a morally relational space shares in the value it imparts. She will focus on this value and will describe it as an attribute displayed in the action of the one who attends on the other. It is important to recognize that this value is *structured into* the center of the ontic relationship that obtains between human beings so that all action partakes of it. Now, in Weil's mind, if attending is to be transforming, one cannot desire to possess its impact. Yet her Platonism suggested to her that when one desires something one actually desires the good. This is a paradox. To reconcile it she evolved her distinctive ontological ethics of sacrificial self-offering. In this account, doing good is always accompanied by some measure of self-abnegation.

The phrase "structured into" may seem to suggest that in Weil's thought there is an original ontological dichotomy comprising two realms: an other-than-worldly one that somehow is juxtaposed against and yet descends into a worldly one where only a lesser good is knowable and doable. From this supposition, one could easily think that Weil was a metaphysical dualist. But instead her language in the early and middle years points away from dualism. It points first to the correlation between the one who attends to the good, the one whose good is being attended to, and to the good that is done. This correlation occurs *within* the domain of human circumstances. Nor does Weil postulate the existence of two principles — good and evil — each operating in a world where human being is trapped on the negative side of the good. Instead of dualism, Weil wanted to argue that the full intelligibility of things and of the good, which is the organizing form of all forms, is displayed and attended to *in and with* appearances in the world between individuals linked to each other through their shared acts.

But Weil was sensitive to the dualist implications of the claim that Plato had in mind two realms. She was aware that such a dualist ontology mistakenly elevated the good — as the form of all forms — beyond the reach of human being and its action in the world. Yet her agenda to give an account of such action required that the good be more than just a worldly satisfaction. It had to be *au-delà*—beyond and above the interests of any one human being—yet *en bas* or *en dessous*—down here, down below—and in the sense of both *entre nous* and *parmi nous*, that is, between and among us. In other words, the good had to be transcendental, immanent, and diffused.[12] In the early and middle years this was an entirely secular ontology of the good as something that is worldly and that is manifested both *across* and *within* instances of action. Though this manifestation can properly be called transcendent because it appears across instances, its display in this period of her career is not that of a religious transcendence.

Thus Weil's early Platonism had the idea that the good in its transcendent mode is the secular sense of the good as something itself by itself (*ti on auto kath auto*), which in the immanent mode is *in but is not captured or limited* by any one instance of attendance to it. Weil was attracted to that part of Plato's account in which he looked for language to describe the forms that instances present in common.[13] She read Plato as saying that instances of things and actions *share* paradigms, that these paradigms are not themselves one of these instances, that they are not confined to any one instance, and that they can be shared by each one because they are a *something itself by itself*.[14] Weil believed that this language made Platonism a viable account of concrete action that attends to the good in the world.

Transcendence and Immanence

Weil's rejection of a separation between transcendence and immanence supported in the early and middle years a secular, a humanist, and something like an existential phenomenology of the good. Her belief that the good was housed in a worldly nexus of this secular transcendence and immanence sustained her political activism in the early years in support of left-wing working-class movements by giving hope to the notion that these movements could realize it. In the middle years, belief in this nexus served also as the critical horizon for her eventual rejection of much of Marxism. Working from this nexus, she became dissatisfied with the reliance of Marx on history as the driving force behind this immanence. But in the late middle years (1935–40), even as she began to adapt her thought to Christian symbols, she did not withdraw into an antiactivist quietism in which the good would be worshiped as something wholly unachievable and outside the confines of human existence.

Like much of the philosophical tradition that preceded her, Weil called the shared paradigms ideas (*idées*) because they are reflected on by the mind. If we recall that the word *idea* comes from the Greek *horaō*, "to see or look," Weil's meaning emerges rather nicely. She was saying that objects present themselves to and for the mind in a certain look. This look of a thing or an action is what the mind simultaneously cogitates as it constructs them for itself.[15] The look of a thing is its intelligibility, and this is what enables the mind to think it — intend it in Husserl's language — as the object that it is. Moreover, the look of the object or its form is the same look that other similarly disposed objects or actions share. But because this look is not possessed by any one of these objects as belonging only to it, it can be said to be something itself by itself. To think the intelligibility of this something itself by itself is to reflect on its generality, to reflect on it as a *one* and a *same*.

This idea or look of a thing conjoins the displayed object to the cogitating subject. This conjunction — a *mariage* Weil called it — is what I have named a correlation.[16] A further implication is that reflection brings out the sense in which this correlation is the locus of secular transcendence and immanence. If *idée* is something itself by itself, then it transcends (climbs across) any one instance. But if it is also shared by each instance, it is immanent *in* it. Throughout her speculations in the early and middle years, she claimed, as many have noticed, that this correlation of transcendence and immanence occurs through intermediaries. In the *Notebooks* she calls these intermediaries *metaxu*.[17] They are sometimes things, more often actions or movements. At the end the of her career, the principal intermediary became the person of Jesus Christ present in religious symbols.

In effect, Weil's thought had two related dynamics of transcendence and immanence, both categorized in terms of correlation and movement. The one who attends and the one whose good is attended to interdependently conduct their actions in the horizontality of time and space. But this mutuality or correlation is also *elevated* so that the good that is done reaches across and therefore beyond the finite action of each mundane encounter. This elevation is the role of the vertical correlation and movement of transcendence and immanence. Here Weil wants us to see that in her version of Plato's theory of form the good is a unifying identity in which every instance of a good action shares as the ground of the goodness it displays. Every instance of earthbound attending passes through and is *elevated* by the vertical dynamic so that it shares in the something itself by itself of the good. Yet in all this, the good is still a perceivable thing, a *concretum* (understood as entity and action), to be found in the world. It is brought forward as the correlate of the consciousness that perceives it.

The sacrificial self-offering that Weil first embraced in her teenage years and which she retained throughout the rest of her life depended on the movements of body and mind correlated in a unity located in the world. This is a unity that restlessly seeks the transcendent good. In *Le Conte des six cygnes dans Grimm* (1925), Weil drew a picture of the worldly dimensions of the self-sacrificing exercises of this good.[18] Throughout her life she believed these exercises were transferable into ordinary social and political life. They are *silent* in the sense of being enacted without complaint and without any attempt to gain reputation or status. They are *difficult* because they require a sacrifice that hands over oneself to the other for the sake of the good. They are *repetitious* so that the one who attends to the good is drawn into his or her sacrifice. Their *difficulty* rises to the level of near but not actual *impossibility*. Together these two latter aspects have the unintended effect of transforming the being of the doer from one who like all human beings desires gain into one who can also desire the good of others when this good is known and understood in the actions that effectuate it. These exercises are also *preoccupying* in that they leave no room for self-absorption. They *command and obligate* in the reflexive sense that they obligate the doer to doing the good in the very act of doing it. They are *disinterested* actions in the sense that they entirely eschew a focus on one's own interests. Finally they are *nonindifferent* because while eschewing personal interest they affirmatively focus on the good of the other.[19]

For Weil, to have interests and to pursue them differentially is to show partiality. Ultimately, showing preference is to be motivated by ends that redound to the gain of the doer. Other-directed actions for her are by definition not actions motivated by interest and difference. Weil's language for sacrificial action—which did not change much over the years—gave to her account of the moral life the sense of being a *vocatio*, or summoning. In the early and middle years this was a calling from the hiddenness of being to a fundamental, whole-life-determining concern or active caring for the good. In the later years it was an activation of grace decreatively received in practices of self-abnegation done for the sake of the good of others. The early discovery of the ontological ethics of self-sacrifice was the key event that eventually allowed her to reconceive as a theological question her ultimate concern with attending to the good.

Now, in the early 1930s, when she was deeply engaged in solving political problems, Weil wondered what *methods* were available for knowing and doing the good. In the background of this question was the Socratic tradition that craft understanding—the unique knowledge that craftspeople display in fashioning an object—was the appropriate model for how to do a philosophy that is about defining and doing the good. In this tradition there was a tendency to think of the achievement of the good as a kind of artful making or producing (*poiēsis*) and to think of the knowing that achieves it as an expertise dominated by mastery of rules (*technē*), albeit intelligible ones (*theoria*). The development of this tradition took many not always compatible twists and turns in Plato, Aristotle, and thereafter. Especially in its Aristotelian version, it eventually passed into Marx and Marxism. The influence of Aristotle on Marx is well documented.[20]

The distinctions Aristotle made between *poiēsis* and *technē*, on the one hand, and *praxis* and *phronēsis* (prudence or thoughtfulness), on the other, are relevant here. Surprisingly, though Weil disdained Aristotle's ethics of the mean and the intermediary, her ideas about ethical and political action resonated more with the tradition of his ideas than has been seen.[21] It was from Aristotelian notions about practical wisdom, as they emerged in the emphasis on *poiēsis* and *technē* in Marx and his followers, that she got her first grasp of the practical understanding that one must have to act on behalf of the good. Up to the publication of "Prospects: Are We heading for Proletarian Revolution?" (1933), the result was a notion of action that emphasized that the good was a product like a created thing. First in "Prospects" and then more clearly in "Reflections Concerning the Causes of Liberty and Social Oppression," her dissatisfaction with Marxism caused her to rethink this focus on *poiēsis* and *technē*.

This change saw a shift in her views about thought and action toward the other Aristotelian tradition of *praxis* and *phronēsis*. In this alternate version of Aristotle's account of the method, action (*praxis*) is embedded in practical wisdom (*phronēsis*). *Phronēsis* is deliberative reasoning that is open to experience and relevant scientific knowledge (*epistēmē*) as it thinks about the means appropriate to achieve a good (*aretē*). In *phronēsis*, the achieved good is not a thing external to and fabricated through deliberation about relevant means. Rather, it is an end continually modified, corrected, and adjusted by the ongoing correlation of thought and action. By contrast to *technē*, in *phronēsis* expertise is less important than gradual training, which inches toward its good though a tradition of this deliberation.

Weil's Platonism

That Weil preferred ideas about ethical deliberation that derived ultimately from the long Aristotelian tradition on method suggests that she was less a Platonist than has been supposed. If we tally the major points on which she agreed and disagreed with Plato and then do the same with regard to certain aspects of the Aristotelian tradition of ethical and political deliberation, the surprising result is that the influence of Plato was less extensive than is ordinarily thought. Weil also made much use of myth, especially the myth of the cave. She saw anticipations of Christianity in Plato's dialogues, adopted the central belief that knowing the good ordinarily leads to doing it, and accepted the idea that the political community can be fashioned by human effort.

But Weil ignored or disagreed with much else in Plato's ethical and political philosophies. To begin with, she had no use for the dialogue format or for the *elenchus* method of reasoning. These philosophical strategies provided no clear way to arrive at rational answers to the urgent questions she and others deeply engaged in politics continuously faced. They offered no such clarity because Plato's account of the relationship between the knowledge these methods yielded and the knowledge needed to do the good was not described in a way that she (or anyone else) could readily use.[22] This is why we ought not to be surprised that she never used Plato's philosophical strategies in any attempt to discover the good in either its transcendent or its immanent mode.

When Weil rejected the theory of the divided line in book VI of the *Republic*, she rejected Plato's account of *theoria* as the way to do political thinking. She rejected also the related rule by expertise in the person of the guardian-philosopher who in Plato's account in the *Republic* is a product of the *technē* of his philosophical education. She denied the legitimacy of all other forms of political elitism that ultimately traced their origins to the *Republic*. This was a disavowal of Plato's basic principle that experts who have attained the highest achievements of rational intelligence should govern the *polis*. Moreover, Weil did not accept the congruence of the tripartite division of the soul with a tripartite order of classes in the state. This division located the capacity for these highest achievements in the natural capabilities of only a few rationally endowed souls.

Accordingly, she had no use for Plato's functionalism, in which the individual types of human souls and their corresponding social classes have unique and appropriate places in the social and political order of the state. The closely related Platonic idea of justice as a proper order of relationships into which individual souls and classes duly fit was also anathema to her. In a strongly non-Platonic way, she associated the social good with release from oppression, not with the acceptance of one's lot in life. Finally, Weil was uncomfortable with the heroic virtues so characteristic of ancient thought and deeply ensconced in Plato's provision in the *Republic* for a class of guardian-warriors—situated one rank below the expert philosophers—whose task it was to monopolize the use of force by the state.

In the political arena in the early and middle period, Weil's distinctive interpretation of Plato's theory of form and of the form of the good made the good a reachable, feasible, potential reality.[23] For her, Plato's myth of the cave was not an excuse for anyone to reject the world as mere appearance, even assuming this is how Plato intended it to be used.[24] We are all cave dwellers. But we live also in the world, and so we are called by our rational intelligence, which shines the light of the sun on our deliberations, not to be fooled by immediately apparent experience. From a political point of view, the myth of the cave is not about the irrelevance of political life or about ignoring the way things evidence themselves to our thinking but about how to live in the *polis*.[25]

Weil would have agreed with Hans-Georg Gadamer that the cave dweller understands social and political life and what actions will be successful even *before* he emerges from the cave into the sunlight. What the cave dweller does not ask about and does not understand until *after* he emerges is the good for the sake of which his practical actions are to be carried out.[26] In fact, what Weil rejected about Plato's use of this myth was not the myth itself but two of its implications: the precedence of *theoria* over *phantasia* and the elite status it seemed to accord the guardian-philosophers trained to recognize this precedence. These elites were the inhabitants of the *polis* who Plato implied through the myth saw the good most clearly in its mode of transcendence and were best able to avoid being fooled like cave dwellers by its mode of immanence. It was Weil's well-known belief that knowledge of the world and of the good to be done in it was available to all, which she first argued in her dissertation, "Science and Perception in Descartes," that forbade her endorsement of the long tradition beginning with Plato that preferred political leadership by expertise.

The Influence of Aristotelianism

It is true that Weil rejected Aristotle's ethical doctrine of the mean. She did so because it was incompatible with her belief in personal sacrifice and in actions on behalf of others that exceed our ordinary capacities. In the early and middle period this morality of excess and sacrifice was a supererogatory ethics. It was not until the later period, especially in "On Human Personality" (1943), that her call for supererogatory action gave way to a call for action on behalf of an impersonal good that was transcendent in the supernatural sense. She rejected also Aristotle's metaphysical naturalism with its attribution of an *aretē* (excellence, good) proper to all natural things, including human being and its actions.[27]

The central theme of Aristotelian thought, as its influence came down through the centuries, is that happiness (*eudaimonia*) is the only completely independent good. Aristotle had claimed that while contemplation of the knowledge of necessary things was the highest achievement of this good, the second best good was practical wisdom, especially as it applied to political life. The subject matter of practical wisdom — *phronēsis* — was defined by him as that which can be otherwise than it is and which is changed by human action. Aristotle had linked *phronēsis* to the ethics of the mean, to the Greek preference for balance in all things, and to a political *praxis* that promoted stability and order in the state. Nonetheless, as Aristotle's own definition suggested, this linkage could be applied to a politics of change.

Weil's reaction to the tradition of eudaimonistic ethics was to pick and choose. This tradition had associated happiness with desire but had also recognized that in virtuous action deliberation must intervene between desire and choice (*prohairesis*). Weil did not single out happiness as the complete end of all attending to the good; she also did not think that one attended to the good of others in the sense of seeking their release from oppression for any other end than their happiness. Her words and action in the early 1930s supported the enhancement of the human dignity of workers so that they could lead fulfilling lives, a notion that suggests the general Aristotelian position that connects human happiness with human flourishing and both with the good. We have seen also that Weil did not reject the legitimacy of desire in human action, just the notion that the ends set by it are the immediate ends of our action. Consistent with the Aristotelian tradition, she argued that rational deliberation — what she called reflection — intervenes between desire and the end of action as the condition of the virtue of this action in the pursuit of happiness.

On the question in the Socratic tradition of *akrasia* in human action (where people do not do what they know to be good) Weil agreed with the Aristotelian tradition, not Socrates or Plato, that one can know but not do the good. In this tradition there are good and bad deliberators. The bad deliberators were the ones who allow their desires to set their ends, thus circumventing deliberation about intermediary actions and overriding what they know to be their good. Such aberrations as dogma, the unthinking acceptance of the authority of leaders, and giving in against one's better judgment to group pressures were evidence for her of bad deliberation in the working-class movements she supported. Weil agreed with the Aristotelian tradition that the point of the intellectual virtues, especially *phronēsis*, was to train people to become good deliberators.

One can even say that Weil's break with Marxian thought was in large part driven by what she perceived as the failure of Marx and his followers to live up to the Aristotelian insistence on the implementation of this virtue in political action. This is the meaning of her insistence in "Reflections Concerning the Causes of Liberty and Oppression" that neither Marx nor his followers have ever fully or properly used Marx's method.[28] As heirs to the Aristotelian tradition, Marx and his followers should have, Weil thought, assiduously adhered to the canons of *phronēsis*. As I have noted, these require that political deliberation pay close attention to the changing experience of *praxis* and that it decide on actions to undertake from within this constantly reinformed and refreshed deliberative process. The failure here was to substitute formulaic thinking for the virtue of deliberation, a failure to which, given Marx's Aristotelian credentials, Weil believed he and his followers should not have succumbed. The failure of Marxists to grasp the nationalism and totalitarianism of the Soviet Union, their failure to recognize the emergence of bureaucracy in all modern forms of social relations, their failure to accurately assess the revolutionary potential of the working class, their failure to see the evidence that oppression is intrinsic to industrial working conditions, and their failure to adjust their political program to these realities were all instances of their general failure to embrace the *phronēsis* and the revised *praxis* that should issue from it.

Weil actually found Plato and the Aristotelian tradition in agreement on several points. She understood both to be saying that right action (*orthē energeia*) is already housed in the practical intelligence that discerns it. Though Plato housed this action in *theoria* and Aristotle in *phronēsis*, the inclusion of end and action in right reason (*orthē logou*) suggested to her that a practical end is actually an intelligible end, one that links desire and end in a chain of deliberation.

Thus *finding* the good in political action was a matter of discerning the way in which it was displayed in deliberation about how to act. This viewpoint was entirely consistent with Weil's disposition to think in terms of correlation.

Weil found additional ground for agreement. The Aristotelian tradition was compatible, she thought, with her phenomenological reading of Plato. Aristotelian tradition's complete or independent good was not, given its rejection of Platonic form, the *idea* of one, ultimate end in which worldly instances participated. Instead, it was the perfect end (*teleis*), the one end that most completely promoted human flourishing, the end that was not pursued for the sake of any other good that might be more conducive to such flourishing.[29] Though Aristotle modified the ground—from *eidos* to *teleis*—for believing that there was a complete good beyond which no other could be identified, he affirmed that there was such a good.[30] The common ground that Weil thought she discerned in Plato and this tradition was this notion that there is an end complete in itself.

Weil's account of the good is rich with ontoethical possibilities. The obligation and the ability to do the good are pregiven as constant *possibilities* of human life. They are rooted in our experience of the good as it appears *in and across* the vast multiplicity of our actions in the world. The obligation and the informed ability to do the good are displayed in every action that allows them to show up, and these actions have a transforming impact on the being of the doer and the other. One can say that such attending actions, finally arising through and from the agency of human being, are *living symbols* that make the good present, thus bringing it out of its hiddenness. Thus attending action has the potential ontological capacity to make the absent good present.

There can be no deeper assertion of what attending to the human good means. It is a call from within human being that the worldly actions capable of evidencing the good become its continuous and unending preoccupation. Weil's interpretation of Plato is joined to the Aristotelian tradition—refracted through Marx—of *phronēsis* as deliberative action. This composite became the major vehicle for her articulation of how the phenomenological and existential call to a constant attending to the good can be achieved.

Notes

1. For the influence of Stoicism on Weil, see Diogenes Allen, with the collaboration of Eric Springsted, "Le Malheur: Une énigme (Simone Weil et Épictète)" *Cahiers*

Simone Weil 2.4 (December 1979): 184–96; Gilbert Kahn, "Simone Weil et le Stoïcisme grec," *Cahiers Simone Weil* 5.4 (December 1982): 270–84; and Martin Andic, "Amor Fati," paper delivered at annual Colloquy of the American Weil Society, University of Chicago, April 23–24, 1999.

2. In *OC* I, see especially "Le Beau et le bien" (60–73), "De la perception ou L'aventure de Protée" (121–40), and "Le Donné et le construit" (225–32).

3. Also in *OC* I, see "Du Temps" (141–58), "Science et perception dans Descartes" (161–221), and "Le Travail et médiation" (243–47).

4. For the influence of Alain and Lagneau, see Rolf Kühn, "Le Devoir-être et la réflexion chez Lagneau," in *Jules Lagneau, Alain et L'École françaises de la perception*, ed. Anne Baudart et al. (Paris: Institute Alain, 1992). See Rolf Kühn, *Französische Reflexions-und Geistesphilosophie: Profile und Analysen* (Frankfurt am Main: Hain, 1993), 50–126, who also considers the influence of Maine de Biran in this tradition.

5. The claim that Husserl's account contributed to the blend of philosophical perspectives that influenced her Platonism and thereby contributed to her composite ontological account of the ethical life as a matter of historical fact cannot be established conclusively. Emmanuel Gabellieri in his *L'Être et Don: L'Unité et l'enjeu de la pensée de Simone Weil* (Louvain: Peeters, 2004), argues for this influence. Kühn, *Französische Reflexions-und Geistesphilosophie*, 129, 135, 142, 148, denies the influence of Husserl and questions the similarity of Weil's account to his. For the French philosophy of consciousness and its connection to German phenomenology, see Ian W. Alexander, "Le Relatif et l'actuel en marge de pensées d'Alain," in *French Literature and the Philosophy of Consciousness; Phenomenological Essays*, ed. A. J. L. Busst, introd. Georges Poulet (New York: St. Martin's Press, 1985), 138–68; and in the same volume "The Phenomenological Philosophy in France: An Analysis of Its Themes, Significance and Implications" (76–103). See also Jean Hering, "Phenomenology in France," in *Philosophical Thought in France and the United States: Essays Representing Major Trends in Contemporary French and American Philosophy*, ed. Marvin Farber (Albany: SUNY Press, 1968), 67–85.

6. Weil does not thematize the concept of intentionality. Instead she thinks in terms of correlations, the connections of consciousness to its objects and the connections that join embodied, conscious subjects to each other's projects. Nor does she have a well-articulated notion of what Husserl called the phenomenological or transcendental reduction.

7. In a passing remark, J. P. Little was the first to apply the vocabulary of *attending* to Weil's vocation for the good. Little uses the phrase to describe what she calls Weil's focus on the "absolute good." She says that Weil "saw her vocation as an attending on that good." This remark can be found in Little's "Simone Weil's Concept of Decreation," in *Simone Weil's Philosophy of Culture: Readings Toward a Divine Community*, ed. and introd. Richard Bell (Cambridge: Cambridge University Press, 1993), 46.

8. See Martin Andic, "One Moment of Pure Attention Is Worth All the Good Works in the World," *Cahiers Simone Weil* 21.4 (December 1998): 352, who discusses

these terms. Andic recognizes the importance of caring in their definitions, but he does not link them to the idea of attending to the human good.

9. See the earliest extant fragment of Weil's student years "Imagination et perception," in OC I 297–98, and in the same volume "De la perception ou l'aventure de Protée" (121–39).

10. Weil's use of these terms seems to have come from the influence of Maine de Biran. This influence derived from a reading of some portion of his collected works, many volumes of which had been and were still being published at the time by Pierre Tisserand. The influence also came indirectly through Biran's influence on Lagneau and Alain. Simone Pétrement, *Simone Weil: A Life,* trans. Raymond Rosenthal (New York: Pantheon Books, 1976), 69, lists Maine de Biran as one of the authors Weil thought she had to "study systematically," though the specific volumes to be studied are not identified. See Michel Henry, *Philosophy and Phenomenology of the Body,* trans. Gerard Etzkorn (The Hague: Martinus Nijhoff, 1975), 11–51, 154–82, for a (partially critical) phenomenological interpretation of Maine de Biran. Henry uses the term *subjective embodiment* to describe Biran's account of the relationship of consciousness to its objects. Weil's correlation of consciousness with its objects—which I suspect she ultimately derived from Biran—has a similar flavor.

11. OC I 60–73.

12. The idea that the good is transcendent, immanent, and diffused is associated with Neoplatonism, especially that of Plotinus and Pseudo-Dionysos. Plotinus is listed by Pétrement (69) as one of the authors Weil thought she had to "review quickly," which suggests that before she began to study for her final examinations she had already read the *Ennead,* his major work.

13. See "Sur L'Idée et les objets: Fragments de dialogues," OC I 306–10, for a text in which Weil mused about the relationship of instances, our ideas (forms), and the names we have for them. She recognized that instances share similarities and that this is a shared something that is not limited to any one instance.

14. Eric Perl, "The Presence of the Paradigm: Immanence and Transcendence in Plato's Theory of Form," *Review of Metaphysics,* 53 (1999): 339–62, for a summary of this interpretation of Plato's theory of Form. See also Perl's "Sense-Perception and Intellect in Plato," *Revue de Philosophie Ancienne* 15 (1997): 15–34. For a similar account, see J. N. Findlay, "Towards a Neo-Neo-Platonism," in *Ascent to the Absolute* (London: Allen and Unwin, 1970), 251–53; and *Plato: The Written and Unwritten Doctrines* (London: Routledge and Kegan Paul, 1974), xi–xii.

15. In OC I, see "Le Donné et le construit," 225–32.

16. In a fragment written in 1925 of Weil's earliest surviving essay, "Imagination et perception" (OC I 297–98), Weil described perception as a *mariage* between us and the world. In "L'Existence et l'objet" (OC I 80–88), she described this correlation in familial terms such as *parente* and *fraternité.* This is also a relationship, she says, in which a thing is the sister (*sœur*) of the mind.

17. Eric O. Springsted, *Christus Mediator: Platonic Mediation in the Thought of Simone Weil* (Chico, Calif.: Scholars Press, 1983), 120, is credited with having been the first to notice the important role mediation and *metaxu* play in Weil's thought. See also chapter 8 in this volume for a discussion of her "metaxology."

18. OC I 57–59.

19. See Emmanuel Lévinas, *Otherwise than Being or Beyond Essence*, trans. Alphonso Lingis (Pittsburgh: Duquesne University Press, 1998), 3–11, who uses this terminology. Weil's dyadic ontology is a correlation of individuals linked in the common enterprise of attending to a good that appears between and to them. It is different therefore from Lévinas's metaphysics in which it is not possible to talk about individual being at all.

20. For an assessment of the extensive influence of Aristotle's metaphysics on Marx, see Scott Meikle, "History of Philosophy: The Metaphysics of Substance in Marx," in *The Cambridge Companion to Marx* (Cambridge: Cambridge University Press, 1999), 296–319. See also Alan Gilbert, "Political Philosophy: Marx and Radical Democracy" in ibid., 168–73. In Joseph Dunne's apt phrase Marxian thought is an "echo chamber" of Aristotelianism (Joseph Dunne, *Back to the Rough Ground: Practical Judgement and the Lure of Technique* [Notre Dame: University of Notre Dame Press], 202).

21. In her *Notebooks* Weil has twelve references to Aristotle. She directly cites the *Metaphysics, On the Heavens,* and *On the Universe.* Most of her references are brief, cryptic, and disparaging, and none of them deal with *phronēsis.* But at one point in the *Notebooks* (453), she says that Aristotle "was the only one of the Greeks of any quality, perhaps, who was not a Pythagorean." There are four references in the *First and Last Notebooks,* none more than passing. In her late essay, "On Human Personality" (SWA 67), Weil is quite disparaging about Aristotle's ethics of the mean. She dislikes this aspect of his ethical theory because he (along with Shakespeare, Racine, and other luminaries) does not grasp the "impersonal good."

22. See Francisco J. Gonzalez, *Dialectic and Dialogue: Plato's Practice of Philosophical Inquiry* (Evanston: Northwestern University Press, 1998), 55–59, who shows just how complex and not easily accessible Plato's teaching is about knowledge and the doing of the good. See also Hans-Georg Gadamer, *The Idea of the Good in Platonic-Aristotelian Philosophy,* trans., introd., and annotated P. Christopher Smith (New Haven: Yale University Press, 1986), 67–68, 81, 99, 103–4, 113, who is skeptical that Plato's account of philosophical inquiry can ever give us applicable knowledge of the good as the principle of all good things.

23. See OL 55, 100.

24. For an interpretation of Plato that affirms what I have been saying about Weil's phenomenological reading of him and particularly in reference to the myth of the cave, see Gadamer, *The Idea of the Good,* 74–78.

25. Gadamer, *The Idea of the Good,* 74–78.

26. Ibid.

27. The notion of the functional ends (*teleion*) and proper excellences of things supported Aristotle's account of the good in which many different goods could function as possible ends of virtuous action. Aristotle imagined these goods arrayed in an ascending hierarchy in which most were pursued solely for the sake of other goods and some were pursued for the sake of a limited number of still other goods on up the ladder until a single, complete end emerged that was pursued for its own sake. This end Aristotle called happiness.

28. See *OL* 46, 56.

29. Gadamer, *The Idea of the Good*, 138–39, argues that the difference between Plato and Aristotle is that in Plato the good is grounded in the principle of number, which is the highest presence and which causes all other things to exist, whereas in Aristotle the ground of the good is the *telos* of what is (*ti estin*). According to him, for Aristotle, *physei onta* are not separated (*chōristos*) from their idea. But in Plato (132–33) they are separated into a level of reality apart from their phenomenal existence. The separation account of the forms, including the form of the good, is avoidable if Plato's account is understood—as I think Weil did—phenomenologically, as a nexus of transcendence and immanence.

30. Sarah Broadie, *Ethics with Aristotle* (New York: Oxford University Press, 1991), 198–202, argues against this so-called grand view, which is that he believed there was an ultimate, culminating, and hierarchical end for the sake of which all other goods were pursued. See Broadie (260 n.12) for those who argue for such a view. See also Richard Kraut, *Aristotle on the Human Good* (Princeton: Princeton University Press, 1989), 155–56, who takes the position that for Aristotle among the many goods of action there is what he calls an ideal good, which he says is the life of theory or philosophy.

CHAPTER 4

Simone Weil

Completing Platonism through a Consistent Materialism

ROBERT CHENAVIER

Alain, Simone Weil's teacher and mentor, wrote that "there is something excessive and even violent in Plato."[1] This statement is equally applicable to Weil, another author of bold statements, not least of which is the following: "Since Greece disappeared there hasn't been such a thing as a philosopher" (NR 246). This assertion with respect to ancient Greece is in line with Weil's claim in 1941 that "nothing surpasses Plato" (PSO 66). Such references to Plato, which are frequent, have given rise to interpretations, notably that of Miklos Vetö,[2] of her religious metaphysics as Christian Platonism.

Still, the central role accorded Plato—and Greece—in critical interpretations of Weil's thought must not obscure what the Greeks lacked for Weil, namely, an appreciation of the significance of work. In both her early and later periods, she makes that claim. For example, in 1934 in *Réflexions sur les causes de la liberté et de l'oppression sociale* she wrote:

The conception of work as a human value is the only spiritual victory of human thought since the Greek miracle; this was perhaps the only lacuna in the elaboration of the ideal of human life that formed the enduring inheritance bequeathed by the Greeks. (OC II.2 92)

At the end of 1943 the following, similar statement appears in *The Need for Roots*:

Our age has its own particular mission or vocation—the creation of a civilisation founded upon the spirituality of work. The thoughts relating to a presentiment of this vocation . . . are the only original thoughts of our time, the only ones we haven't borrowed from the Greeks. It is because we have been unequal to this mighty business which was being conceived in us that we have thrown ourselves into the abyss presented by totalitarian systems. (NR 91–92)

These citations also remind us of the importance of Marx in Weil's thought, an importance underlined by the claim, "[A] philosophy [of labor] remains to be worked out. It is perhaps more particularly a need of our time" (OL 169). Nonetheless, for Weil, in this regard even Marx "did not begin the sketch of a sketch. All he supplied were a few indications" (OL 169). But if Weil was willing to criticize Marx, curiously, despite her long-standing Platonism, she does not do so for having been a materialist but for failing to be consistent in his materialism and in his ideal of justice, an ideal that should have led him to recognize the reality of the supernatural.

Here we find ourselves at the intersection of two strands in Weil's thinking whose point of convergence defines the very origin of her philosophy. The first strand is concerned with a lacuna in the Greek conception of the ideal of life, and could be summed up by the following enigmatic note in Weil's *Notebooks*: "Art/Science/labor/philosophy first. Plato only said half of it" (OC VI.1 424). According to the second strand, Marx gave "some indications" for a philosophy of labor, and the basis of his materialism was justified because "if one leaves the supernatural out of account, one is right to be a materialist" (OL 177). All the same, a materialist must also be consistent; in Weil's opinion Marx was not.

In short, for Weil, Platonism cannot be complete unless it allows for a philosophy and a spirituality of labor, and materialism cannot be consistent if it rejects the reality of the supernatural. Consequently, this chapter examines Weil's attempt to elaborate a philosophy that takes account of such contradictions.

From Levels of Being and Degrees of Knowledge to a Philosophy of Labor: Weil's Interpretation of the Divided Line

A reading of Weil's early works shows that very early on she gravitated toward a philosophical analysis of the notion of labor.[3] The starting point for this analysis was Alain's philosophy of perception. But Weil's method also owed a great deal to Plato. For example, the development of her philosophy of perception depends on a progressive distinguishing of levels of being and degrees of knowledge evocative of Plato's divided line in book VI of the *Republic*.

This philosophy of perception begins with a problem addressed by Alain: how does one rise from imagination to understanding? Like Alain, Weil holds that we begin in illusion because imagination is primordial. Consequently, "when we see the world, the image we see is not only a reflection of the world, it is also a reflection of us" (*OC* I 298). The starting point of Weil's philosophy is thus the ambiguity of the limits between one's self and the world.[4]

Moreover, before the world manifests itself before us, given and ordered, it is already *within* us in the form of constantly evolving impressions. From this initial condition of the human being, plunged into the world like a wave in the ocean (a situation described as "the reign of Proteus"),[5] Weil goes on to describe the first degrees of knowledge as an awakening of the mind. From the barely awakened mind—one that perceives but does not yet think—we progress to the dream, described by Alain as this "naive perception formed from insufficient facts."[6] Subsequently, the awakening mind "demands an account of what it sees" (*OC* I 131), but it first awakens in idealism, the childlike state in which the world is simply interpreted and never encountered.

The next stage is unrefined perception, when the mind "outfits [its impressions] with ideas" (*OC* I 123) (by organizing the series of qualities perceived and especially by organizing the perceived forms). However, perception remains unrefined as knowledge is still mixed with beliefs that correspond to bodily affections. Consequently, the ambiguity of the limits between world and mind remains.

A pure perception of things would rid appearance of all admixture of emotion, impression, and illusion. This stage, defined by Weil as "Cartesian clear-sightedness" (*OC* I 134) allows us to think, like Descartes, that "extension is the substance of all things" (*OC* I 134). This clear-sightedness is the condition required for thinking the world through the idea of exteriority, that is, to think the world in a way other than through the form of our own existence immersed in the world. For all that, this Cartesian clear-sightedness poses two problems: maintaining this point of view is difficult, and it is useless without an *art* of perceiving. Emerging from the cave through "reflection on geometry" is not enough if outside this geometry, if in everything else, we remain childlike victims of emotion and credulity. To counter this, a sort of "geometrical gymnastics," as Plato suggested in book VII of the *Republic*, is needed, that is, an ordered exercise of both body and mind that makes us alert to our condition.

In addition to this gymnastics, Weil posits art, as Plato posited music, as a second intermediary to develop "privileged perceptions" (OC I 137). Art teaches us how to purify appearances, and aesthetic perception disciplines the emotions. Gymnastics and art lead to an art of perceiving that protects us from the "reign of Proteus," while at the same time dispensing with the need to maintain us permanently at the level of pure extension—something beyond our condition.

At the end of this trajectory of different degrees of perception, we finally reach perfect perception: the presence of exteriority. Now what is to be done with this exteriority? The athletic body and the geometrical mind do not suffice to define a wisdom for our condition of being in the world. What, then, is lacking in the trajectory we have traced to this point—a trajectory Plato himself would doubtless not have rejected? We have, of course, only "said half of it." So far we have the methodical activity of the body and the disciplining, privileged perception of art. We also have necessity as conceived by geometry and by science. However, to be completely in the world, we still need the experience of real necessity; in other words, our *thought*, purified and disciplined, needs to be checked by something exterior. That can only be through action undertaken in accordance with the thought of methodical changes produced according to laws. Only action mediated by thought can make one experience reality in this way; hence the "leap" to labor that occurs in Weil's analysis. Geometry expresses "the conditions that necessity imposes on specific actions to make these actions labor" (OC I 135). In this way reality is experienced. The law that makes all our actions labor is not "imagined, nor supposed, nor proven, but constantly experienced" (OC I 126). The law of labor imposes on projected actions "the conditions laid down by the universe with respect to its own changes" (OC I 155).

An important consequence results from this. We do not proceed from first impressions to the *reality* of the world by judgment, by imaginative synthesis, or by the Kantian schema alone. *The* formative action that allows us to progress from the impression to the object is primarily labor: labor is the true schematism. "This schema is the form of all our actions in the sense that it is a condition of all our actions to be labor, that is to say, to be totally lacking in immediacy" (OC I 154).

Let me make a brief observation on this point. For Alain, the image is "a representation of the object through which we anticipate the influences of which it would be the source if we entered into contact . . . with it."[7] According to Weil, it is not simply the object that is represented. The imagination also renders the "law of labor" perceptible through mimed movements.[8] This function of the imagination would correspond fairly well to Alain's description of the order introduced by the mind into perception by way of what he called "the drawing imagination."[9] "To perceive the object is to draw it by anticipatory attention, attention that is mimed by some corporeal gesture."[10] This idea dates from Kant's *Critique of Pure Reason:* "In order to cognize something in space, e.g., a line, I must draw it, and thus synthetically bring about a determinate combination of the given manifold."[11] Literal drawing, the "mark resulting from a controlled action," is a prime example of this sort of cognition,[12] but so too is labor. Geometry refers to perceived space insofar as imagination makes the geometer feel that all figures are drawn. Imagination makes geometrical law perceptible, which in turn expresses the laws of labor. According to Weil, these reflections illuminate "Kant's remarks regarding synthetic *a priori* propositions, for although geometry does not need to be verified by a specific experience, those who do not experience the presence of an antagonistic term in their actions are not geometers" (OC I 136). When working, I experience "the presence of an antagonistic term" that resists me through the laws of its exteriority expressed by geometry. The laborer is the person who, when acting according to the necessities of geometry, experiences the truth of these conceived necessities; in other words, she experiences real necessity. The sciences are merely the theoretical expression of vanquished Proteus. Practical victory is in labor. This is why "the worker can be taken out of the cave [and why] the members of the Academy of Sciences can move amongst the shadows" (OC I 136–37). This is Weil's completed Platonism.

From Weil's early writings one may conclude that labor is not presented as a social category. Rather, it is envisaged as the activity through which the form of the human condition is discovered.

Going Beyond the Philosophers, "from within Their Thinking"

Independently of her social commitment, it seems philosophically quite natural that Simone Weil should end up dealing with Marx in order to get to what Rolf Kühn has called "an integration of historical materialism into a certain type of geometrical and labor idealism."[13] In Weil's opinion, Marx posits "a conception that shows reality appearing at the intersection of thought and the world" (OC II.1 306). She interprets his philosophy as a search for the understanding in action. If labor is human activity par excellence, it is because it is first and foremost thought that, Weil thinks, is a disposition to act. When she claims that "the philosophy of labor is materialism" (OC I 378–79), she does so in order to insist that "materialism is inconceivable without the notion of the mind" (OC I 379). The "necessary gesture" that labor requires of action is imposed by matter but originates from the mind. "Matter is something that imposes an inevitable order on our actions. Matter is everything, except thought, which grasps necessity" (OC I 379). But by adding the following, Weil avoids any idealist interpretation of thought that would see it acting independently of contact with real necessity: "Thinking and working are not divorced; labor is no less thought than reflection. It is no less an absolute act of the mind" (OC I 379).

This is why Marx's thought is *philosophy*. Early on, Weil defines philosophy as "the only study that requires the subject as the starting point, 'provided that one does not forget that the subject is empirically determined'" (OC I 379). Marx is a philosopher of the "empirically determined" subject, grasped in the search for understanding in action, that is to say, in labor.[14] For this reason Weil includes Marx among those philosophers whose method qualifies them as the "successors of Platonism, Descartes [and] Kant."[15]

But according to Weil, in their method of investigation the philosophical descendants of Plato, Descartes, and Kant "were not sufficiently aware [of this empirical determination of the subject], which harmed their work."[16] As we have seen, "Plato only said half of it." Descartes, Weil affirms, "says explicitly what Plato only suggested" by pressing for the notion of a geometry "turned towards the world" (OC I 96). But "Descartes stopped halfway" (OC II.2 270); there is something "lacking" in his method.[17] He saw that the question of signs was essential for thought, but he did not prevent signs from replacing the signified and becoming their own end (as is the case in algebra). In short, Descartes failed to discover the way to understand without at the same time ceasing to perceive.

With regard to Kant, Weil took Alain's lesson for granted. Kant was the first to show the relationship between understanding and intuition by revealing it in its real exercise, but one must think of the formative activity by which the subject passes from impression to object more in terms of the body's mediation than Kant did: one has to go as far as the body's hold on external existence through labor.

Marx for his part discovered the explanation of the historical process in the relationships that exist between individuals, the products of their activity, but he hypostasized the real conditions of this activity[18] and made of them an essence to be realized. So, as an investigation of the condition of an empirically determined subject, Marx betrays his own philosophy when he claims that "social existence determines consciousness," as though social existence could be separated from the consciousness of individuals who act. Marx is unfaithful to his method and his initial philosophy, a philosophy of labor.

Weil's crossing of a spiritual threshold after her first contact with Christianity (in 1935)[19] introduces no "turning" (in Heidegger's sense of *die Kehre*) in her philosophical itinerary, or any denial of her previous position on Marx. For Simone Weil, the only appropriate images for describing the movement of thought are images of mediation, images of passage between different levels, excluding nothing and abandoning nothing.[20] This implies the elaboration of a method of reading allowing one to cross thresholds between one level of reality and another (natural, social, supernatural) in order to determine the meaning and value of each of these levels. We can get an idea of how these levels are distinguished by examining the place of materialism in Weil's thought.

The Right Use of Materialism: Knowing How to Be a Materialist

An "incomprehensible solution" (*OL* 176) must not be given to problems that defy human faculties, in particular, to the problem of unity between the necessary and the good.[21] One must avoid "fabricating a fictitious, mistaken equivalent of this unity" (*OL* 174) because of the risk of falling to "the bottom of the inferior forms of the religious life" (*OL* 174). Yet among all the "inadequate solutions" that have been proposed, the only ones that perhaps "contain some fragments of pure truth" and that are "by far the best, the most useful," are the "materialist solutions" (*OL* 177). "Materialism accounts for everything, with the exception of the supernatural" (*OL* 177). From this point of view, Marx's writings contain "an extremely valuable indication," but he scarcely makes "any real use of it" (OL 177).

One must know how to be a good materialist, and the right use of materialism consists in not falsifying it through vague syntheses with the ideal of justice or goodness: "If the materialist could set aside all concern for the good, he would be perfectly consistent" (OL 173). Marx had set out with the intention of being a consistent materialist by applying to social science the notion of "conditions of existence" that Darwin had applied to the structures and transformations of living beings.[22] But his theory that the unlimited development of productive forces would automatically create the *best* adapted structures for their development shows Marx to be closer to Lamarck than to Darwin. All Weil's writings between 1933 and 1937 criticize Marx for failing to recognize that if social existence is interwoven with external relations, with necessary relations, any introduction of a principle of inherence transforms the materialist approach into a form of mythology.

Later, in her London writings (1942–43), Weil would intensify this criticism of Marx. By making a "fictitious equivalent" of the unity between justice and force, Marx revealed he was an "idolator" (OL 160). He was not wrong to want to combine idealism with materialism, "for they have to be combined," but he placed "this combination at too low a level; for their unity dwells . . . outside this world" (OL 164).

If one wants to elaborate a science of social structures, one must first be exclusively materialist: "Marx was right to begin by positing the reality of a social matter, of a social necessity, of whose laws one must at any rate have caught a glimpse before venturing to reflect on the destinies of the human race" (OL 179–80). Because he tried to explain through materialism everything that could be explained, Marx was led to introduce into the material process an inherent power and an aspiration for the better. Consequently, he provided an overhasty solution to lurking contradictions that he had not yet fully developed.

From an authentically spiritual point of view, Marx stands accused of idolatry; from an authentically materialist point of view, he sins by the religious form of his thought. But it is important for us to note that for Weil herself, *materialism occupies the same place* in the texts produced during 1933–34 as it does in the London writings. Philosophically or spiritually, one must be a materialist when studying necessity because, as Weil wrote in 1943, "materialism accounts for everything, with the exception of the supernatural" (OL 177). This is not so far from what she wrote in 1934: "Everything can be explained by matter, except thought itself which grasps and understands the role of matter. If it is at-tempted, materialism degenerates into a kind of popular pragmatism" (*OC* II.1 353). This means that forms of thought are reduced to forms of action with a view to their success.

In 1943 Weil wrote: "This universe, minus the supernatural, is only matter. In describing it solely as matter, one seizes upon a particle of truth. In describ-ing it as a combination of matter and of specifically moral forces belonging to this world . . . , one falsifies everything" (*OL* 177). One must not grant to the course of events powers that belong only to the mind that conceives.

From the materialist conception that can (and must) explain everything, except for the mind that understands and masters matter through labor, to the kind of materialism that can (and must) explain everything, except for the super-natural that operates "decisively, but in a hidden manner" (*OL* 177), a thresh-old is certainly crossed, but the direction of thought remains unchanged. That is, far from putting genuine materialism into eclipse, authentic spirituality broadens its domain. Ultimately, the spiritual perspective permits an under-standing of what is most valuable in Marx's thought: "In his works there are compact fragments whose truth is unchanging [and that] are not only com-patible with Christianity, but of infinite value to it" (*OL* 170). In Weil's opinion, such are the fragments that represent the pure materialism contained in Marx's thought.

> The works of Marx contain one extremely valuable indication . . . —the idea of non-physical matter. Marx, rightly regarding society as being the human fact of primary importance in this world, directed his attention only to so-cial matter; but one may similarly consider in the second place, psycho-logical matter. (*OL* 177)

It is not a reductive materialism that renders different domains uniform. On the contrary, it is an extension, under certain conditions, of the legitimate use of the notion of *matter*, as the following comment illustrates: "Under all the phenomena of a moral order, whether collective or individual. There is some-thing analogous to matter properly so called. Something analogous; not matter itself" (*OL* 177–78).

Within the notion of matter we find the notion of real necessity (so impor-tant in the early writings), developed as much as possible thanks to the spiritual point of view. In the notes from her philosophy classes dating from 1931–32,

Weil affirmed that "reality and necessity are the same thing" (*OC* I 376), and in a fragment written in 1943, she confirms that "everything that is real is subject to necessity" (*OL* 178).

Reality, Necessity, and the Supernatural

One can never be enough of a materialist when studying reality. It is in this way that one will understand that "the wretchedness of our condition subjects human nature to a moral form of gravity that is constantly pulling it downwards" (*OL* 166). Moral phenomena themselves are not governed by the arbitrary. Like everything that is real, they are subject to a "specific necessity," "only [this necessity] is harder to know" (*OL* 178). So Weil insists: "[W]hen studying [these moral laws], one cannot be too cool-headed, too lucid, too cynical. In this sense, to this extent, one must be a materialist" (*OL* 166).

Even the part played by the supernatural here below, its silent and decisive intervention, does not escape that law of the real that is necessity. "Those who think that the supernatural, by definition, operates in an arbitrary fashion, incapable of being studied, are as wrong about it as those who deny its reality" (*OL* 167). To deny that "the influence of the supernatural on human societies [might] also be studied" (*OL* 167) as a specific form of necessity leads to a denial of the *reality* of the supernatural: "The true knowledge of social mechanics implies that of the conditions under which the supernatural operation of an infinitely small quantity of pure good, placed at the right point, can neutralise gravity" (*OL* 167).[23] If materialism is the best of the "inadequate solutions," it at least allows an in-depth examination of the supernatural force according to the laws of specific necessity that govern it in this world. In this way, the gap separating Plato's spirituality from materialism reveals itself as being "infinitely small" (*OL* 175), for between true materialism and authentic spirituality no real contradiction exists, only a paradox for human intelligence, which has difficulty recognizing in its *reality* the part of the supernatural in this world.

If the contradictions allowed by Marx are not sources of truth in his work, it is because he uses contradictions badly, by transposing them into things and by expecting a resolution in and by the things themselves. Plato, on the contrary, makes legitimate use of contradiction by turning it into dialectics so that contradiction is something by and for thought, that awakens thought, and is not the essence of reality proper. If the resources of intelligence collapse before contradiction, contradiction "must be recognised as a fact," and it must be "used . . . like a pair of pincers, so that through it direct contact may be made with the transcendent sphere of truth beyond the range of human faculties" (OL 173). Contradiction "as a fact" must be used so that it allows us to connect with this level that we cannot reach through intelligence:

> The contact is direct, though made through an intermediary, in the same way as the sense of touch is directly affected by the uneven surface of a table over which you pass, not your hand, but your pencil. The contact is real, though belonging to the number of things that by nature are impossible, for it is a case of a contact between the mind and that which is not thinkable. It is supernatural but real. (OL 173)

The image of the pencil evokes Descartes's image of the blind person's stick used by Weil in her early writings. The stick is a tool of perception that allows the blind person to feel things directly "as though the stick were feeling and were part of one's body" (OC I 210). In the same way, contradiction is used as a tool of perception that allows us to make contact with the supernatural. The stick makes up for the absence of vision, and allows blind persons to touch an object as though they were seeing it, since feeling is at the end of the stick. In the same way, contradiction makes up for the shortcomings of human intelligence that render it incapable of grasping "the transcendent domain of truth" and allows us to experience the reality of the supernatural as intelligence would grasp it. In the same way that the blind person's sense of the unreal becomes real through touching with the stick, that which is supernatural because of intelligence's inadequacies is reached through contradiction.

The extension of the materialist method finally allows us to move beyond a major contradiction in Marxism. Thanks to his method, Marx provided an insightful view of the reign of necessity. But in stepping back from the hopeless consequences of the reign of force in social matter, he tweaked both his materialism and his ideal of justice in order to render them commensurate. For Weil, by studying materialism's legitimate domain of investigation, one ought at the same time to establish hope but without changing direction in the ideal of justice. The idea, developed in 1943, that "there is a unity between the necessary and the good . . . outside this world" (OL 160) is expressed in similar terms as early as 1934 but from a philosophical perspective. In *Réflexions sur les causes de la liberté*, for example, we read: "When the past is studied, the notion of progress . . . only misleads the mind. It must be replaced by a value system conceived outside time" (OC II.2 86–87). In 1937 Weil writes that insofar as thought "constantly constructs a value system that is not of this world, it is an enemy of the forces that dominate society" (OC II.2 132).

To remain a coherent materialist and to be consistent in one's perception of the good, and in order not to distort them by making hasty syntheses, thresholds must be crossed. The spiritual point of view finally reached is not reductionist. Rather it is a corrosive force in respect of the order of the world, insofar as this order is governed by force. But the spiritual perspective is also a factor of order insofar as it sheds as much light as possible without dispelling the shadows our intelligence encounters (unlike the dialectic that, when it is illegitimately used, claims to explain everything conceptually).[24]

Rather than lead to an abstract conciliation, the crossing of the spiritual threshold reveals the gap that exists between the necessary and the good, and their unity "outside this world" remains "incomprehensible" for our intelligence (OL 160). Could supernatural knowledge allow this gap to be overcome? If we were to study this, it would be important to remember that Simone Weil's philosophy is—consistently—a philosophy of the human condition, that is, a philosophy of experience that tests the laws of real necessity, as in labor for example, but that also tests the experience of affliction.

If affliction is a fundamental experience of the "human condition" it is because the efforts of thought needed to resolve the contradictory spheres of experience that continually try us and to understand the paradoxical operations of the supernatural in this world are never enough. Those supernatural operations decide the shape of the world but are also so "secretive" and "silent" that they are "almost invisible" (OL 167). The gap between the necessary and the good and their unity outside its world remain obscure to the intelligence. Thus in the year she died, Simone Weil wrote to Maurice Schumann: "I feel an ever-widening rift which is present both in my mind and in the very centre of my heart because I find myself unable to reconcile in truth the affliction of mankind, the perfection of God, and the link between them" (EL 213). Yet, she adds: "I have an inner certainty that if this truth is ever granted to me, it will be when I myself physically experience affliction, one of the forms of the affliction of our age" (EL 213).

It is almost as though consenting to extreme affliction were capable of unveiling the back side of necessity, cracking "the shell of the world," and giving access to that rarest form of discernment: *simultaneous reading on different levels*. Weil describes this in the following way: "It is one and the same thing, which with respect to God is eternal wisdom; with respect to the universe, perfect obedience; with respect to our love, beauty; with respect to our intelligence, balance of necessary relations; with respect to our flesh, brute force" (*NR* 281).

This allows us to understand that the reasons that led Weil to expose herself to danger so often in her life depend as much on her method as on her psychological makeup. Wherever there is danger, war, oppression, nothing provokes more horror from her "than the situation of those who find themselves at the rear," as she wrote to George Bernanos in 1936 on the subject of her involvement in the Spanish Civil War (*EHP* 221). At the end of 1934 she gives a similar reason for her decision to work in a factory: "To enter into contact with real life" and "to find myself beside real people."[25] Finally, in 1942, she agreed to leave for New York and then London because she planned to be parachuted into France in order to participate in the Resistance. As soon as she was in New York she wrote to Schumann:

> Because of my frame of mind, pain and danger are indispensable. . . . I am obsessed with the affliction that reaches across the globe . . . , and I cannot . . . rid myself of this obsession unless I have a large share of danger and suffering. . . . I beg you to find me . . . the quantity of useful suffering and danger that will prevent me from being consumed unproductively by despondency. . . . It is sad to have a character like mine; but really, this is the way I am and there is nothing I can do . . . ; all the more so because it is not just a question of character, but of vocation. (*EL* 199–200)

Indeed, Weil resumed the essential quality of the sage or saint's vocation by commenting on the allegory of the cave:

> When the saint has torn the soul from the body . . . he must incarnate himself in his body in order to shine the reflection of supernatural light on this world, and make this world and this earthly life a reality—because until now they have only been dreams. In this way he must finish creation. The perfect imitator of God first disincarnates himself, then incarnates himself. (*SG* 106)

This is why Weil affirms, "There is no need for a new Franciscan order. The monk's order and the convent are a barrier. The new *élite* must be a part of the mass and in direct contact with it" (*SE* 216). Spiritual conditions must be created at the heart of our civilization and they must take account of what is most particular to it, labor and technology: "Everybody is busy repeating . . . that what we suffer from is a lack of balance, due to a purely material development of technical science. This lack of balance can only be remedied by a spiritual development in the same sphere, that is, in the sphere of work" (*NR* 94).

This explains why she confides in her *Notebooks*: "The object of my research is not the supernatural, but this world" (*OC* VI.2 245). If "good descends from heaven upon earth only to the extent to which certain conditions are in fact fulfilled on earth" (*NR* 252) it must be accepted that "the plenitude of the reality of a man is in this world, should this man be perfect. The model is to be found in the *Timaeus*" (*OC* VI.3 51).

Why the model of the *Timaeus*? Because "the *Timaeus* is the book of the man who has re-entered the cave" (*SG* 129). Undoubtedly, Weil would have wished her work to be that of "the man who has re-entered the cave" in the very conditions of our civilization, and that her philosophy be a response to the surprise she expresses in her *Notebooks*: "A strange question of historical materialism: why such an absence of 'Platonism' in our day?" (*OC* VI.1 121)[26]

If an age without precedent such as ours requires, to emerge from its confusion, a Marx "overtaken from within his thinking" by Plato, and a Plato who has absorbed Marx, it is possible to understand that "[t]oday it is not enough merely to be a saint [or a sage], but we must have the saintliness [or wisdom] demanded by the present moment, a new saintliness [or wisdom], which is itself also without precedent" (*WG* 45).

The philosophical expression of this saintliness depends on the elaboration of a "completed" Platonism that would include a philosophy of labor and on a materialism that would recognize the reality of the supernatural. It is less the combining of Christianity and Platonism—which in the final analysis is quite a traditional combination—that defines the originality of Simone Weil than the articulation of a Christian Platonism together with a consistent materialism. To my mind, these were the philosophical and spiritual vocations of Simone Weil; each of these vocations was "new [and] without precedent."

Translated by Aedín Ní Loingsigh,
revised by E. Jane Doering and Eric O. Springsted

Notes

1. Alain, *Les Passions et la sagesse* (Paris: Gallimard, Bibliothèque de la Pléiade, 1960), 919.

2. Miklos Vetö, *The Religious Metaphysics of Simone Weil,* trans. Joan Dargan (Albany: SUNY Press, 1994).

3. This section is a synopsis of the analysis presented in my *Simone Weil: Une philosophie du travail* (Paris: Éditions du Cerf, coll. "La Nuit surveillée," 2001).

4. See *Premiers écrits philosophiques,* in OC I 185. See also Betty McLane-Iles's comments in *Uprooting and Integration in the Writings of Simone Weil* (New York: Peter Lang, 1987), 15.

5. See OC I 127.

6. Alain, "Définitions," in *Les Arts et les dieux* (Paris: Gallimard, Bibliothèque de la Pléiade, 1958), 1086.

7. Georges Pascal, *L'Idée de philosophie chez Alain* (Paris: Bordas, 1970), 167. The author quotes the following passage from *Quatre-vingt-un chapitres sur l'esprit et les passions:* "For example, what I perceive as being in relief is not a real relief that is known at the moment of touching. It is signs that I know, and that allow me to perceive as though I had my hands outstretched." (See Alain, *Les Passions et la sagesse,* 1084.)

8. The Weilian idea of the imagination that "makes the law of labor perceptible for me" through "movements begun and remembered" corresponds to Lagneau's thinking: "We represent the exterior world to ourselves only through movements or through the anticipation of our movements and their effects." *Célèbres leçons et fragments* (Paris: Presses Universitaires de France, 1964), 197.

9. Florence Khodoss, "Le poème de la Critique," *Revue de Métaphysique et de Morale* 2 (April–June 1952): 226.

10. Ibid.

11. Kant, *Critique of Pure Reason,* trans. and ed. Paul Guyer and Allen W. Wood (Cambridge: Cambridge University Press, 1998), 249.

12. Khodoss, "Le poème de la Critique," p. 228.

13. Rolf Kühn, "Dimension et logique interne de la pensée de Simone Weil," in *Simone Weil, philosophe, historienne et mystique,* ed. Gilbert Kahn (Paris: Aubier, 1978), 338.

14. This formula—applied to the consciousness of our existence—comes, of course, from Kant's *Critique of Pure Reason,* 327: "The mere, but empirically determined, consciousness of my own existence proves the existence of objects in space outside me."

15. Simone Weil, "Une chronique philosophique à Marseille en 1941," *Cahiers du Sud* 235 (May 1941): 288–94. Reprinted in *Cahiers Simone Weil* 9.3 (September 1986): 234.

16. Ibid.

17. Simone Weil, Letter to Robert Guihéneuf, *Cahiers Simone Weil* 21.1–2 (March–June 1998): 8.

18. See *OC* II.2 120.

19. Weil speaks more precisely of the "three contacts with Catholicism that really counted" in *Waiting on God*, trans. Emma Craufurd (London: Routledge, 1951), 19: Portugal in 1935, Assisi in 1937, and Solesmes in 1938, a trip that led shortly afterward to her first mystical experience.

20. See J. P. Little, "Le Pont, le seuil et la porte: Trois images de la médiation chez Simone Weil," in *Question de*, ed. François L'Yvonnet (Paris: Albin Michel, 1994), 148–56.

21. See *OL* 174.

22. See *OC* II.1 330–31.

23. This is what Simone Weil would try to do in her "Project for the training of front-line nurses" (*EL* 187–95).

24. In a short piece dating from 1928–29, Weil remarked: "When I find order where mankind has not passed I do not conclude that the world is also capable of creating an order. Rather I see this order as a strange mark in the world by a being who is close to my mind" (*OC* I 237).

25. Simone Pétrement, *La Vie de Simone Weil*, vol. 1 (Paris: Fayard, 1973), 440. See also Simone Weil's *La Condition ouvrière* (Paris: Gallimard, coll. "Folio Essais," 2002), 33.

26. Note, for example, the following fragment dating from 1929: "The thinking of our age is dominated by technology, and individuals frequently surrender themselves to intoxicating pleasures reminiscent of the age of Proteus. On the contrary, the religious, and even philosophical ideas of the Greeks, which often seem inferior to ours, are doubtlessly considerably more advanced than ours in respect of wisdom" (*OC* I 128).

CHAPTER 5

The Christian Materialism
of Simone Weil

PATRICK PATTERSON
AND LAWRENCE E. SCHMIDT

> Human nature is so arranged that a desire of the soul, unless it passes through
> the flesh by means of actions, movements and postures that naturally corre-
> spond to it, hasn't any reality for the soul. It dwells there only as a phantom.

Simone Weil, *The Theory of the Sacraments*

The familiar caricature of Platonism as otherworldly, dualist, idealist, anti-
cosmic and antimaterialist—in short, as simply Gnostic—dominates and provides the straw man for much postmodern philosophy informed by the Heideggerian interpretation of Nietzsche and his epigones such as Derrida and
Foucault. Leslie Paul Thiele argues that, according to Heidegger, "metaphysics
began with Plato's separation of Being, the unchanging forms or ideas, from becoming, the changeable and the timely."[1] In his commentary on Nietzsche, Heidegger wrote: "For Plato, the supersensuous is the true world. It stands over all as

what sets the standard. The sensuous lies below, as the world of appearances. What stands over all is alone and from the start what sets the standard. It is therefore what is desired."[2] Our purpose here is to argue that Simone Weil's Christian Platonism represents a complete rejection of this caricature. Although it is true to say that her explicit conversion to Christianity compelled her again and again to reject every hint of the otherworldly dualism so often ascribed to Plato, and to emphasize instead the particularity and materiality of his thought, she was certain that her Platonism was consistent with Plato's. Her sacramental ontology, her world-affirmative epistemology (or *via positiva*) and her ethics of engagement within the world all counter the current prejudice that Platonism is inevitably set against the material world in favor of what is said to be "spiritual," as if the spiritual could be understood in abstraction from the corporeal.

Authentic Mysticism

To claim that Weil and Plato are not engaged in a flight into an other world that pits the material against the spiritual is not to deny that their mysticism is rooted in a stark dualism.[3] Throughout her entire corpus of writings, before and after her explicit conversion to Christianity, Weil asserted that Good and necessity, as Plato said, are separated by an infinite distance: "They have nothing in common. They are totally other. Although we are forced to assign them a unity, this unity is a mystery; it remains for us a secret" (OL 174). Thus at the heart of the mystical experience is a contradiction, a paradox. Ontologically it is acknowledged in the Platonic and Judeo-Christian belief in the infinite qualitative difference between God and the world. The eternal and the realm of becoming, the Creator and the creation, are essentially different. Whatever may be said in terms of their unity, it will never dissolve itself into absolute identity. "'God does not mingle himself with man'" (IC 125, quoting Plato's *Symposium* 202e).

This difference is initially felt by the mystics not as a metaphysical but as a moral contradiction, and with devastating effect. Weil writes:

> There is only one time when I really know nothing of ["the certitude of perfect security in God"] any longer. It is when I am in contact with the affliction of other people, those who are indifferent or unknown to me as much as the others, perhaps even more, including those of the most remote ages of antiquity. This contact causes me such atrocious pain and so

utterly rends my soul, that as a result the love of God becomes almost impossible for me for a while. (WG 42)

How to think together human affliction and the perfection of God? Again and again Weil gives eloquent testimony to her own experience of the paradox, the intensity of her descriptions suggesting that it was profoundly constitutive of her inmost self.[4]

Weil asserted that Plato's familiarity with this experience, and even more, his refusal, learned above all from Homer and the fifth-century tragedians, to evade "the contemplation of human misery in its truth implies a very high spirituality" (IC 75). The caricature of the mystic as one who hides from the harsh realities of life in a sentimental mist of evasion and denial describes what Weil calls "spurious mysticism" (NR 150). The authentic mystic resists the ever present temptation to retreat, determinedly realist in holding to both poles of the contradiction.

Like Plato, Weil uses the term *necessity* to denote the pole that consists of all that appears to eclipse the perfection of God. Necessity is most basically the ordered character of the material world, described by scientific laws.[5] It is also the determinative dynamic of human corporate social life. Society, politics, the media, the judiciary, the church, but also all of the more informal communities we inhabit, all are comprehensively ordered by necessity. In this realm, the realm of the great beast, necessity expresses itself as the collective mind and will of society driven by the quest for prestige in the face of public opinion, and mistaking the order of necessity for the order of the good, "call[ing] the just and the beautiful the things that are necessary, being incapable of discerning and teaching what a distance separates the essence of what is necessary from the essence of what is good" (NR 132). But necessity also reigns supreme in the psychological and moral realm. The counterintuitive character of this claim only renders it the more provocative. Weil and Plato are sure that where human beings think their freedom is greater, they are in fact deceived. Psychology has shown us that, subconsciously, unconsciously, we are driven by "monsters within us . . . all sorts of monsters" (LOP 98). Or, borrowing from Plato, we are "wooden horses" indwelt by "warriors (thoughts) which live an independent life" (LOP 97). And Weil claims that this psychological necessity is complicated by a moral necessity, our consistent tendency to repression. "The essence of repressed tendencies is lying; the essence of this lying is the repression of which one is aware" (LOP 98). The effect of our self-deceptive repression is that we become the victims of the monsters within. They determine our actions. "This mechanical necessity holds all men in its grip at every moment" (WG 42). Might, raw force, injustice, ugliness are some of the names Weil gives to this sovereign dynamic at work in the order of necessity.[6]

Nevertheless, as a still small voice in the midst of omnipotent necessity, there may be heard an ever-present summons to recognize and to hearken to the good that is truly good, a summons that issues from the world outside, but also from within, in our minds and souls. In other words, paradoxically juxtaposed to the omnipresent reality of raw might there is another reality, or rather the same reality seen from a different perspective, the world imbued by grace. With her eyes wide open to the universality of necessity, Weil insisted with equal passion on the graced character of all things. As the vision of necessity most often issues in anguish, so the vision of grace brings with it ecstasy. Ecstasy describes the mystic's experience and the accompanying conviction of the invisible reality of an order that is other and higher than the order of necessity. Viewed from the perspective of that higher order, the world is known and loved as good. As mystical experience it comes to a person not as the conclusion to rational argument or on the basis of experimental investigation but mysteriously, from above, as a gift, as grace and ecstasy. And it is in particular the dual nature of the experience, the coterminous vision of necessity and the good, infinitely distant from one another and yet equally true and real characterizations of the world, that Weil identifies by the term *mystical*.

But it is important to note that such ecstatic mystical experience does not remove us from the necessity or materiality of the world. Rather it is the experience of God's obligatory summons to do justice, or what for Weil is the same thing, to love the Good in the midst of, even embodied in, the all-pervasive necessity of the world. Weil calls it supernatural justice because at every step of the way it is in direct contradiction to the logic of the great beast that, within and without, seduces us to its ways. It is in the doing of this supernatural justice that the infinite contradiction and cost of the love of God come into focus, the pain and effort required for allegiance to the Good in the midst of ubiquitous necessity and over against the great beast. The call to do justice entails a demand to be engaged within the necessity of the world. For Weil, the world and God, necessity and the Good, are never mutually exclusive. Human life is not a ceaseless struggle to escape the prison of the world here below and to rise to our true home in the pure and ordered reality of heaven. Rather the love of the Good that absolutely transcends the created order is evoked and sustained by the very created order it transcends.

Weil emphasizes the particularity and materiality of Plato's thought in three ways, which we explore below. What we call her sacramental ontology, her world-affirmative epistemology, and her politics of engagement in the world are all descriptive of a Platonism that runs counter to that caricature in which the so-called spiritual is invariably set over against the material world and sought through escape from the corporeal.

Sacramental Ontology

The beauty of the world is an image, a sacrament, of the face of God. Citing Plato as her authority, she says that the world's beauty, "indistinguishable from its reality[,] . . . is really an incarnation of God" (FLN 341). God has so ordered the world that it summons us, on God's behalf, to attend to and to live according to the character of God to which the world bears constant and silent testimony. "Beauty is a providential dispensation by which truth and justice, while still unrecognized, call silently for our attention" (*FLN* 341).

Characteristic of the Platonist is the emphasis on the silence of the sacramental appeal of the beauty of the world, a silence that renders it liable to being ignored, unrecognized.[7] Faith is the prerequisite for seeing it. "We must have faith that the universe is beautiful on all levels" (WG 97). Perhaps mindful of the typical interpretation of Platonism, Weil adds that we must believe that the world's beauty is "in relation to the bodily and psychic structure of each of the thinking beings which actually do exist" (WG 97). The world's beauty is transcendent, it opens on to the original and eternal beauty of God, but "the part of this beauty which we experience is designed and destined for our human sensibility" (WG 97).

The "transcendent character of the beauty of the world" is not an invitation to engage in an idealist flight into fantasy. It is true that God is other than the world. But God "created" it, and "created the beauty of it for us" (WG 97). We do not therefore need to escape it to come to him; rather he has so made it that it is the way by which he comes to us. "Love came down into this world," Weil writes, "in the form of beauty" (FLN 71). In that sense, as the means of his making himself known to us and drawing us to himself, the world is a sacramental mediating of God to us, and of us to God. "The beauty of the world is Christ's tender smile for us coming through matter. He is really present in the universal beauty. The love of this beauty proceeds from God dwelling in our souls and goes out to God present in the universe. It is also like a sacrament" (WG 97).

We might well suspect that this wholehearted "Yes" to the created order in all its materiality betrays a revisionist reading of Plato in the light of Christian or other influences that cannot be supported by the Platonic texts. But Weil insists that it is precisely Plato that has taught her this "Yes," and that while it is consistent with the New Testament, it has been almost altogether ignored in the Christian tradition.[8] St. Francis and St. John of the Cross are the most notable representatives of an exceptional minority, what she calls the Platonic tradition, within Christianity. In reflections on Plato's *Phaedrus* she finds the invitation to the joy of "a total and pure adherence of the soul to the beauty of the world" (*FLN* 83). When the world is so adhered to, "it is a sacrament[,] . . . the sacrament of St. Francis" (*FLN* 83). In a similar vein, and in deliberately physical terms, inspired by Plato's *Timaeus*, she writes that the sacramental beauty of the world summons us to the knowledge that "all that we touch, see and hear is the very flesh and the very voice of absolute Love" (*IC* 103). Weil is careful to distinguish this Platonic Christian perspective from all forms of pantheism.[9] The world is neither to be identified with nor altogether separated from God. Yet God "penetrates the world and envelopes it upon all sides, being . . . outside space and time yet being not entirely distinct from these but governing them" (*IC* 103).[10]

Affirmation of the World

Weil's sacramental account of reality undergirds her affirmation of the material world that it implies. But the common prejudice that Platonism is inevitably set against corporeality in favor of what is said to be immaterial and spiritual is deeply ingrained not only in the popular mind but in academic circles too. Even so sympathetic and sensitive a commentator as George Grant has misleadingly reinforced the prejudice. In conversation with the Canadian writer and broadcaster, David Cayley, Grant observed that there have been two traditions within Christianity. One he called the positive tradition, defining it as moving to God "through the world," and associating it with Aristotle; the other he called the negative tradition, identifying it with Platonism and defining it as moving to God "by negating the world."[11] He then asserted that "certainly Simone Weil is on the side of the negative tradition." Though what Grant seems to want to say here about Weil is correct, namely, that the contradiction be-

tween the perfection of God and the affliction of the world lies at the root of
her mysticism, nevertheless we are convinced that Weil herself would have rejected his particular way of saying it. Material reality is comprehensively to be
identified with the wisdom and goodness, the love, of God. God comes to us,
and draws us to himself so that we come to him, in and through the world. Furthermore, Weil is sure that her account is consistent with that of Plato. In other
words, she and Plato are passionately committed to what Grant calls "the positive tradition," which we prefer to call "the affirmative way." The phrase is borrowed from Charles Williams in his reflections on Dante's *Divine Comedy*.[12]
Williams notes that those who, like Dante, take the affirmative way know that it
includes the strictest discipline and a profound dimension of negation. Dante
comes to Paradise through his love for the creature, Beatrice. Through her he
is drawn into the presence of God. But true affirmation of God's creature, and
thereby of God, is reached by Dante only through his arduous journey of purgation through Hell and Purgatory. Similarly, for Weil, the godly affirmation of
created, material reality is achieved through the costly negation of the deceptions
that assault us both from within and from without. Affirmation includes negation, but it is not the negation of matter as such. Rather created matter is the
means by which God reveals himself.

Revelation is really just another word for love, the love of God manifest in
a particularly remarkable way in Christ but manifest also in and through all of
created reality. "This Love, which is God himself, acts, since he is God, but he
acts only so far as he obtains consent. It is thus that he acts upon the souls of
men" (*IC* 118). We should take particular note of this point in contrast to those
who say that Plato's God does not act. What Plato and Weil rule out is any suggestion that God's acting is by force, by might, by compulsion. Plato's God, according to Weil, is the God whose way of acting is most profoundly revealed in
Christ, above all, in the crucified Christ.

That creation is revelatory is but another way of describing its essentially
sacramental character. God manifests himself in and through the universe, as
an artist in his work. He is no more to be identified with the universe than the
artist is to be identified with his creations. Weil is equally opposed to any suggestion that the supernatural love of the natural implies a lessening of the
reality and worth of the natural. This again is the typical criticism of what is
taken to be Plato's dualist bias against the visible in favor of the invisible. Weil
confronts this criticism head-on in her treatment of the famous cave analogy in
Plato's *Republic*. Yes, wisdom is found by escaping from the unreality of life in

the cave and being carried "beyond space, and beyond the world, to God" (*IC* 134). But this escape from unreality, this being carried beyond the world, she insists, neither assumes nor implies a contrast between the relative unreality of this world and the perfect reality of God. Rather it is a contrast between true and false perspectives on the same reality with a view to "escap[ing] from the errors of a false perspective" (*IC* 134). Weil writes in a terse and brilliant countering of the traditional dualist position: "The unreality of things, which Plato so powerfully depicts in the metaphor of the cave, has no connection with the things as such; the things in themselves have the fullness of reality in that they exist. It is a question of things as the object for love" (*IC* 134).

The Platonic Christian's quarrel is not with those who wish to safeguard the inherent worth and significance of the world in which we live. Rather it is with those who would define that inherent worth in terms of some ulterior purpose, some end that we humans bring to the world and in terms of which the world, or any particular part of it, is defined. Purpose and worth belong to the world and to everything within it including human beings before ever we have anything to do with it. We are under an obligation consistently to attend to, discern, and honor that God-given purpose. That is what Plato and Weil mean by loving the world: intellectual and affective attention to it simply for *what* it is and for the fact *that* it is. Such discerning love for the created order in general and for the particular beings within it, both human and other, permits and invites the world, as a whole and in its parts, to disclose its intrinsic worth and meaning to us, so that we in turn will attempt to act *with* or *on behalf of* any being only on the basis of having first come to an appreciation *of* that being and the various relationships, human or other, within which it is set.

This means that our response to created things must undergo as profound a transformation as our response to God, and in the same direction. No longer defining them on our terms and for our own ends, we must attend to them on their own terms, according to their God-given integrity and purpose. "God," she writes, "has entrusted to every human being the function of treating all creatures in the same way as God" (*FLN* 339). Immediately preceding and following these words are two quotations from the Gospels regarding Christian discipleship as stewardship in a master's household. The created universe is God's household and God's "goods"; it has been entrusted into the care of humanity. That we should treat it "as God" implies a humility and respect toward the world bordering on worship: the discerning delight, the appreciative contemplation that is the hallmark of Weil's epistemology.

In another passage Weil applies this same way of perceiving and knowing God and the world specifically to other human beings. Again, it is a willingness to appreciate the sheer facticity of an other, to take delight in, and to acknowledge the infinite worth of every fellow human being simply on account of their being alive, that is to inform and define all subsequent aspects of our relation to them. "It is a weakness to seek from those we love, or to wish to give them, any other comfort than is given by works of art, which help us by the simple fact that they *exist*. To love, and to be loved, simply makes one another's existence more concrete, more constantly present to the mind" (*FLN* 47). The comparison of another person to a work of art corresponds to the comparison of created reality to God. God and the work of art are intrinsically worthy of our attention.

Obligation to Act Politically

We have argued thus far that Simone Weil's ontology was sacramental and her epistemology world-affirmative. It remains for us to articulate the political implications of her approach. It has often been suggested that Weil moved from the political activism of an early Marxist phase to a political withdrawal that characterized her Platonist-Christian period. As theoretically plausible as such a schematization might appear, its truth is contradicted by the facts of her life and the writings of her final years. Her unconditional offer of service to General De Gaulle in the interests of the rebuilding of postwar France and her writing of *The Need for Roots* as a programmatic treatise for that work of reconstruction, together with the extreme asceticism of the last months of her life for the sake of complete identification with her compatriots in war-ravaged France, testify to her continuing engagement with and dedication to political involvement, critique, and reconstruction.

At the end of her life Weil was engaged in developing what might be called a metapolitics. As such, it is distinguishable from Weil's practical political proposals as articulated, for example, in *The Need for Roots*. Her metapolitical commitments may be taken to have a certain permanence, and are foundationally constitutive of her particular, practical, political commitments. Weil believed that the shape of practical political action is dependent on the context in which that action is to take place. Historical situations are by definition "unprecedented" (*NR* 181). Not even Plato could provide her with the particulars of the political reconstruction of postwar France.[13] Nevertheless, her particular proposals are informed by certain metapolitical convictions that transcend historical particularities, that Weil would wish should inform political action always and everywhere. These convictions require an engagement with the world rather than a withdrawal from it. That engagement will be characterized by obedience, valor, and love.

Authentic political action will always be obedient action. Its character as obedience is seen first in the fact that political involvement is an obligation that is given in and with the Platonic-Christian vision of God and of the eternal realities of truth, goodness, and beauty. In the opening petition of the Lord's Prayer Weil says that we "[tear] our desire away from time in order to fix it upon eternity, thereby transforming [our desire]" (WG 138). The transformation of our desire is necessary because otherwise we remain addicted to the beast of public opinion and prestige. Only eternity can transform that. But the course of events in time is not left behind forever. On the contrary, we return with our desire for eternity "in order to apply it once more to time" (WG 138). We pray for, and are intent on, nothing less than "the infallible and eternal conformity of everything in time with the will of God" (WG 138).

This movement from time to eternity and back to time, with its accompanying sense of obligation with respect to the course of events in time, is present also in Plato. As we have seen, wisdom is gained through leaving the cave of false perspectives in which we see and know things only superficially, according to their capacity to satisfy our own appetites and passions, and learn instead to see and know things as they are, on their own terms and according to their intrinsic purposes, or which is to say the same thing, know this world "in its relationship to eternity" (LOP 220). Such true knowledge of the world brings with it an inescapable political obligation: in Plato's terms, "the wise have to return to the cave, and act there" (LOP 221). The obligatory character of this political action is borne out by the fact that it is not something that the wise person seeks or wants. At the same time, only those who cannot refuse the obligation to ensure the satisfaction of the essential bodily and psychic needs of every human person may be entrusted with political and social power.[14]

Weil, like Plato, is deeply pessimistic in her assessment of society as something ordered *against* those who pursue wisdom and justice, a pessimism that she thinks is justified and borne out by the state executions of Socrates and Christ. It is this context of inevitable hostility that gives rise to the need for valor, the second outstanding feature of authentic political engagement. Valor (other terms Weil uses are *courage* and *moral stamina*) is required of anyone who has consented to the claims of justice in the face of the oppressive mediocrity and aggressive forcefulness of the great beast that is human society. Over against the politics of justice the politics of the beast is informed by the effort to satisfy the mediocre and often contrived needs and pleasures to which the majority of people have succumbed.

In a memorable passage Weil draws a provocative contrast between Marxists and Christians with respect to what she calls the "self-awareness" that is the necessary condition for the courage required to resist the beast. Rigorous, uncompromising analysis of contemporary society along the perceptive lines laid down by Marx must go hand-in-hand with a correspondingly rigorous self-awareness on the part of the would-be analyst, something Marxists, she insists, all too often shy away from.[15] Human self-awareness must take cognizance of eternity. But, again exploding the dualist caricature, Weil is convinced that supernatural justice and the vision of society granted from above are not in conflict with natural justice and happiness.[16] The problem is that natural justice pursued on its own, apart from the vision of eternity and an appreciation of its sacramental mediation by the natural, does not in itself have the power to sustain itself. Initially it will stimulate the will to moral action. But sooner or later, and inevitably, "fatigue forces [one] to find illusion" (IC 181). Turning from the demanding pursuit of natural justice and happiness to which the soul aspires, human beings construct personal and societal goals that are more easily realizable, and only indirectly or not at all connected to justice. Justice, as an absolute and objective end having its own integrity, is perverted through being reduced to a manipulable instrument for the satisfaction of the private interests of individuals and special interest groups intent on their right to self-realization on their own terms. In the face of the might of necessity, the wiles of the beast, fatigue, and the slide into mediocrity, the vision of eternity sustains the valor of the just person by disclosing the fact that natural justice is the image of eternal justice, and natural happiness, the image of the eternal *telos* that belongs essentially to human nature.

The link between the vision of eternity and persistence in doing justice is faith. Specifically, the vision of eternity instills a certainty about the obligations of justice. The just person persists in doing justice because of that certainty. But here Weil identifies a paradox. Only faith in the certainty of the obligations of justice (and conduct informed by that faith) discloses or achieves the certainty that justifies that faith.[17] Such faith is not a way out of the world but a way through the world in the light of eternity.

Weil's third metapolitical commitment is to political action, the pursuit of justice, as love. This love expresses itself in three ways: as consent, as madness, and as martyrdom. Consent to necessity derives from the God's-eye perspective on necessity as obedience. While seeming to commit Weil to an essentially conservative political agenda, this is not the case, because a particular society's conception of the world and corresponding ordering of itself may be, indeed probably is, other than the way the world actually is. Societies serve the will of the great beast. Conservatism, then, when it is nothing more than maintenance of the status quo, serves not God and the obligations of justice but the will of the great beast.

But radicalism, when it is the will to power by those not served by the status quo, also only serves the great beast because it neglects patient attention to the God-given character of the world and continues to reconstruct society according to an account of political and social order defined by power, competitive rights, and acts of will. Over against such revolutionary reconstruction stands consent as discernment, patient attention to the world until it discloses its true character and purpose, so that one acts *for* something or someone only on the basis of having first come to an appreciation *of* that something or someone. Justice as love, then, entails consent to necessity.

Weil says, secondly and provocatively, that justice that is rooted in loving consent is, or at least appears to be, madness. Plato's "just man" is perceived by his contemporaries, not as the just person that he is, but as the contradiction of justice (*IC* 137 f.). Christ was believed to be out of his mind and possessed of the devil. For Weil, the supreme act of justice is the passion of Christ. In obedience to the Father, Christ consented to be mocked, scourged, humiliated, and crucified; or, what for Weil is the same thing, he consented to the brute force of necessity. "This consent is madness" (*IC* 182).[18] Weil in turn describes a human person's consent to the obligations of justice in the world—entailing as it does consent to necessity, perceptive attention to the God-given order of the world, and almost universal misunderstanding and contempt—as "man's own particular madness" that corresponds to the madness of Christ (*IC* 182).

The third way that the pursuit of justice as love expresses itself is martyrdom. As Christ's madness entailed a kind of martyrdom, so too does the madness of the just person. A favorite passage of Plato for Weil is the description of the just man and in particular of his end: "the just man shall be whipped, given over to torture, to chains, his eyes shall be burnt out and, at last, having been inflicted with all possible sufferings, he shall be hanged" (*IC* 138, quoting *Rep.* 361e in her own translation).

Weil's rejection of dualism ascribed to her teacher is perhaps nowhere clearer than in her comments on Plato's just man. Plato, she says, knew that the reproduction of just people in the world could never be achieved by a mere ideal. Citing at length passages from the *Timaeus*, the *Theaetetus*, the *Phaedrus*, the *Symposium*, and above all the *Republic*, she demonstrates that for Plato "the ideal model for relatively just men can only be a perfectly just man"; never a mere "abstraction" (*IC* 141). It is the mystical genius of Plato that he "refused to demonstrate that such a thing [the perfectly just man] could be possible" while at the same time being certain of its reality because "the perfect is more real than the imperfect" (*IC* 141). Being real, the perfectly just man "must have an earthly existence at a certain point in space, and at a certain moment of time. . . . There is no other reality for a man" (*IC* 140 f.).

The climax of this explosion of the dualist caricature is one of the most re-markable and provocative passages in all of Weil's corpus. She is sure that Plato anticipated nothing less than the eternal God enfleshed on earth as the actuali-zation of the perfectly just man: in her own words, Plato "demonstrates the idea of divine incarnation more clearly than any other Greek text" (*IC* 140). She confirms this assertion with the following extraordinary citation from Plato: "in order that a man 'in no way differs from justice itself . . . divine Justice, from be-yond the skies, must descend upon earth'" (*IC* 140). It need hardly be added that Weil made the closest possible connection between what she perceived to be Plato's insistence on the historical particularity of the perfectly just man and the New Testament witness to Jesus Christ.

Conclusion

A careful reading of Weil's corpus, especially texts from the years following her experiences of Christ in 1937, does not confirm the all too common assumption that her Christian Platonism is conducive to "otherwordly mysticism." On the contrary, what Weil appropriates from Plato and the Gospels is what we have chosen to call Christian materialism. Her conversion to Christianity only deep-ened her determination to reject every hint of a dualism that privileged the spiri-tual at the expense of and in retreat from the material. She was allergic to that dualism. So too, she insisted, was Plato. She consistently emphasized the particularity and materiality of his thought. Her quarrel was never with those who sought to safeguard the inherent worth and significance of the world in which we live. Rather it was with those who would define that inherent worth in terms of some ulterior purpose, some end that we humans bring to the world and in terms of which the world or any part of it is defined. Purpose and worth belong to the world long before we have anything to do with it. The world, material reality, the order of necessity, is comprehensively to be identified with the wisdom and goodness, the love of God.

That identification is finally mysterious, even paradoxical. It cannot be reduced to a philosophical system (*IC* 85) or to a set of foundational principles or to ideological commitments; it constitutes the vision and vocation of the true mystic: a way of seeing marked by passionate attention to what has been given to see; a being called which lays one under the strictest obligation and the most absolute allegiance. Vision and vocation are inextricably bound up with one another. That which is seen issues the call, while obedience to the call renders what is seen ever more luminous.

But is this mystically discerned identification a mysterious paradox or sheer confusion? Can Weil's faith in the sacramental beauty of the world as an "incarnation of God" (*FLN* 341) be reconciled with her profound respect for Plato's recognition of the absolute sovereignty of might "in all of nature, including the natural part of the human soul, with all the thought and all the feelings the soul contains," as "an absolutely detestable thing" (*IC* 116). The force of mechanical necessity is *the* dominant principle in the universe. It threatens the mystic with the agonizingly total eclipse of the beauty and perfection of God. How then can the same universe be sacramentally beautiful, so that she can write of "Christ's tender smile for us coming through matter" and "God dwelling in our souls and present in the universe" (*WG* 97)? There is no easy answer, but we must begin by acknowledging that though it is true in more than one passage that Weil agrees with Plato that the comprehensive and sovereign rule of force in all of nature is absolutely detestable, the weight of her argument, discernible in the rest of her writings, relativizes the absoluteness of the offensiveness of necessity, both for her and for Plato as she reads him.

This gives rise to a second more general question, whether Weil's Christian materialism has served to deepen and enrich her reading of Plato, or has compromised it by introducing material that is other than and even alien to the actual content of Plato's texts. She was quite sure that she had not read extraneous matter into her master's work. In the end we must leave that question to Plato scholars to judge whether she was right. But we may observe that she has for company numerous patristic authors who, similarly impressed by the correspondence between Plato and the Gospels, were convinced that Plato must have met and been influenced by Moses, or that a common source lay behind both Plato and the Bible, most notoriously, the writings of Hermes Trismegistis. Though the attempted explanations have been shown to be groundless, it is the discernment of a remarkable correspondence between Plato and the New Testament by so many early Christian writers that is worthy of note. Perhaps they, and Weil with them, discerned that correspondence because it is actually there to be discerned.

Notes

1. Leslie Paul Thiele, *Martin Heidegger and Postmodern Politics* (Princeton: Princeton University Press, 1995), 225.

2. Martin Heidegger, *Nietzsche. Volume I: The Will to Power as Art* (San Francisco: Harper & Row, 1979), 201.

3. Weil was drawn to those whom she called mystics. Within Christianity they were an exceptional minority who alone had preserved "the truly Christian inspiration" (*NR* 265). But mystics were not confined to the Christian tradition. Transcending the barriers of race and religion, "mystical truth is one," so that we should not be surprised by, for example, "the close analogy between Plato and St. John of the Cross" (*FLN* 243). "What is Plato?" Weil once asked herself, and answered, "A mystic," "an authentic mystic and even the father of Occidental mysticism" (*IC* 74, 76).

4. She wrote to her friend Maurice Schumann: "I feel an ever increasing sense of devastation, both in my intellect and in the centre of my heart, at my inability to think with truth at the same time about the affliction of men, the perfection of God, and the link between the two" (*SL* 128).

5. "The universe we inhabit is a network of geometrical relations, and . . . it is to geometrical necessity that we are in fact bound" (*NR* 66).

6. And the spectacle is ugly. Weil vividly depicts it in terms of "the well-known phenomenon which makes hens rush upon one of their number if it is wounded, attacking and pecking it" (*WG* 42). Human beings are similarly determined: "All men bear this animal nature within them. It determines their attitude towards their fellows, with or without their knowledge and consent. . . . This mechanical necessity holds all men in its grip at every moment" (*WG* 42). Weil believed that Homer had described this mechanical necessity with consummate skill in the *Iliad*, thereby bequeathing to ancient Greece its "innate grandeur" (*IC* 116). That grandeur consisted not only in their uncompromising

recognition of "might as an absolutely sovereign thing in all of nature, including the natural part of the human soul, with all the thoughts and all the feelings the soul contains," but also in their depiction of it as "an absolutely detestable thing" (*IC* 116).

7. The same theme is to be found in the Hebrew Scriptures. "The heavens are telling the glory of God; and the firmament proclaims his handiwork. Day to day pours forth speech, and night to night declares knowledge. There is no speech, nor are there words; their voice is not heard; yet their voice goes out through all the earth, and their words to the end of the world" (Psalm 19.1 ff.). "All people who were ignorant of God were foolish by nature; and they were unable from the good things that are seen to know the one who exists, nor did they recognize the artisan while paying heed to his works. . . . From the greatness and beauty of created things comes a corresponding perception of their Creator" (Wisdom 13.1, 5).

8. "Christianity has almost lost the beauty of the world" (*FLN* 83).

9. "There is in this conception no hint of pantheism" (*IC* 103).

10. Weil speaks of the universe, albeit with particular and even exclusive reference to its beauty, as "the body of the Word" (*FLN* 83). And she writes, "[God's] soul allows it to be perceived by us through our sense of beauty, as an infant finds in its mother's smile, in an inflection of her voice, the revelation of the love of which itself is the object" (*IC* 103).

11. George Grant, in David Cayley, *George Grant in Conversation* (Concord: Anansi, 1995), 177.

12. Charles Williams, *The Figure of Beatrice* (London: Faber and Faber, 1943), 63 f.

13. "If Plato, for example, had devised a general solution . . . we should require to do more than make a study of his solution in order to get ourselves out of the quandary; . . . even if we knew how an inspiration can be breathed into a country, we should still not know how to proceed in the case of France" (*NR* 181).

14. "All forms of power are to be entrusted, so far as possible, to people who effectively consent to be bound by the obligation towards all human beings which lies upon everyone, and who understand the obligation" (*SE* 223). Weil never explains how it might come about that power in a society would rest with those whose consent to obligation qualifies them to hold it.

15. Marxists will not "look at themselves in the mirror" because it "would be too painful an operation"; only "the specifically Christian virtues . . . are able to supply the necessary courage" (*NR* 63).

16. "The experience of, and desire for, supernatural joys do not destroy the soul's aspiration to natural happiness, they confer a fullness and a significance upon it" (*IC* 180).

17. "Certainties of this kind are experimental. But if we do not believe in them before experiencing them, if at least we do not behave as though we believed in them, we shall never have the experience which leads to such certainties. There is a kind of contradiction here. Above a given level this is the case with all useful knowledge concerning spiritual progress. If we do not regulate our conduct by it before having proved it, if we

do not hold onto it for a long time only by faith, a faith at first stormy and without light, we shall never transform it into certainty. Faith is the indispensable condition" (WG 54).

18. Christ's consent corresponds to the madness of the consent of the Father in his creation of the world. Weil understands the act of creation to have entailed God's withdrawing of himself, permitting "what is other than himself" to come into being, thereby "consenting to the possibility of being destroyed." That possibility was realized in the crucifixion of Christ. As such, creation "constitutes God's own madness" (IC 182 f.).

CHAPTER 6

Simone Weil and the Divine Poetry of Mathematics

VANCE G. MORGAN

> Poetry; passing through words into silence, into the nameless. Mathematics; passing through forms into the formless.
>
> Simone Weil, *Notebooks*

Simone Weil frequently makes claims about mathematics and science that are very odd, so odd that a reader as astute as Rush Rhees says that in the face of such claims, "I have just to back away and sit down."[1] For instance, Rhees writes, "Simone Weil could see in mathematical (geometrical) ratios a representation of the Incarnation and of the role of Christ as Mediator. And it is clear that she does not think of this as a far-fetched representation."[2] Further:

> She sees in geometry what most of us do not and cannot see there, especially in the idea of arithmetic proportion. . . . She is not thinking of a

mean proportional as an abstract symbol which happens to present certain analogies, or just happens to be suitable as a symbol. She is taking it as involving an idea which *is* the idea of mediation between God and his creation or creatures.[3]

Ultimately, Rhees suggests, Weil's insights concerning mathematics are "an expression of something which could not be understood except by someone who had known the grace of God as she did. It needs not only religious faith, but a kind of religious insight, in order to understand the phrases or the figures or the grammar of what she writes."[4]

If what Rhees says is true, I am undoubtedly not up to the task I have set for myself here. Still, it is important to investigate what Weil might have had in mind when in a letter to her brother she asks, "I wonder how many mathematicians today regard mathematics as a method for purifying the soul and 'imitating God?'" (*SL* 118). Not many, I would venture to guess. My aim is to lay the groundwork, at least, for an understanding of Weil's claim that "mathematics . . . is a symbolical mirror of supernatural truths" (*NR* 280) and an "image of the mysteries of faith" (*FLN* 90).

I

> Geometry . . . is really a manifest assimilation to one another of numbers which are naturally dissimilar, effected by reference to plane areas. Now to a man who can comprehend this, it will be plain that this is no mere feat of human skill, but a miracle of God's contrivance.
>
> Plato, *Epinomis*

"With the Greeks, the science of nature was itself an art, with the world for material and the imagination for instrument" (*NB* 27). This notebook observation is a characteristic expression by Simone Weil of what she considered the unique energy behind Greek science. Whereas contemporary science is increasingly concerned with technology, utility, and mastery of nature, the aim of Greek science was "to conceive more and more clearly an identity of structure between the human mind and the universe" (*SL* 117). Science conceived in this way is a spiritual exercise, as Weil writes in a letter to her brother, André, in early 1940: "In the eyes of the Greeks, the very principle of the soul's salvation was measure, balance, proportion, harmony; because desire is always unmeasured and boundless. Therefore, to conceive the universe as an equilibrium and a harmony is to make it like a mirror of salvation" (*SL* 125). In Greek thought, "science, art and religion are connected together through the notion of *order of the world*" (*NB* 248); equilibrium, harmony, and proportion were central, because in such relationships are revealed divine truths. Thus "they searched everywhere—in the regular recurrence of the stars, in sound, in equilibrium, in floating bodies—for proportions in order to love God" (*SN* 21).

Thus mathematics, particularly geometry, also possessed spiritual importance in Greek thought.

> Purity of soul was their one concern; to "imitate God" was the secret of it; the imitation of God was assisted by the study of mathematics, in so far as one conceived the universe to be subject to mathematical laws, which made the geometer an imitator of the supreme lawgiver. (*SL* 117)

Although Weil's conception of mathematics is clearly Platonic, she frequently identifies the Pythagoreans as a common source of the mathematical vision that she shares with Plato. Scattered throughout her notebooks and various essays are references to shadowy figures such as Pythagoras, Philolaus, Archimedes, and Eudoxus, sources of cryptic claims including, "All is number," "Justice is a number to the second power," "God is ever a geometer," and Plato's famous "None enters here unless he is a geometer." It is in the geometrical discoveries of the Pythagoreans, for whom "mathematical truth was originally theological" (*FLN* 85) that Weil finds a profoundly prophetic source rooted in "a supernatural revelation" (*SN* 142). To understand how Weil can viably claim that these early, mystic mathematicians "saw in geometry the image of the Incarnation" (*NB* 441), it is necessary to consider some of the fundamental Pythagorean notions and how they are expressed in geometry.

In general, the Pythagoreans considered pure mathematics as simultaneously a formal calculus and discipline, a theory of nature and natural events, and a religious mystical doctrine. The following fragments from Philolaus, quoted by Weil in various writings, state the Pythagorean doctrines most important to my considerations here.

> The order of the world and of things contained therein has been brought into harmony starting from that which limits and from that which is unlimited.

> All that is known involves number. For without number nothing can be thought or known.

> Unity is the principle of everything.

> Harmony is the unification of what was mixture. It is the common thought of what is separately thought. (*IC* 153–54)

Number, limit, unity, harmony, equilibrium, balance—these are some of the foundational elements of Pythagorean thought. If tradition is to be trusted, the Pythagoreans not only established arithmetic as a branch of philosophy; they made it the basis of a unification of all aspects of the world around them. Numbers were represented by lines, each expressed as a natural number according to the ratio (*logos*) it has to another line when both have a common measure. A fraction was looked upon not as a single entity but as a ratio or relationship between two whole numbers.

Weil writes, "The Pythagoreans considered all created things as having each a number as its symbol. . . . [A]mong these numbers, some have a particular bond with unity" (*IC* 159). This bond is proportion, or harmony, established between one and another number by a "mean proportional," as, for instance, 3 is the mean proportional between 1 and 9 in the relationship $1/3 = 3/9$. For the Pythagoreans, "harmony is defined . . . as the unity of contraries" (*IC* 95), contraries such as 1 and a number that is not 1 (9). The numbers that have a "special bond with unity" are the numbers "which are of the second power or square," numbers such as 4, 9, and 16, that can be placed in proportion with unity with their square root as the mean proportional.

Even at this rudimentary level, the notion of harmony between contraries takes on great significance. The Pythagorean dictum "Justice is a number to the second power" (*IC* 159) sounds less ridiculous when it is seen that the clearest mathematical example of mediation between contraries is the relationship of x^2 to 1 by the mediating activity of x, as illustrated by the example in the previous paragraph where x equals 3. Here, Weil argues, there are intimations of some-

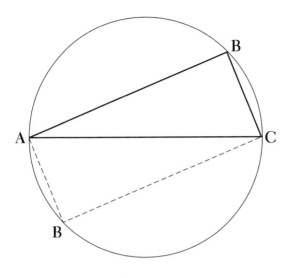

Figure 1

thing greater than mere numbers, since "the key . . . is the idea of a mean proportional and of mediation in the *theological* sense, the first being the image of
the second. It is known that among the Pythagoreans one is the symbol of God"
(*IC* 159). As she suggests in a notebook entry, "Justice is a number raised to the
second power. The just man is the one between whom and God mediation is
possible" (*NB* 603). These intimations can be brought into sharper focus by
considering some of the foundational Pythagorean discoveries in geometry.

   One of the great discoveries of the Pythagoreans was that the circle is the
locus of the apices of the right-angled triangles having the same hypotenuse.
According to tradition, this momentous discovery prompted Pythagoras to sacrifice a bull (some say one hundred bulls) and celebrate with a religious feast.
To illustrate, consider a circle with diameter AC (Fig. 1). The Pythagorean discovery shows that if one specifies a point B anywhere on the circumference of
the circle and draws lines AB and BC, resulting triangle ABC will always be a
right-angled triangle, with AC as its hypotenuse. In other words, the apex of
any right-angled triangle that can be constructed with hypotenuse AC will fall
on the circumference of the circle with diameter AC. Given the related theorem
bearing Pythagoras's name that tells us that the area of a square constructed on

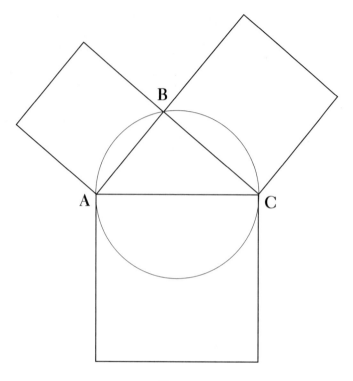

Figure 2

AC will be equal to the sum of the areas of squares constructed on AB and BC ($AC^2 = AB^2 + BC^2$) (Fig. 2), a striking relationship among lines, triangles, squares, and circles is revealed.

These geometrical properties can be used to address what turned out to be an earth-shattering crisis in the Pythagorean worldview, a crisis in which Weil finds remarkable foreshadowings of the Christian doctrines of the Incarnation and Passion. It was a fundamental tenet of early Pythagoreanism that the essences of all things, in geometry as well as in the practical and theoretical affairs of human beings, are explainable in terms of the intrinsic properties of whole numbers or their ratios; as Philolaus stated, "All that is known involves number" (*IC* 153). This faith in whole numbers, however, was demolished by the discovery that in geometry itself the whole numbers and their ratios are inadequate to account for even the simplest geometrical proportions. For in-

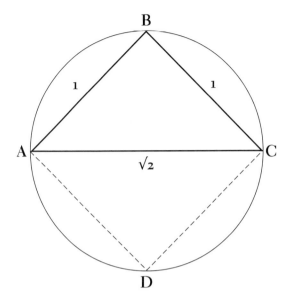

Figure 3

stance, the hypotenuse and the side of an isosceles right-angled triangle do not have a common measure, no matter how small the unit of measure chosen: they are *incommensurable*. To illustrate by returning to our figure, if AB = BC, for instance, then the relationship of either AB or BC to hypotenuse AC is 1/$\sqrt{2}$ (Fig. 3). In other words, the side and the hypotenuse are incommensurable because they do not have a ratio such as a whole number has to a whole number; they have no lowest common denominator. This raises havoc with mathematical theorems involving proportions and, Weil argues, with far more.

Recall Weil's discussion of the special relationship of the numbers such as 4, 9, and 16 to unity. As it turns out, these numbers are far less common than those that cannot be so linked. This, Weil believes, is a reflection of the human condition itself.

If one considers whole numbers, one sees they are of two sorts; those that are linked to unity by a mean proportional, such as 4, 9, 16 on the one hand, and on the other hand all the others. If the first are an image of perfect justice, as the Pythagoreans say, we resemble the others, we who are in sin. (*IC* 161)

Justice is that between which and God there is naturally mediation. On the other hand, there is not naturally mediation between sinners and God (they are numbers "not naturally similar"), just as there is not between unity and numbers other than square. (SN 144)

If, as the Pythagoreans believed, "all is number," then the fact that the most foundational relationships cannot be described in terms of whole numbers is a truly world-shattering revelation.

Among the Pythagoreans the words *arithmos* and *logos* were synonyms. They called the irrational relationships *logoi alogoi*. To bind those numbers which are not square to unity requires a mediation which comes from outside, from a domain foreign to number which can only fulfill this function at the price of a contradiction. This mediation between unity and number is in appearance something inferior to number, something indeterminate. A *logoi alogoi* is a scandal, an absurdity, a thing contrary to nature. (*IC* 162)

In Weil's estimation, the genius of Greek geometry lies in the possibility that it was motivated by precisely the search for mediation that would resolve this scandal.

Was it by force of so intense a search for a mediation of these wretched numbers that the Greeks discovered geometry? . . . Whether or not geometry had since its first origin been a search for mediation, it offered this marvel of a mediation for the numbers which were naturally deprived of it. (*IC* 161–62)

Geometry is the science of the search for the proportional means by way of the incommensurable proportion. (SN 142)

One of the most profound discoveries of Greek mathematics, one attributed to Eudoxus, is that the mediation of "these wretched numbers" can be achieved by, as Eric O. Springsted writes, "extending the sense of *logos* to cover the relative magnitude of lines," thus including "the natural numbers and the irrationals in the one real number system. A *logos alogos* is not definitely ex-

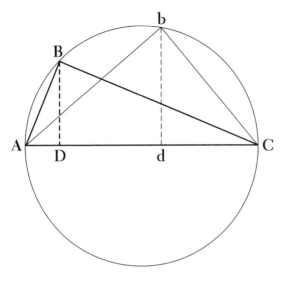

Figure 4

pressible . . . but it is a perfectly rigorous relation between incommensurate numbers."[5] Furthermore, the mean proportional between any two magnitudes, commensurate or incommensurate, can be constructed via a simple geometrical operation. Returning to our right-angled triangle inscribed in a circle (Fig. 4), drop a perpendicular from apex B to point D on the hypotenuse of the triangle (AC). If point B is placed in motion around the circumference of the circle, obviously the lengths BD, AD, and DC will be constantly changing. Eudoxus's discovery is represented by the remarkable fact that BD is always a mean proportional between AD and DC. Regardless of whether AD and DC are commensurate or incommensurate, BD always serves as the mean proportional. As Weil describes in a notebook entry, "through the destination reserved for plane figures—which is a supernatural marvel—there is mediation between unity and any number whatever" (NB 603).

It is this discovery of a geometrical solution to the problem of the mean proportional between incommensurables that, arguably, Weil finds the most profound in all of Greek mathematics: "The discovery of incommensurables, so far from being a defeat for the Pythagoreans as is so naively believed, was their most wonderful triumph" (SN 142), a triumph that is the source of Plato's definition of geometry as "a manifest assimilation to one another of numbers which are naturally dissimilar, effected by reference to plane areas" (*Epinomis* 990d). It is this discovery that serves as a bridge between mathematics per se and larger applications, for, "since it was possible in this way to equalize the ratios in the case of two completely different pairs of magnitudes, one could hope to be able also to apply the notion of ratio to psychological and spiritual matters" (*NB* 161). As Weil writes elsewhere, "The notion of real number, arrived at by the mediation between any number and unity . . . forces the mind to deal in exact terms with those relationships which it is incapable of representing to itself. Here is an admirable introduction to the mysteries of faith" (*IC* 161).

II

There are a few texts which indicate with certainty that Greek geometry arose out of religious thought; and this thought appears to resemble Christianity almost to the point of identity.

Simone Weil, *Seventy Letters*

In several important documents, Weil reflects on some of the implications of Eudoxus's discovery, reflections that serve as entrance into consideration of what she perceives as a direct connection between Greek geometry and Christianity. With reference to figure 4,

The alternating movement of the point [D] which comes and goes upon the diameter enclosed by the circle, is the image of all becoming here below. . . . This becoming is indeed the projection of divine life upon earth. As the circle encloses the moving point upon the diameter, God assigns a term to all the becomings of this world. . . . The segment [BD] on the right angle which joins the point of the circle to its projection upon the diameter [AC] is, in the figure, an intermediary between the circle and the diameter. . . . [I]t is, like the mean proportional, the mediation between the two parts of the diameter [AD and DC] which are on either side of the point [D]. This is the image of the Word. (*IC* 192)

The Word, the *Logos*, is the mediator both in the triangle and in the universe of contraries in need of mediation. "If we say that harmony, which is the union of opposites, is the same thing as proportion, which is the proportional mean, then we have exactly the idea of the Mediation of the Word" (*NB* 587). Indeed, Weil writes that "instead of Word, one should always translate *Logos* as Mediation" (*SN* 139), suggesting that the most accurate translation of the first verse of the Gospel of St. John would be "In the beginning was the Mediation, and the Mediation was with God, and the Mediation was God" (*SN* 143). Mediation, proportion, and harmony provide the link between mathematics and our contact with the divine.

> In a general way, and in the widest sense, mathematics, including under this name all rigorous and pure theoretical study of necessary relationships, constitutes at once the unique knowledge of the material universe wherein we exist and the clearest reflection of divine truths. . . . It is this same mathematics which is first, before all, a sort of mystical poem composed by God himself. (*IC* 193)

In the *Gorgias*, Socrates states that "the heavens and the earth, gods and men, are bound together by fellowship and friendship, and order and temperance and justice, and for this reason they call the sum of things the 'ordered' universe" (*Gorgias* 507e). He chides Callicles, "[Y]ou pay no attention to these things[,] . . . you are unaware that geometric equality is of great importance among gods and men alike, for you neglect geometry" (*Gorgias* 508a). This, Weil believes, provides a prophetic link to Christianity that is impossible to mistake, a link that raises pure mathematics and geometry from the "interesting" to the "sacramental."

> By inscribing over the door of this school "Let no one enter who is not a geometer," Plato was doubtless affirming in the form of an enigma, and therefore as a pun, the truth which the Christ expressed in the saying, "No one cometh unto the Father except by me." The other Platonic equation, "God is a perpetual geometer," obviously has a double sense and refers at the same time to the order of the world and to the mediatory function of the Word. To sum up, the appearance of geometry in Greece is the most dazzling of all the prophecies which foretold the Christ. (*IC* 171)

In her essay "The Pythagorean Doctrine," Weil identifies at least five ways in which the Pythagorean doctrine "Friendship is an equality made of harmony" (*IC* 166) can instruct us concerning the internal relations of the Godhead, the communion of God and human beings, and the relationships of human beings with each other, "provided that the Pythagorean sense of the word harmony is taken into account" (*IC* 166). Let us consider Weil's contention that contemplation of geometrical proportion and harmony can provide insights into the fourth of the relationships she discusses, that of justice and friendship between human beings.

Recalling that for the Pythagoreans, harmony and proportion are synonyms, reflecting the unity of contraries, Weil writes:

> The Pythagorean definition of friendship, applied to God and to man, makes mediation appear as being essentially love, and love as being essentially the mediator. . . . The same definition applies also to friendship between men, although there is more difficulty in this since as Philolaus said: "Things of the same species, of the same root, and of the same station, have no need of harmony." (*IC* 172)

The Pythagorean notion of friendship as an equality made of harmony (a union of opposites) applies to human interaction because "although they [humans] are in fact of the same species, of the same root, of the same rank, they are not so in their thought" (*IC* 172). In human relationships such as justice and friendship, the contrariety that requires mediation, proportionality, and harmony is the opposition between the "I," whether individual or collective, and every other human being. In each person, "I" is "the center of the world" — for the most part, "everyone disposes of others as he disposes of inert things, either in fact, if he has the power, or in thought" (*IC* 173). Hence it would appear that in order for the supernatural friendship of justice to occur, "one must renounce . . . this illusory power which God has accorded us, to think in the first person" (*IC* 174).

According to Weil, the key factor in mediating between the "I" and the "other" is mutual *consent*; she notes in her essay "Are We Struggling for Justice" that "the Greeks defined justice admirably as mutual consent," and quotes the passage from the *Symposium* in which Plato writes that "where there is agreement by mutual consent there is justice, say the laws of the royal city" (*SWW* 121). There are instances in which human beings need each others' consent and in which they are, for all practical purposes, "equal" in terms of need or power. In such cases, justice can be established between them without sacrificing the "I": "justice then occurs as a natural phenomenon" (*IC* 173). Such justice is valuable and should be sought as often as possible, but such "natural" justice "does not constitute harmony, and it is a justice without friendship" (*IC* 173). The cryptic Pythagorean notion that "justice is a number to the second power" illustrates such a situation. Just as 9 has a special bond with unity through 3, so justice can occasionally be established on a natural basis.

More often than not, however, the natural relations between human beings do not reveal equal need for consent, just as more often than not, the numbers needing mediation with unity are irrational or "wretched." To illustrate the more common dynamic between human beings, Weil draws our attention to the familiar interaction between the Melians and the Athenians described by Thucydides, an interaction that, according to Weil, "perfectly defines the natural relations between human beings" (*IC* 174). In response to the Melian call for justice and fair treatment, the Athenians, who are in a position of power, reply:

> The human mind being made as it is, the justice of a matter is examined only if there is an equal necessity on both sides. Contrarily, if one is strong and the other weak, what is possible is accomplished by the first and accepted by the second. . . . Of the gods, we believe, as of man, we certainly know, that it is a necessary law of their nature to rule wherever they can. (*IC* 174)

Just as there is no "natural" mediation between numbers that are incommensurable, so there is no natural basis for consent between human beings when there exists neither equal need nor equal power. There is no natural reason for the Athenians to seek the consent of the Melians: "it would be absurd and mad for anyone at all to impose upon himself the necessity of seeking consent where there is no power of refusal" (*SWW* 123).

Weil believes that Eudoxus's discovery of the mean proportional between incommensurates provides us with a direct picture of the only possible source of the mediation needed between human beings that are "incommensurate." Just as the mediation of "those numbers which are not square to unity requires a mediation which comes from outside, from a domain foreign to number which can only fulfil this function at the price of a contradiction" (*IC* 162), so the mediation between human incommensurates, whether the strong and the weak or the I and the Other must come from a domain or source that is "outside." The mediator must be truly other, or "divine." This is why Weil insists that ultimately "human consent is a sacred thing" (*SWW* 122), elaborating: "Supernatural justice, supernatural friendship or love, are found to be implicit in all human relationships where, without there being an equality of force or of need, there is a search for mutual consent. The desire for mutual consent is charity" (*IC* 177). It is precisely this supernatural source of mediation between contraries that is at the heart of the Christian faith. To the Athenian claim that "Of the gods, we believe, as of man, we certainly know, that it is a necessary law of their nature to rule wherever they can," Weil movingly responds that "the Christian faith is nothing but the cry affirming the contrary" (*SWW* 122).

The mediation of incommensurables on the human level requires an "abdication" of the I, an abdication modeled by the Christian doctrine of the Incarnation, according to which Christ "assumed the state of slavery. . . . He humbled himself to the point of being made obedient unto death" (*SWW* 123). Here is an example of what is truly of most value, the Divine itself, choosing voluntarily to become equal to, even lower than, what is truly lower than itself. Weil observes, however, that such an argument would hardly have been convincing to the Athenians. "These words could have been an answer to the Athenian murderers of Melos. They would have really made them laugh. And rightly so. They are absurd. They are mad" (*SWW* 123). Their absurdity and madness arises because the required mediation is impossible without an "invasion" from a domain other than the natural. "When one applies the formula "Friendship is an equality made of harmony" to men, harmony has the meaning of the unity of contraries. The contraries are myself and the other, contraries so distant that they have their unity only in God" (*IC* 175).

It is beyond the scope of this chapter to do more than sketch some of the practical signs of such a supernatural mediation between human beings. The absurdity and madness of a perpendicular invasion of a mean proportional between horizontal incommensurables, just as it transformed geometry and mathematics, can be expected to transform "the modalities of action and thought" (*SWW* 123). Weil suggests variously that "men struck by the madness of love need to see the faculty of free consent spreading throughout this world, in all forms of human life, for all human beings" (*SWW* 124) and that

[t]he madness of love draws one to discern and cherish equally, in all human milieux without exception, in all parts of the globe, the fragile earthly possibilities of beauty, of happiness, and of fulfillment; to want to preserve them all with an equally religious care, and where they are absent, to want to rekindle tenderly the smallest traces of those which have existed, the smallest seeds of those which can be born. (SWW 130)

Most simply, the ability to renounce "the power to think of everything in the first person . . . grants to a man the knowledge that other men are his fellows" (IC 175), opening the possibility of discovering that "some particular human being really exists" (SWW 124), a possibility simply and beautifully described in the following passage from "Reflections on the Right Use of School Studies with a View to the Love of God":

The love of our neighbor in all its fullness simply means being able to say to him: "What are you going through?" It is a recognition that the sufferer exists, not only as a unit in a collection, or a specimen from the social category labeled "unfortunate," but as a man, exactly like us, who was one day stamped with a special mark by affliction. For this reason it is enough, but it is indispensable, to know how to look at him in a certain way. (WG 115)

III

To restore to science as a whole, for mathematics as well as for psychology and sociology, the sense of its origin and veritable destiny as a bridge leading toward God[,] . . . that would indeed be a task worth accomplishing.

Simone Weil, *Notebooks*

Simone Weil, writing in the midst of World War II, found striking similarities between the crises of our contemporary world and that of fifth-century B.C. Greece, as she describes in "Reflections on Quantum Theory":

It is as though we had returned to the age of Protagoras and the Sophists, the age when the art of persuasion—whose modern equivalent is advertising slogans, publicity, propaganda meetings, the press, the cinema, and radio— took the place of thought and controlled the fate of cities and accomplished coups d'état. . . . Only today it is not the fate of Greece but of the entire world that is at stake. And we have no Socrates or Plato or Eudoxus, no Pythagorean tradition, and no teaching of the Mysteries. We have the Christian tradition, but it can do nothing for us unless it comes alive in us again. (SN 64)

In this final section, I place the considerations of the previous two sections into the larger framework of the crisis referred to in the above passage, a crisis that, in Weil's estimation, only a reawakening of the Greek vision of reality can address.

At the heart of human existence, of reality itself, is contradiction, the seemingly endless conflict of incommensurable properties.

> Our life is impossibility, absurdity. Everything we want contradicts the conditions or the consequences attached to it, every affirmation we put forward involves a contradictory affirmation, all our feelings are mixed up with their opposites. It is because we are a contradiction—being creatures—being God and infinitely other than God. . . . We are beings with the faculty of knowing, willing and loving and as soon as we turn our attention towards the object of knowledge, will and love, we receive evidence there is not one which is not *impossible*. (GG 86–87)

Although such contradictions pervade all of reality, our task is not to resolve or eliminate them, "because in this world man cannot release himself from contradictions, he can only make good use of them" (SN 60). Furthermore, the proper use of contradictions is of paramount value, for "contradiction is what pulls, draws the soul, toward the light" (NB 34); "contradiction is our path leading toward God" (NB 386). The Greeks, believing that the fabric of reality was woven from the constant tension between the limited and unlimited, equilibrium and disequilibrium, defined the divinely imposed order of the world as the harmony and proportion between apparently contradictory elements of reality. As Philolaus claimed, "[T]hings that are not alike, nor of the same root, nor of the same station, need to be locked together under key by a harmony capable of maintaining them in the world order" (IC 154).

The beauty of mathematics and geometry, for Weil as well as for the Greeks, lies in their ability to reveal the links, the bridges, between contradictories, so that "the contemplation of the first principles (hypotheses) of geometry and kindred sciences should be contemplation of their contradictions" (NB 34). Throughout mathematics and the universe that operates according to mathematical relationships, contradictory quantities and conflicting elements abound.

> The universe provides these images thanks to a divine favor accorded to man which allows him to make use of number in a certain way as intermediary, in Plato's terms, between the one and the unlimited, the indefinite, the indeterminate—between unity, as man is able to conceive it, and everything that opposes his attempt to conceive it. (SN 18)

Mathematics ultimately serves as a model of the link between the ultimate contradictories, creature and Creator.

> Since the highest is beyond the reach of thought, in order to conceive it we must conceive it *through* that which is within the scope of thought. A link is necessary. Mathematics supply us with a model of such a link. (NB 62)

Just as the mean proportional mediates numbers that are not similar by nature, Christ is the mediator between God and human.

What, then, is the "crisis" that Weil speaks of in the passage from "Reflections of Quantum Theory" quoted at the beginning of this section? Briefly put, a crisis arises because we have lost sight of the true value and purpose of mathematics and have failed to preserve for science "its true destiny as a bridge leading toward God" (NB 453). Weil suggests in a letter to her brother that even at the time of Socrates, Plato, and Eudoxus, the negative effects of failing to understand these truths were evident. Even though the problem of incommensurables led to the most important discovery in Greek geometry,

> there *was* a drama of the incommensurables and its repercussions were immense. The popularization of that discovery brought the concept of truth into a discredit which still endures today; it brought to birth the idea that it is equally possible to prove two contradictory theses; this point of view was

diffused among the masses by the sophists, along with a learning of inferior quality, directed solely towards the acquisition of power. (SL 115)

When it is not understood that contradictions, such as those revealed by the problem of incommensurables, "reflect the contradictions of the human condition" (SN 36) and are to be seen as opportunities for mediation from a higher plane, as illustrated by the discovery of the mean proportional, such contradictions are invariably misinterpreted. If incommensurables are interpreted to indicate that "it is equally possible to prove two contradictory theses," relativism is a natural result; and "so soon as truth disappears, utility at once takes its place" (SN 63); the pursuit of power replaces the pursuit of truth. As it was in fifth-century B.C. Greece, so it is today.

Weil's critique of both classical (Renaissance through nineteenth-century) science and contemporary (twentieth-century) science, a critique that is well beyond the parameters of this chapter, is traceable back to her contention that just as in ancient Greece, we have misunderstood and ultimately forgotten that "a science which does not bring us nearer to God is not worth anything" (NB 191). We have failed to understand the sacred purpose of Greek mathematics and science, even though we have inherited and built on their discoveries.

The bridges of the Greeks. We have inherited them. But we do not know what use to make of them. We have imagined that they were for building houses upon. So we have erected sky-scrapers thereon to which we are continually adding fresh storeys. We do not realize that they are bridges, things made to be crossed over, and that is the way leading to God. (NB 370)

Although she never did more than preliminary work toward justifying her claim that "not much would be required to bring us back from contemporary science to an equivalent of Greek science" (NB 69), it is clear that a recovery of a sacramental vision of mathematics and science would require a powerful sense that "reality represents essentially contradiction[,] . . . [that] the beauty in mathematics lies in contradiction" (NB 387). This contradiction does not imply relativism, is not to be eliminated, but rather is "the lever by which [humanity] raises itself above its natural habitat" (SN 60).

A science and mathematics envisioned as a bridge leading toward God would undoubtedly eliminate barriers between various human enterprises such as science, art, and spirituality that we have come to take as self-evident. These barriers are exemplified in Weil's description of the dilemma of Pascal, who, "when he was on the point of discovering the algebraic form of the integral calculus, abandoned algebra and geometry because he desired contact with God" (SN 47). Similarly, in our contemporary world, "we cannot imagine that the same man could be a scientist and a mystic except at different times in his life" (SN 47). This is because in the classical and contemporary scientific pictures of the world,

> the good is altogether absent; it is absent to the point where one cannot even find a trace of its absence. . . . [C]lassical science is without beauty; it neither touches the heart nor contains any wisdom. . . . It was quite different among the Greeks, those fortunate men in whom love, art, and science, were three scarcely separate aspects of the same movement of the soul towards the good. Compared to them we are wretched; and yet the thing that made them great is close to our hand. (SN 16)

Weil considered Christianity, understood not as a collection of doctrines and formulas, but as the most profound expression of mediation between contraries, the miraculous divine creation of a proportional mean between God and humanity, as the ultimate coming to fruition of what Greek mathematics and science intimated.

> The allusion is evident. Just as the Christ recognized himself as Isaiah's man of sorrows, and the Messiah of all the prophets of Israel, he recognized himself also as being that mean proportional of which the Greeks had for centuries been thinking so intensely. (IC 161)

Science and mathematics, conceived in this manner, thus become human enterprises most likely to approach the transcendent.

> Correlations of contraries are like a ladder. Each of them raises us to a higher level where resides the connection which unifies the contraries; until we reach a spot where we have to think of the contraries together, but where we are denied access to the level and which they are linked together. This forms the last rung of the ladder. Once arrived there, we can climb no further; we have only to look up, wait and love. And God descends. (NB 412)

Notes

1. Rush Rhees, *Discussions of Simone Weil,* ed. D. Z. Phillips. (Albany: SUNY Press, 2000), 88.
2. Ibid., 65.
3. Ibid., 67.
4. Ibid., 64.
5. Eric O. Springsted, "Contradiction, Mystery and the Use of Words in Simone Weil," in *The Beauty That Saves: Essays on Aesthetics and Language in Simone Weil,* ed. J. Dunaway and E. Springsted (Macon: Mercer University Press, 1996), 16. See also his *Christus Mediator: Platonic Mediation in the Thought of Simone Weil* (Chico, Calif.: Scholars Press, 1983), 165–93, for a continued discussion of Pythagorean mathematics in Weil's thought.

CHAPTER 7

To On

A Nameless Something over Which the Mind Stumbles

FLORENCE DE LUSSY

In taking up the immense and virtually insoluble problem posed by the notion of the "real," I limit my examination to Simone Weil's remarks on this subject in *cahiers* 7 (end of the notebook), 8, and 9 in the series from Marseilles.[1] It is precisely at the end of *cahier* 7 that the philosopher, who has reached in vaulting strides a summit of meditation, confronts, in almost triumphal tones, the question of the real. And Plato is referred to immediately, as well as the word that he uses, *to on*, meaning "what is":

> Joy (pure joy is always joy of beauty) is the sense of the real. The beautiful is the manifest presence of the real.

> It is just that and nothing else that Plato says — *to on*.[2]

Everything here evokes an obvious joyousness. A veil has been rent. Hesitation and doubt have vanished. On the following page another step is taken. *To on* is the name that Plato gives to transcendent reality, a term in which Weil has a personal investment: "Beautiful, manifest presence of reality, of a transcendent reality. But it is implied. Reality is only transcendent. For the appearance alone is given to us. *To on*."[3] More soberly, and as if in conclusion (she has come to the end of the notebook), Weil draws the consequences of these assertions : "In Plato, translate *to on* by the real."[4]

"Real": a word of modest appearance and a dull sonority. Equally modest is the Greek, *to on*, with the same contrast between the limited phonic brilliance and the immense semantic field, the neuter, substantive participle of the verb *to be*. In so translating the word, Weil walks in the footsteps of one of the fathers of Greek philosophy, the great Parmenides, for whom, Hans-Georg Gadamer has said, *eon* means "what is possible, namely that which possesses the power of being."[5] The Greek *on* is substantial, firm, and resistant, and Weil always gives it strong meaning.

One cannot avoid here a confrontation with the Lévinasian notion of "there is" (*es gibt*); there is the same sort of minimal outfitting of an expression in order to approach the very sources of being. But with this philosopher, the expression occurs at the opposite end of the semantic spectrum. Lévinas means by this "raw and indeterminate existence, which has neither the strength to pierce through to "the other than being," or, inversely, the strength of being."[6] The *es gibt* that Heidegger saw as a generosity, as a sign of joy and abundance, is understood by Lévinas as a neutral impersonal mode of being, and hence without meaning.[7]

Despite Weil's certainty about the fullness of reality of *to on*, it can only be expressed in "neutral" modest terms. Modeling her formulation on the Greek language, she uses the expression "something," which says exactly the same thing, although less succinctly:[8] "That world order is entirely human, except for this nameless 'something' which the mind butts into and surrounds with names" (K9, ms. 10).

This "something" exists to the highest degree, but we stumble over it and words fail us. "Impossibility" will, in a way, be its mark of existence. Thus we realize that for Weil *to on* is the exact opposite of the category of the fictive, which in her vocabulary she calls the "dream": "Existence is only a shadow of reality. Necessity is a solid reality. Impossibility is a manifest reality. Necessity, being conditional, leaves room for 'ifs.' Impossibility asserts itself" (K8, ms. 68).[9]

That quote is too rich, as is often the case with our philosopher whose thought, of extreme density, is constructed on different levels. The layers need to be peeled back, unfolded carefully.

What Are We Bumping Into? The Problem of Perception

"Why these things and not others?" (K8, ms. 67). Given its vastness and difficulty, we have here an almost unbounded question. As soon as we pose the problem of the relation of the Self and the World, there immediately arises a manifold number of corollary questions: What do we grasp? Do we apprehend the "real" by the intermediary of the senses or by that of the intellect? What are the conditions for attaining it? And so on. Having followed the teachings of Alain and been deeply influenced by him, Weil had already confronted this set of problems for some time, both as a student and as a professor. But they emerged again, more nagging than ever. The need to see clearly was again pressing, imperative. The clarity that resulted from the methodical examination, however, was not as great as the difficulties that were uncovered—truly unfathomable. A little further in notebook 9, Simone Weil evokes the "mysteries" that are enclosed in this notion. It is indispensable to bring them out in the open. The equilibrium of her thought represents a difficult compromise between convictions and a cluster of doubts: "Nothing is more essential than the analysis of perception and the unveiling of the mysteries it encloses" (K9, ms. 35).

In attempting to respond to the challenge, Simone Weil will show daring. Leaving aside the information of the senses, whose testimony is so often blemished by error and illusion, she will favor the exercise of the intellect for apprehending the real, to the point of seeing intellectual grasp as the highest guarantee of veracity. "Demonstration imposes itself upon us more than sensation does," she writes in notebook 8 (ms. 62).[10] Some pages later, she continues, "What is real in perception and distinguishes it from dream is not the sensations but the necessity that is present" (ms. 67).[11] This is the lesson taught by Lagneau (taken up again by Alain), based on the example of the cube that offers the eyes only successive appearances but whose essence (its reality as a cube) necessitates, to be perceived, an act of intellect (just as one perceives an invariable amid a multiplicity of variables). That famous example will be used over and over by the philosopher who makes it a touchstone of her way of thinking. She nevertheless goes further than her predecessors. In her construction, the sensible (perception) loses its characteristic of being purely sensible (which is to say graspable only through the senses). The sensible for her is impregnated, indeed overflowing, and even at its most basic, by its subservience to the *logos:* "No experience, even in perception, without the notion of necessity, which is that of limit. Think sensible nature mathematically."[12]

Having arrived at this point, we feel relatively close to a conception of perception like the one forged by the ancient Greeks, under the name *aisthēsis*. Both Plato, in the *Theaetetus*, who speaks of knowledge as *aisthēsis*, and Weil (working from a reversed perspective), who sees perception as an act of intelligence, are getting at the notion of the *evident*, in the mathematical sense of the word. In both instances it is an immediate grasp that is not subject to the intercession of a demonstration. That immediacy of the grasp, that contiguous fusion between the thing perceived and the act of perception, which keeps the sensible and the intelligible indissolubly linked, sheds some light on the beginnings of Greek speculative reflection. This was shown in the admirable analyses of Gadamer in the courses he gave in 1988 at the Institute for Philosophical Studies in Naples.[13] More precisely, his commentary on Parmenides gives an account of the full force of the word *noein*, which is not dissociated from contact with the thing it is expressing; he uses, to make himself better understood, a striking expression: the *noein* is, according to him, the result of an "écoute pensante [thinking listening]" of being.[14] Apparently, Weil assimilated this Greek message, in its fullness, with that excess of confidence in the *logos* which, to my mind, that position implies.[15]

A new step could now be taken that Weil did not fail to take. One can indeed go further and link up with a sort of "pure perception," "without mixing any dream in," to which she held the secret from her adolescence, but which she rediscovered through reading, at the beginning of March 1942, the *Essays on Zen Buddhism* by Daisetz Teitaro Suzuki.[16] This was a reading that was surprising for her at first[17] but which then illuminated and forcefully revived memories of her seventeenth year when she was in her first year of *cagne*: "Idea of Zen Buddhism: perceive *purely*, without any mingling of dream (my idea at age 17)" (K8, ms. 64).[18]

Weil found in the notion *Yathabutham*[19] ("splendid word," she exclaims [K8, ms. 65]) a conception that lived within her without her actually knowing it—that of a vision relieved of all idea or affect, what she called thereafter "*non-lecture* [nonreading]." By that she meant a contact with raw reality, in all its clarity and transparency. This is not unrelated to emptiness, but this emptiness is not nothingness. The world is not annihilated; things are looked at as they are. Suzuki translates that as "suchness" (*tathata*).[20] It is precisely under the effect of that inspiration that Weil composed, again while very young, the poem "Éclair":

> May the pure sky blow on my face,
> This sky swept by long clouds,
> A wind so strong, bearing a fragrance of joy,
> So that all may be born, cleansed of dreams.[21]

Weil herself recognized it in one of the most remarkable pages of notebook 7 (a fragment of which has been cited above), where for the first time this little word *to on* appears associated with Plato: "That was what I was thinking, at the age of twenty, when I was writing 'Éclair,' but I didn't know that Plato was that. Real presence."[22]

With that absence of "noise" (as one would say today in the field of communication) and this dismissal of the "self," do we arrive at the ultimate step in the approximation of an inkling of the real? And yet the presence of the sensible is not lacking, in the form a "sense of reality" that signals the passage to another order of reality during completely exceptional experiences. Here the difficulty of appreciation—on the speculative level—is immense. Simone Weil not only saw the problem, she had formulated very clear warnings: "There is a *sense of reality* that is the very color of the imaginary. There is another, very different, that is really real. To be analyzed in perception."[23]

The first Greeks had had the presentiment of that alliance between the intelligible and the sensible which opens the way to a showdown where the perceptive power, allied to a form of wonder-full listening, would encounter— would touch, as it were—"that which is." This, however, leads us, as interpreters, down the perilous path that goes by the name of mystical. Let me simply note that locked up inside is the specter of a host of acceptations for the notion of perception where "contact" and "reading" (to use Weil's terminology) combine and form allies in different doses.

But how do we know that we have passed from a fallacious order of reality (that of pure sensation) or one encumbered by illusions, to a more real reality? It must impose itself on us, and that supposes a shock, a collision, which will alone permit the mind to leave the torpor of thought. Commenting on the theory of perception in the *Theaetetus*, Gadamer likes to emphasize that Plato conceived of it as a "collision with reality, or a meeting with it."[24] Weil, for her part, speaks rather of "shock," as, for example, here: "Mathematics. When by clear perception one stumbles on the inconceivable, that is the shock of the real" (K8, ms. 34).[25] She takes up this proposition in a similar fashion in the following: "This is the shock of the real, when one is surprised at nothing being arbitrary" (K9, ms. 33).[26]

The work of D.T. Suzuki apparently put Simone Weil on this trail. The doctrine of Zen Buddhism makes great use of the notion of the *koan*.[27] Perceiving the operative value of such a confrontation with the absurd, Weil annexes the word to her own vocabulary, introducing it in varied contexts. The effect is arresting and the reader surprised. (In reality, her detour through Far Eastern thought led her back to her origins: the exercise of thought centered on the concepts of obstacle and labor, inherited from Alain.)

The practice of mathematics multiplies in an exemplary way the opportunities for eliciting this type of salutary shock, which wakes up intelligence by confronting it with requirements that are contradictory to reason.

The Privileged Path of Mathematics

> The non-reading of geometry. Geometry as *koan*.
>
> Weil, *Oeuvres complètes*, vol. VI.3

Weil embraced the study of mathematics with excitement. By initiating again the analysis of finalities and uses of science, she knew—or foresaw—that she would encounter true obstacles, ones that oblige the intellect to suspend its action. The *impossible* encountered in an almost pure state precipitates us into the transcendent. Mathematics as purification and as a privileged path for penetrating the domain of the supernatural is the program envisaged.[28] Notebook 9 will be the theater of a prodigious ascension of thought on this theme. Nonetheless, the new deal of the cards is already announced in notebook 8 as a program:

> The appearance of an obstacle that causes the mind to stumble is the worth of demonstrating by the absurd in mathematics. Value of impossibilities. One cannot find a common measure between the diagonal and the square. One cannot pass from one side to the other of a straight line without traversing it. (Ms. 65)[29]

On starting a new notebook, notebook 9, Weil continues to address the main themes, but more deftly and with even more vigor. The mind mounts a new assault. She hammers away: "Return to the analysis of perception according to Lagneau and Alain—Plunge into that purification, to the very bottom" (ms. 5); then on page 32: "Define the *real*. Nothing is more important."[30] Finally, since the resistance is extreme and she does not succeed with those conceptual obstacles, she brings into her vocabulary *inflated* and highly connotative words, whose use she had forbidden up until then, such as *miracle, Providence, mystery*, to the point that she will uproot them from their traditional fields of application. For her, it is the field of mathematics that offers the most obvious examples of the intervention of the inexplicable. "The application to physics of a complete mathematical theory before all application is a testimony to Providence more brilliant than a miracle. But mathematics itself, the study *a priori* of nature, is already a miracle" (ms. 33).[31]

The Irreducible in Mathematics

Henceforth, it is in mathematics, that hard and crystalline subject, which most resists the observing mind, that Weil will search out the source of the inexplicable, or rather a way of forcing the passage. She flexes her intelligence to the limits. The game is played out in a few pages (78–85); she multiplies the questions, presses ever farther; she tests resistances; she wants to understand, and proceeds methodically: "Suppose one makes a list of everything that is or seems inexplicable in mathematics" (ms. 75).[32] The reflections on page 78 turn out to be decisive: here she throws up an argument that she will use frequently thereafter: "It is incomprehensible, but by the same token certain." Then she describes the limits of intelligence:

> Only mathematics tests the limits of our intelligence. One can always believe that an experience is inexplicable because we don't have all the facts. There we have all the facts, combined in the full light of the demonstration, and yet we do not understand. It is always the contemplation of human misery.[33]

And to conclude: "[W]e constantly come up against the irreducible." The demonstration is more necessary to us than the sensation. But the demonstration itself in its limpid perfection is unsatisfying. It can present all the characteristics of legibility and yet enclose a mystery (K8, ms. 79). "It encloses a part of convention. One must grasp the nonconventional in mathematics" (ms. 62).[34] This is precisely the key point. What, then, is that thing that the intellect cannot grasp?

Harmony and Mystery

Weil will give a name to the ungraspable, where the essential is played out. She will use a word with delicate sonorities, whose mundane acceptations evoke the conventions propounded by human groups, namely, the word *convenance* (suitability, fitness). She subverts its meaning, and reinvests it with its primary underlying meaning that is congruent with its etymology; she transplants the word into another soil. Notably, she passes from the word *coïncidence* to one that is etymologically close, *convenance*. She is prowling around the notion of providence, to which again she wants to give a nontraditional usage.

   Convenance, in the new connotation that she gives it, is the concept of what is outside all concept. The word marries two notions that are mutually enriching and complementary: harmony and mystery. Harmony as mystery; mystery as the keystone of harmony and, consequently, that mysterious key that coherently maintains the world and its order. It goes without saying that Weil understands the word *harmony* in the same way that the Pythagoreans did. The source is the section devoted to Philolaos in the *Fragmente der Vorsokratiker* (vol. 1), fragment 6 in particular, which she uses to conclude notebook 8 and begin notebook 9.[35] She also uses a segment of the fragment 10, as is seen on page 79, where she combines in a somewhat forced adaptation the *dicha phroneontōn sumphronēsis* of Philolaos[36] with the process of formation of the Pythagorean gnomon: "Harmony in the Pythagorean sense is always mysterious. Simultaneous thought of what is thought separately. For example the series of odd numbers and the series of squares. The demonstration is very clear, and yet it is a mystery" (ms. 79).[37]

   That there is harmony *and* mystery in the very notion of world order is easy to understand; but that there should be *convenance* at the very heart of mathematical necessity "is harmony and mystery to the second degree" (ms. 81).[38] In writing that, Weil is thinking for example of "a locus of points equidistant from the center" (ms. 82). She adds then: "[T]hat *convenance*, translated so, also remains mysterious. The possibility of that translation is an additional mystery."[39] She had already evoked, in an earlier notebook, the fitness expressed by the essential asymmetry of "the formula dx dy ≠ dy dx," by which she summarizes a paragraph from the book by Louis de Broglie, *La Physique nouvelle et les quanta*.[40] And to mark that resistance which formulas exert as we try to penetrate them, she does not hesitate to speak of the density of mathematics: "What strength is to the will, the impenetrable density of mathematics is to our intelligence" (ms. 78).[41] It is hardly surprising that henceforth Simone Weil introduces in this context the term *weight*; "One can find the nth power, not the nth root. Etc. There is thus a weightiness in mathematics" (ms. 84).[42] And, precisely, that "weight" is partly linked with *convenance*. Thus *convenance*, which has a relationship with the Good, and also with the Beautiful, is linked here with everything that, for us, is *unpredictable* and *given*. The use of this word is not exempt from ambiguity, however. Weil, who experiments and invents, tests new modes of thought and new names. Time is precious for her, as she is about to leave Marseilles, and these notebooks that she fills day after day play the role of laboratory notebooks.

Crossing yet another threshold in her thought, and arriving at the summit of her meditation, Weil evokes the "providential" aspect of the World Order (the term being used according to a very special acceptation, as we shall see): "The essence of reality is beauty or transcendental *convenance*" (ms. 83).[43] These effects of *convenance* oblige the passage from the knowledge of the "2nd genre to that of the 3rd genre" (ms. 78). One could not have the full mastery of the real: "In spite of telescopes and microscopes, we cannot step outside our scale. All that we see, by definition, is at our scale" (ms. 83).[44] There follows on the next page an admirable development, probably inspired by the myth of Protagoras in the *Theaetetus*,[45] using the concentric circles on the trunk of a freshly felled tree as a metaphor:

> Our universe is a cross section in the universe, cut at a place that corresponds to the dimensions and to the structure of our body. Thus the universe is only known to us subjectively; our organism also; *but the* convenance *between the two is a fact*. (Ms. 84; my emphasis)[46]

Here the master word is loosed: the *convenance* is a FACT. We have, I think, enough trump in hand now to attempt an analysis of a stunning expression, constituting in any case a striking example of an oxymoron, namely, that of "*a priori* facts," which is found for the first time on page 105 of notebook 7: "AFFIRMATION in mathematics. *Anupothetos.*[47] A *priori* facts. Where does the value of an *a priori* fact reside?"[48]

Weil immediately reactivates the notion of an a priori fact at the beginning of notebook 8. She is perhaps more explicit in that she refers to Kant. It would seem that here she is taking, consciously and not without a certain provocation a position opposed to that of Kant and his *Erkenntnistheorie*:

> Notion of an *a priori* fact. Kant barely glimpsed it; the framework of his system kept him from linking up with it. How is the *a priori* fact more precious than the observed fact? And the harmony in the *a priori* facts? Harmony that we do not put there, which is given to us. (Ms. 6, taken up again in ms. 10)[49]

It is remarkable that immediately after having noted these reflections, Simone Weil lays down the absolute character of the real: "Plato. Translate *aei on* by *eternally real.*"

As concerns Kant, Weil may have in mind, more specifically, the preface he wrote for the second edition of his *Critique of Pure Reason* (1787): "Experience itself is a mode of knowledge which requires the aid of understanding, whose rule I must suppose in myself before objects be consequently given to me *a priori* and this rule is expressed in concepts to which all objects of experience must necessarily adjust themselves and be conformed." Weil seems to respond to that argumentation in an older notebook (dating from the beginning of the stay in Marseilles), using with magisterial aplomb the argument of reciprocity. One reads here, with regard to "*a priori* evidence" (the expression has a certain consonance with that of "*a priori* facts"), "those necessities that are imposed on our thought by the world": "But why look at them as a structure in our mind, as subjective, as so many who have commented on Kant have done? They are a property of the world as an object of thought, or of our thought as it is applied to the world, as one wishes."[50]

And the most direct echo of that confrontation with the *Erkenntnistheorie* of Kant is found, in my opinion, in the extract cited earlier and to which I can return now that the discussion has been given a bit of muscle: "Our universe is a cross section of the universe . . . [etc.]." For us, *at our scale*, and by an effect of divine Providence (understood here in its strongest sense), the observed and the observing are in accord, or at least they have the possibility of being in accord. Here there is harmony and fitness in the sense that the philosopher understands the words. The notion of World Order proclaims this accord and presupposes it.[51] From then on, one is better able to understand the adjective *anupothetos* forged by Plato,[52] and which qualifies the "principle" to which one accedes only by dialectic. "It is necessary to grasp the non-conventional in mathematics," Weil notes in K8, ms. 62, which is to say, one must pull back farther than the hypotheses and postulates. She evidently refers here to the *Republic* (533b–d), which she translates as follows in *La Source grecque* (107):

> The sciences that we have said participate in being—geometry and the others that follow—we see that in a way they dream about being, but are incapable of seeing it when awake. It is because they use hypotheses (*i.e.*, axioms and postulates) which they can neither touch and nor be aware of. The dialectic method alone suppresses the hypotheses and directs the eye and the soul toward the principle itself.[53]

"Les sciences rêvent . . . [The sciences dream . . .]." The real is transcendent and it is hidden. We can only sound it out, determine the contours of an absence. The approximation can only be made in the violence of a vocabulary, which will vary according to the different registers of the impossible, for example:

> What throws us into a sort of stupor: contradiction, absurdity
> What browbeats and humiliates intelligence: the unrepresentable, the inexplicable, the inconceivable
> What quickens our thirst for the real: the unattainable, the ungraspable.

That power of the negative can, all the same, present a less brutal countenance: following a certain gradation, the real is what escapes from the demonstration, what one cannot deny, what is imposed on us, what is given from without. The access to knowledge "without words,"[54] the access to nonreading—when intelligence finally gives in and agrees to stop being master—will take place in an atmosphere of repose. Pride yields.

> To resolve is to understand that there is nothing to resolve; that existence has no meaning for the discursive faculties, and that these must not be allowed to go beyond their role of the simple exploratory instrument of intelligence seeking out contact with raw reality. (K8, ms. 116)[55]

In the notebooks of Simone Weil, brilliant formulations abound; they are often the result of a sudden tightening of thought; but she does not always take the time (she doesn't have the time) to reconcile her abrupt intuitions. Thus she writes: "Necessity is a network of conditions, thus of possibilities, and yet it is the basis of reality" (K9, ms. 35); but elsewhere, taking up the problem of the "*sine qua non* of the real's appearance (avoid putting oneself in the center of space)," she evokes the "passage to the eternal" (K12, ms. 27). A leap has been made in thought, a change of level. There has been an "elevation to a superior ontological condition," to use Gadamer's expression.[56] In effect, when Weil leaves Marseilles and France definitively, she is possessed by the conviction that there exist several ontological levels, several degrees of reality: the order of nature and that of super-nature. The synthesis that she composes in one flow, in the space of a few days, during the stopover in Casablanca before the transatlantic journey, leaves no room for ambiguity on this point. "The reality of the universe is for us nothing other than necessity."[57] And to continue: "The necessary connections, those constituting the very reality of the world, have themselves reality only as the object of intellectual attention in action."[58] The conclusion bursts forth on the next page: "This intellectual attention is at the intersection of the natural and supernatural parts of the soul. Having conditional necessity as its object it only arouses a *half reality*" (my emphasis).[59] She gives in notebook 12 (the one that will cross the Atlantic) this résumé that slams the door shut and terminates the immense chapter of meditations in Marseilles: "Intelligence, intersection of nature and the supernatural (conditional necessity). Love (consent) produces reality" (ms. 35).[60]

The transcendent alone is "really real." However, one of the consequences of Simone Weil's conceptual strong-handedness is the 180-degree about-face in the usual thinking about the notion of providence: "Providence is the proper object of science, and reciprocally there exists no study other than science — the most exact, precise and rigorous science" (K9, ms. 11).[61]

Let us understand her properly; she is asking that one exercise trenchant discernment: "Reason should exercise its function of demonstration only in order to succeed in stumbling up against the true mysteries, the true undemonstrables, which are the real" (K11, ms. 42).[62]

Translated by Patricia Stirneman and Chris Callahan

Notes

1. The original manuscripts of Weil's notebooks are referred to as K (with the number of the notebook) followed by *ms.* which gives the page number. As of this writing notebook 7 (K7) has been published in *OC* VI.2 and references are given; notebooks 8 and 9 are in *OC* VI.3, which was published afterward. They are referred to by the noted signs, K8, K9. The passages in question in the English translation start at *NB* 360.

The translations provided here are original; however, because the argument follows the text and its linguistic nuances closely, the original French is provided in the notes. — *Ed.*

2. "La joie (la joie pure est toujours joie du beau) est le sentiment du réel. Le beau est la présence manifeste du réel.

C'est cela même et non autre chose que dit Platon — *to on*" (*OC* VI.2 485). To mark the importance of the sentences she had just written, Weil sets them off in the margin with several vertical lines.

3. "Beau, présence manifeste du réel, d'une réalité transcendante. Mais cela est impliqué. La réalité n'est que transcendante. Car l'apparence seule nous est donnée. *To on*" (*OC* VI.2 486). Again, Weil sets these sentences off in the margin.

4. "Dans Platon, traduire *to on* par le réel" (*OC* VI.2 491). Weil gives this name "real" the fullest density possible: "real" is the opposite of "apparent, illusory, fictive," also of "relative," taking its consistency from what is "given" and not "constructed."

5. See *Au commencement de la philosophie: Pour une lecture des Présocratiques*, translated from German into French by Pierre Fruchon, reread and corrected by Dominique Séglard (Paris: Éditions du Seuil), 143.

6. "L'existence brute et indéterminée qui n'a ni la force de percer vers *l'autrement qu'être*, ni, inversement, la force de l'être." See François-David Sebbah, *Lévinas: Ambiguïtés de l'altérité* (Paris: Les Belles Lettres, 2000), 138.

7. See *Autrement qu'être ou Au-delà de l'essence*, 2d ed. (The Hague: Martinus Nijhoff, 1978), 178: "As impersonal goings-on, as incessant lapping of waves, as muted rustling, as *'es gibt'* — does not the essence drown out the meaning which gives it birth? The insistence of this impersonal noise, is it not the menace felt in our time of an end of the world?"

8. "Cet ordre du monde est entièrement humain, sauf ce quelque chose sans nom sur quoi l'esprit bute et qu'il entoure de noms." Weil takes up the same expression a few weeks later, in "Formes de l'Amour implicite de Dieu," to evoke the supremely real that is given for contemplation in the Eucharist: this "quelque chose que nous ignorons totalement, dont nous savons seulement, comme dit Platon, que c'est quelque chose, et que rien d'autre n'est jamais désiré sinon par erreur [something of which we are entirely ignorant, of which we know only, as Plato says, that it is something, and nothing else is ever desired except by error]" (*AD* 195).

9. "L'existence n'est qu'une ombre de réalité. La nécessité est une réalité solide. L'impossibilité est une réalité manifeste. La nécessité étant conditionnelle laisse place à des 'si.' L'impossibilité s'impose."

10. "La démonstration s'impose à nous plus que la sensation."

11. "Ce qui est réel dans la perception et la distingue du rêve, ce n'est pas les sensations, mais la nécessité qui y est présente."

12. "Pas d'expérience, même dans la perception, sans la notion de nécessité, qui est celle de la limite. Penser mathématiquement la nature sensible."

13. They were brought together and published first in Italy, then in France. See Gadamer, *Au commencement de la philosophie*, 143.

14. Ibid.

15. Tempered, however, by the presence of that "sensitive" quality that perception preserves in the pure exercise of the act.

16. London: Luzac and Co., 1934. The three series were translated into French, under the direction of Jean Herbert. René Daumal, who introduced Weil to Sanskrit, was the translator of the second series. It was thus Daumal who suggested she read the book.

17. Her reading notes, in her current notebook, attest to the difficulty of integrating into her "doctrine" elements that were so basically foreign.

18. "Idée du bouddhisme zen: percevoir *purement*, sans mélange de rêve (mon idée à 17 ans)." Compare this reflection noted at the end of the notebook: "When I was in *cagne*, my 'ultra-Spinozian meditation'; look fixedly at an object with the thought: what is it? without taking into account any other object, without relation to anything else, for hours. This was a *koan*" ("Quand j'étais en cagne, ma 'méditation ultra-spinoziste'; regarder fixement un objet avec la pensée: qu'est-ce que c'est?, sans tenir compte d'aucun autre objet, sans rapport avec rien d'autre, pendant des heures. C'était un *koan*") (K8, ms. 116).

19. See the definition that Suzuki gives in his *Essays:* "the Prajna is seeing into the essence of things as they are (*yathabutham*); that the Prajna is seeing things with their nature empty; that thus seeing things is to reach the limit of reality, i.e. to pass beyond the realm of the human understanding; that, therefore, the Prajna is grasping the ungraspable; attaining the unattainable, comprehending the incomprehensible; that when this intellectual description of the working of the Prajna is translated into psychological terms, it is not becoming attached to anything whether it is an idea or a feeling." *Essays in Buddhism*, 3d series (London: Luzac, 1934), 250.

20. "Suchness (*tathata*) is an uncouth term, but in Buddhist phraseology one of the most expressive terms. . . . Suchness is not to be confounded with the sameness or oneness of things. When 'the vanishing of pluralities' is talked of, one may imagine that they are ignored or annihilated in order to reveal their aspect of oneness. But what the Prajna devotees mean is that they are understood in their true relations, not only to one another but to that which makes up their reason of being."

21. Que le ciel pur sur la face m'envoie,
Ce ciel de longs nuages balayé
Un vent si fort, vent à l'odeur de joie,
Que naisse tout, de rêves nettoyé. (See *P* 21.)

22. "C'est cela que je pensais, à vingt ans, quand j'écrivais 'Eclair', mais je ne savais pas que Platon c'était cela. Présence réelle" (notebook 7, ms. 101). See OC VI.2 485. See above.

23. "Il y a un *sentiment de la réalité* qui est la couleur même de l'imaginaire. Il y en a un autre, très différent, qui est réellement réel. A analyser dans la perception" (notebook 7, ms. 54). See OC VI.2 452.

24. *Theaetetus*, 153 e. See Gadamer, *Au commencement de la philosophie*, 76.

25. "Mathématique. Quand par la perception claire on se heurte à l'inconcevable, c'est le choc du réel."

26. "Qu'il y ait surprise là où il n'y a aucun arbitraire, c'est le choc du réel."

27. Suzuki gives a definition in his work, *Essays*, 1st series, 394 n. 1. The *koan* consists of a paradoxical situation engendered by a gesture or a word provoking an abrupt rupture in the mind, which can allow access to another reality.

28. She already had that in mind when she wrote to her brother in Spring 1940. It was there like seeds that she scattered on paper.

29. "Dans la mathématique, prix de la démonstration par l'absurde: c'est le signe d'un obstacle où la pensée se heurte. Valeur des impossibilités. On ne peut pas trouver une commune mesure entre la diagonale et le carré. On ne peut pas passer d'un côté à l'autre d'une droite sans la traverser."

30. "Revenir à l'analyse de la perception selon Lagneau et Alain—Se plonger dans cette purification une fois à fond." . . . "Définir le *réel*. Rien de si important." The latter injunction had such importance to her that she drew a frame around it.

31. "L'application à la physique d'une théorie mathématique complète avant toute application est un témoignage de la Providence autrement éclatant qu'un miracle. Mais la mathématique elle-même, étude *a priori* de la nature, est déjà un miracle."

32. "Si on faisait la liste de tout ce qui est ou paraît inexplicable en mathématique." It is remarkable that she posed questions on the golden number at precisely this moment.

33. "La mathématique seule nous fait éprouver les limites de notre intelligence. Car on peut toujours croire d'une expérience qu'elle est inxplicable parce que nous n'avons pas toutes les données. Là nous avons toutes les données, combinées dans la pleine lumière de la démonstration, et pourtant nous ne comprenons pas. C'est toujours la contemplation de la misère humaine."

34. "Elle enferme une part de convention. Il faut saisir le non conventionnel dans la mathématique."

35. Fragment 6 Diels Kranz [Weil's translation]: "Les choses semblables et de même race n'ont nul besoin d'harmonie; celles qui sont dissemblables et ne sont pas de

même race ni de même ordre, il est nécessaire qu'elles soient enfermées ensemble sous la clef d'une harmonie propre à les contenir dans un ordre du monde. [Similar things and of the same race need not be in harmony; for those that are dissimilar and not of the same race or the same order, it is necessary that they be enclosed together, under the key of a particular harmony that contains them in an order of the world.]"

36. This is an expression to which she attaches great importance. She will go so far as to give theological and even trinitarian readings.

37. "L'harmonie au sens pythagoricien est toujours mystérieuse. La pensée simultanée de ce qui se pense séparément. Par exemple la suite des nombres impairs et la suite des carrés. La démonstration est très claire, et pourtant c'est un mystère." See *OC* VI.2 488.

38. "c'est harmonie et mystère au second degré."

39. "cette convenance ainsi traduite reste aussi mystérieuse. La possibilité de cette traduction est un mystère de plus."

40. Paris: Flammarion, 1937: "[D]ans le produit de la matrice correspondant à une coordonnée par la matrice correspondant à la composante conjuguée de la quantité de mouvement, l'ordre des facteurs n'est pas indifférent, et la différence entre le produit effectué en rangeant ces deux facteurs dans un ordre et le produit effectué en les rangeant dans l'ordre inverse est égal à la constante de Planck. [In the product of the matrix corresponding to a coordinate by the matrix corresponding to the conjugate component of the momentum, the order of the factors has to be taken in account, and the difference between the product obtained by arranging these two factors in an order and the product obtained by arranging these two factors in the inverse order is equal to Planck's constant.]" See on this subject, *OC* VI.2 652; K7, n. 276.

41. "Ce qu'est la force à la volonté, l'épaisseur impénétrable de la mathématique l'est à notre intelligence."

42. "On peut trouver la puissance nième, non la racine nième. Etc. Il y a donc une pesanteur dans la mathématique."

43. "L'essence de la réalité est beauté ou convenance transcendante."

44. "Malgré les télescopes et les microscopes, nous ne pouvons pas sortir de notre échelle. Tout ce que nous voyons, par définition, est à notre échelle."

45. With the idea of "platform," where medium-sized, measurable realities appear.

46. "Notre univers est une coupe dans l'univers, pratiquée à un endroit qui correspond aux dimensions et à la structure de notre corps. Ainsi l'univers ne nous est connu que subjectivement; notre organisme aussi; mais la *convenance entre les deux est un fait*."

47. This term, borrowed from Plato, is taken up here for the second time; it appears for the first time two pages earlier: "ce dont parle le *Banquet: la beauté de la mathématique*. Cela est *anupothetos*. C'est (dans le vocabulaire de Guénon) la *réalisation* qui correspond à la théorie mathématique. Mystique mathématique [what the *Banquet* talks about: *the beauty of mathematics*. That is *anupothetos*. It is (in Guénon's terminology) the *realisation* which corresponds to mathematical theory. Mystical mathematics.]" (*OC*

VI.2 486–87). On the notion of the "beauty of mathematics," see in K9, ms. 97, a very beautiful and rich synthesis. It will be noted that in citing the *Banquet*, Weil furnishes the proof that she always links up with the thought of Plato in the end.

48. "La CONSTATATION dans la mathématique. Anupothetos. Faits *a priori*. Où réside la valeur privilégiée d'un fait *a priori*?" This notion is particularly dear to her. As proof, we have it again in K12, ms. 7, where, on the point of confiding her notebooks to Gustave Thibon, believing that she was on the eve of her departure for America, she notes in haste certain points or reflections that she judges important not to lose. "Mathématique et distinction des niveaux—*h*-et constatation. Faits *a priori*. [Mathematics and distinction of levels—*h*- and *constatation* (establishment of facts). A *priori* facts]." She uses a telegraphic style to express what she had noted in K7. Note the abbreviation of "Relationship of *h* (Heisenberg) and of dxdy ≠ dydx."

49. "Notion de *a priori*. Kant l'a entrevu à peine; les cadres de son système l'ont empêché de s'y attacher. En quoi le fait *a priori* est-il plus précieux que le fait constaté? Et l'harmonie dans les faits *a priori*? Harmonie que nous n'y mettons pas, qui nous est donnée."

50. "mais pourquoi les regarder comme une structure de notre esprit, comme subjectives, ainsi qu'ont fait tant de commentateurs de Kant? Elles sont une propriété du monde en tant qu'objets de pensée, ou de notre pensée en tant qu'elle s'applique au monde, comme on voudra" (*OC* VI.2 177–78).

51. Already in K9, ms. 11, Weil echoing the "ordre saisissable pour nous [graspable order for us]," had evoked the World Order "comme condition d'existence d'une créature pensante [as a condition of existence of a thinking creature]." In the measure of the man, Protagoras would have said.

52. *Republic* 510 b.

53. "Les sciences dont nous avons dit qu'elles participent à l'être, la géométrie et celles qui suivent, nous voyons qu'elles rêvent en quelque sorte au sujet de l'être, mais sont incapables de la voir éveillées. C'est du fait qu'elles se servent d'hypothèses (*i.e.* axiomes et postulats) auxquels elles ne touchent pas et ne peuvent pas rendre compte. La méthode dialectique seule supprime les hypothèses et dirige l'œil de l'âme vers le principe lui-même." Translation into English is difficult here, because Weil does not quote Plato exactly (sentences are shortened, for example), and she bends Plato's words to fit her personal "doctrine." Consequently, we must confront this translation with the best that are available in English, for instance, that of Paul Shorey (Cambridge, Mass.: Harvard University Press; London: William Heinemann, 1969).

54. See K9, ms. 108.

55. "Résoudre, c'est comprendre qu'il n'y a rien à résoudre; que l'existence n'a pas de signification pour les facultés discursives, et qu'il ne faut pas laisser celles-ci sortir de leur rôle de simple instrument explorateur de l'intelligence en vue du contact avec la réalité brute."

56. Gadamer, *Au commencement de la philosophie*, 69.

57. *IPC* 143. "La réalité de l'univers pour nous n'est pas autre chose que la nécessité."

58. "Les connexions nécessaires, lesquelles constituent la réalité même du monde, n'ont elles-mêmes de réalité que comme objet de l'attention intellectuelle en acte" (*IPC* 154). Weil seems to adopt here the position of Kant, for whom it is no more than "the sum of the object linked by laws." See on this subject, Sebbah, *Lévinas*, 84.

59. "Cette attention intellectuelle est à l'intersection de la partie naturelle et de la partie surnaturelle de l'âme. Ayant pour objet la nécessité conditionnelle, elle ne suscite qu'une DEMI-REALITÉ."

60. "Intelligence, intersection de la nature et du surnaturel (nécessité condition-nelle). L'Amour (consentement) produit la réalité."

61. "La providence est l'objet propre de la science, et réciproquement il n'en existe pas d'autre étude que la science—la science la plus exacte, précise et rigoureuse."

62. "La raison ne doit exercer sa fonction de démonstration que pour parvenir à se heurter aux vrais mystères, aux vrais indémontrables, qui sont le réel."

CHAPTER 8

Reconstructing Platonism
The Trinitarian Metaxology of Simone Weil

EMMANUEL GABELLIERI

Since Nietzsche and Heidegger, a considerable number of contemporary philosophers have rallied under the banner of "dismantling metaphysics" (Hannah Arendt), a program most clearly expressed by Gilles Deleuze as "overthrowing Platonism."[1] I argue that Simone Weil's thought is of major significance not only for contemporary philosophy but also for the history of philosophy because she offers a counterargument, and perhaps the most coherent and profound alternative, to this program of overthrowing Platonism.

But I must be more explicit. If her thought constitutes a counterargument, it is not because she defends the type of Platonism that, from Nietzsche to Heidegger, Deleuze, or Derrida, contemporary philosophy seeks to challenge but because she invites and forces us to read Plato differently. Indeed, the Platonism targeted by contemporary critics of metaphysics and by deconstructionist doctrines *is* a philosophy of concept, essence, and being as presence without relationships, freedom, events, and, most significantly, love. The Platonism of Simone Weil, however, is a philosophy of the constituent bond between reason and love, a philosophy of being as *metaxu*, link, mediation, and finally, a philosophy of the fullness of being as supernatural love.

The first question that arises is whether this Platonism is more revealing of Weil as a reader of Plato than it is of Plato's thought. This question is even more pointed in Weil's case than in traditional Christian Platonism since, in addition to the metaphysics of grace, the most central dogmas of Christianity—the Trinity, revelation, the Cross—are linked in her work to Platonism. Assuming the viability of her reading of Plato, even given the most audacious aspects of her interpretation, a second wider question then arises concerning what is at stake for her, both on a historical and a conceptual level. Might not this new shape given to Platonism, while a key to the meaning and unity of Weil's thought as a whole, also be a key to contemporary debates about the end of metaphysics and the relationship between philosophy and theology? This implies acknowledging the intrinsic speculative originality of Weil's thought, a claim that has not been made with sufficient vigor until now.

These two questions guide this chapter. I first strive to reconstruct Weil's Christian rereading of Platonism undertaken in Marseilles, thus "Reconstructing Platonism." Second, I propose that if this reading of Plato is of value, it is so with respect not only to the potential rehabilitation of Platonism in contemporary philosophy but also, on a deeper level, to the possibility of reconstructing metaphysics. This would be a "metaxological" metaphysics that would be fitting of Christian inspiration, thus "the Trinitarian Metaxology of Simone Weil." Here I seek to demonstrate the fecundity and relevance of Weil's thought by comparing her ideas to those of Heidegger, Lévinas, Blondel, and Hans Urs von Balthasar, among others.

The Platonism of Simone Weil

The Synthesis of Marseilles and the Problem of the Internal Unity
of Weil's Texts

I leave a complete reconstruction of Weil's relation to Plato and the entire genesis of this relation, beginning in Alain's classroom, to Michel Narcy's chapter in this volume. Here, I focus only on Weil's global rereading of Platonism effected in Marseilles in 1941–42.[2] Her synthesis was effected through the establishment of an explicit relation between Greece and Christianity, a relation that was especially well illustrated by Weil's linking of Plato with St. John of the Cross and her speculatively rooting it in the Pythagorean doctrine of mediation, as she reread it in the light of the Christian Trinity and Incarnation. But the full scope of this synthesis is difficult to grasp, first because of the fragmentary nature of the texts at our disposal and second because of what I propose to call the double exposition of Platonism developed in the most essential texts of this period.

Until now, one of the major obstacles for interpretation has been that Weil's analyses from this period seem to be highly disorganized textually. We have both the bulky *cahiers* and the fragments and major essays contained in *Intimations of Christianity in the Ancient Greeks*.[3] The whole has the appearance of a massive jumble of notes and of multiple drafts attesting to the evolution of her thought and making all search for unity appear fruitless. This apparent disorder, however, is not due to a lack of unity or to the incompleteness of Weilian thought, as if essential unifying elements were missing. Above all, the perception results from the conditions in which Weil drafted and completed those different texts. By focusing on their continuities and connections, we should be able to reconstitute the logical unity of Weil's thought. The first task is to identify and study as accurately as possible the correlations between the two types of texts—those of the *cahiers* and those of *Intimations*. Clearly the fundamental cohesion of the *cahiers*—which, as Florence de Lussy demonstrates, covers a wide range of topics—confirms the maturity of thought that flows from the first discussions held in the crypt of the Dominican convent in Marseilles to the final, written texts. These correlations between the *cahiers* and the essays of *Intimations* prepare us for understanding the finished ones because the *cahiers* were themselves preparatory for those essays.[4] But the most important task is to determine what internal connections exist in the major texts. The central connection is that which links the two most fundamental texts of Weil's "Christian Platonism" composed in Marseilles: "God in Plato" and "Divine Love in Creation." In what follows, I argue that these two texts offer a dual but complementary exposé of Platonism; together they constitute, for Weil, an integral whole.

"God in Plato": The Three Phases of Platonism

"God in Plato" details Weil's understanding of the logical progression of ideas in Plato's main dialogues concerning the soul's relation to God. Her primary purpose is to put into perspective the various stages of the relationship between the human and the supernatural as they are found in Platonism. We can distinguish three fundamental phases whose essential progression is also the link between the *Republic* and the *Timaeus*.

The first phase consists in categorically opposing two ethics: one purely worldly, concerned with virtue and visible rewards in society, and the other supernatural, which does not provide for worldly reward but rather seeks pure good and the salvation of the soul, thus radically transcending social concerns. The soul that escapes the tyranny of opinion and of the great beast prefers to suffer evil rather than inflict it. This soul is symbolized by the image of the "crucified just man" in the *Republic*.[5] For Weil, this image embraces the teachings of the Greek tragedians[6] and the Platonic critique of the social great beast, as well as her own experience of politics, oppression, and barbarism. She synthesized these elements into her formulation of the rule of "force" in her meditation on the *Iliad* of the previous year. The crucified just man of the *Republic* as well as Aeschylus's *Prometheus* are prefigurations of Christ, for like him, they preferred suffering, the "nakedness of death,"[7] condemnation by humankind, and apparent forsaking by God to the acceptance of evil. Weil's conclusion is thus noteworthy because the "loosening of worldly attachments" (SG 75) implied in the double image of death and nakedness is intimately related to St. John of the Cross's thought. Thus: "If justice requires that we be naked and dead in our lifetime, then it becomes obvious that this is impossible for human nature, even for the supernatural, to achieve" (SG 77).

This conclusion seems to introduce for Weil the second stage of Platonism, that is, the experience of Grace. This experience itself has at least two moments. The first, an implicit one, is the recognition that resisting the power of evil is already a sign of supernatural love and of the gift of grace. For example, in the *Republic* 493a, after declaring that "human" teaching entails submission to the social great beast, Plato writes that "anyone who is saved" from evil in spite of this must "be saved by the effect of a predestination ordained by God" (SG 78) (In the manuscript housed in the Bibliothèque Nationale, this passage is highlighted by three large vertical strokes in the margin, following which Weil states: "N.B. One could hardly assert more categorically that grace is the only source of salvation, and that this salvation comes from God, not from human kind" (SG 79). Similarly, the passage is twice underlined in which Plato asserts that anyone who submits to society is unaware of "how much the essence of necessity differs from the essence of good," and Weil adds the term *revelation* in the margin, underlining it three times (SG 80). The Platonic longing for good, defined subsequently as the implicit love of God (SG 85–86), seems to be interpreted similarly to what classic Christian theology would call "prevenient grace."

But the purpose of these reflections is to introduce a second moment, the direct experience of grace that Weil sees described in the myth of the cave. It is here that the parallel with St. John of the Cross is most striking. This parallel, already intimated by a similar orientation of the "entire soul" toward detachment in both thinkers' works, is also confirmed by the parallels between the emergence from the cave and St. John of the Cross's two "nights." The prisoner's liberation inside the cave (consisting of breaking the chains and walking in darkness) corresponds to the first night, "the dark night of sense" (SG 94), through which, by turning away from all finite objects, one desires good with all his strength but, not finding it, "believes himself lost" (SG 93). Then the blinding of the eyes that occurs when the prisoner, once out of the cave, is "stunned by the light" corresponds to John of the Cross's "dark night of the soul" (SG 93–94). Thus the "two thresholds" of mystical experience are limned in Plato's work. Moreover, those thresholds, often defined in the Marseilles *cahiers* (NB 2.299), leads finally to the contemplation of the sun in the *Republic*, and to "what John of the Cross calls spiritual union." Therefore, the longing for good, the night of the senses, the night of the soul, and mystical union represent the four stages of what I call the second phase of Weil's Platonism.

But this is still only a second phase. Immediately after referring to John of the Cross's spiritual union, Weil states: "But in Plato this is not the final stage; there is one more" (SG 94). We therefore reach the third phase of Platonism in Weil's work, which corresponds to the return to the cave described in the *Republic*. During this phase, "the saint, after crossing the valley of death to reach God, must somehow be incarnated in his own body in order to cast a reflection of the supernatural light over this world, this earthly life" (SG 96). Consequently, an essential paradox, which is at the heart of our debates on Christian Platonism, lies in the fact that Platonism does not conclude with a disincarnation, an escape from the world, but with an orientation toward incarnation. Two remarks are in order here. First, this return to the cave is a third phase, not a retreat to an earlier one, in the human relation to grace and the supernatural, because it is *supernatural light* that must be shed over the world. So, second, the supernatural should not be seen as a kind of surface layer that could be added to a reality whose substance is self-sufficient. The saint must "make this earthly life and this world real because, thus far, they have only been dreams. It is incumbent on him to finish his own creation" (SG 96). Thus the return to the cave has not only ethical but also ontological and eschatological dimensions.

From the Republic *to the* Timaeus

The goal of the remainder of "God in Plato" is to delineate these dimensions by leading directly to Weil's metaxology. Based on her analysis of the soul's orientation toward God as developed in the first part of the text, we need to consider the world as a series of *metaxu*, or bridges, between us and God. For Plato, the two main *metaxu* are knowledge and love. Thus Weil distinguishes "the intellectual path" of knowledge, as defined in the *Republic* or the *Theaetetus*,[8] from the "other path to salvation indicated by Plato as the non-intellectual path," namely, beauty and love as represented in the *Phaedrus* and the *Symposium*.[9] Weil places the greatest emphasis in "God in Plato" on the "non-intellectual path."[10] The "shock of beauty" described in the *Phaedrus* is the same as that "nameless force in the *Republic* which causes chains to fall and which forces us to walk."[11] So the longing for beauty, the excited irritation of the awakening soul's wings, is related to John of the Cross's "alternation between the periods of dark night and the periods of sensible grace" (SG 111). The *Symposium* is then treated by Weil as the dialogue in which Plato "reveals a bit more" about the path of "love which leads to the highest knowledge" (SG 116). It reveals that what "follows" the sciences "along the path described in the *Republic* is the connection between the beauty of knowledge and beauty itself" (SG 116), with love playing the role of a *metaxu* between the human and the divine. Plato develops this role in "the theory of mediation" (SG 117).

But still, all these developments lead to the *Timaeus*, which, in the last pages of "God in Plato," is presented as the text in which the dual path of knowledge and love attains its unity and its most perfect form.[12] The *Timaeus* "does not resemble any other of Plato's dialogues . . . between the other dialogues and this one something has occurred. . . . He has emerged from cave, stared at the sun, and returned to the cave. . . . Thus the tangible world no longer looks like a cave" (SG 119). Therefore, the *Timaeus* is the extension of the *Republic*, but it brings the revelation contained in Platonism to a level never before attained. Its originality lies in its being a "story of creation" (SG 119), which describes the world as a work of art created by "a trinity: the Worker, the Model of Creation, and the World Soul" (SG 119). But Weil does not justify this assertion here. She resumes her analysis at the beginning of "Divine Love in Creation" and finally brings it to a conclusion as part of her reflections on the Pythagorean doctrine of mediation.

"Divine Love in Creation": The Heart of Platonism

In 1990 Francis Heidsieck noted that the reading of the *Timaeus* contained in "God in Plato"[13] precedes the reading of the *Timaeus* in "Divine Love in Creation," which is later, more mature, and more developed. Heidsieck emphasized that the *Timaeus*, the "Omega of the first study," was the "Alpha of the second."[14] Further, he noted a remarkable switch: in "God in Plato" Weil moves from the *Symposium* to the *Timaeus*, whereas in "Divine Love in Creation" she goes primarily from the *Timaeus* to the *Symposium*. This would make "the themes of divine love and divine order . . . the mainstays of her Platonism."[15] But we must go beyond these remarks, even correct them. First, the reading of the *Timaeus* she reaches at the end of "God in Plato" is more than the starting point of "Divine Love." It is implicitly or explicitly present *throughout* "Divine Love," especially in the final section, "The Pythagorean Doctrine."[16] Second, saying that the *Symposium* and *Timaeus* are the "two pillars" of Weilian Platonism fails to take into consideration her numerous reflections on the theme of "the crucified just man," which permeate both works. This is a theme that comes from the *Republic* and even Aeschylus's *Prometheus* (as well as *Electra* and *Antigone*), and on which she has far more significant commentary (*IPC* 71–108). This parallel is crucial, for it reveals the *third* pillar of Weilian Platonism: the theme of "the suffering of the perfect just man."[17] The parallel between the two texts is even more important than Heidsieck realized because it shows a Platonic Christology in which the three *metaxu* of suffering, beauty, and world order (each a modality of love) are hidden figures of Christ the Mediator.

This parallel should also make us avoid the conclusion that "God in Plato" is more developed than "Divine Love in Creation." Only "Divine Love in Creation" fully reveals the three mediations: the World Order (*Timaeus*, 20 pp.), Beauty (*Symposium*, 30 pp.), and Suffering (*Republic* and *Prometheus*, 30 pp.). Also, and more important, this work alone develops, in its final section, the fundamental principle of this triple mediation, that is, the "Pythagorean doctrine of mediation" (70 pp.). Thus the three phases comprising the first major part of the text (based on the *Timaeus*, the *Symposium*, the *Republic*) converge in the second part where the Pythagorean theory appears as the key to understanding all types of mediation.[18]

Following Eric O. Springsted's example in *Christus Mediator*, I have shown elsewhere how this second part developed—according to a more rigorous order than is apparent in a text without visible subdivisions—the five levels of mediation that constituted for Weil the truth of being: (1) the Trinity, (2) the relation between God and creation, (3) friendship between God and humans, (4) friendship between humans, (5) "number," which gives its own internal order (*logos*) to material necessity itself.[19] At each of these levels, being proves to be "mediation" or "relation" (the two terms most often used by Weil). But whereas the Trinity is the perfect mediation whose terms are coequal, the other four levels of mediation can only constitute a perfect unity if a "proportional mean" brings together the distant terms. Weil sees this proportional mean in Christ, the *logos* of creation. (See chapter 6 in this volume.)

The annotations made in her own copy of the *Timaeus* (now in the Bibliothèque Nationale)[20] shows the evolution of these concepts. One of the key texts in which Weil sees the Pythagorean theory of mediation exposed is *Timaeus* 31c, where Plato declares that for there to be perfect unity between two terms there must be a third one "between them, in the middle, and the link that will lead them to union."[21] In Weil's copy of the *Timaeus*, this passage (highlighted by three vertical strokes in the margin) is linked first to a note in the left margin: "necessity of a mediation with three terms," then to a second one at the top of the page: "Proportional mean. Proportion image of the Trinity?"[22] We see clearly here the starting point of the speculations that are developed at the beginning of "The Pythagorean Doctrine." There, however, the question mark has disappeared and Platonic proportion has become identified with John 17.23: "I in them and you in me, that they may be completely one" (IPC 120–21).

Such an identification makes sense only if 31c is subjected to an analogical reading that reveals the Trinitarian schemas and personae of the dialogue. Weil's annotations illustrate this clearly. I simply call attention to those concerning the Trinity of the Artificer (Demiurge), the Model, and the World Soul.[23] All Weil's commentary and the emendations in her translations emphasize the personality and the spiritual singularity of these three divine beings. Thus the Model that is contemplated by the Artificer as "the living, eternal one," the source of creative inspiration, must be related to the Holy Spirit.[24] Similarly, Weil underscores the phrase "the goodness of the Artificer," then, crossing out Rivaud's translation, writes: "NB: It is dishonest to translate *o theos* by 'the' God for when the Gospel mentions God it always says *o theos.*"[25] Or concerning heaven as "the only one of its kind," she adds in the margin: "But also only Son" (*monogenes*), a translation that she takes up again at the end of the dialogue concerning the uniqueness of the world ("Only begotten, only Son").[26] All these remarks are compiled in *cahiers* 6 to 9 and summarized in "The Pythagorean Doctrine" by Philolaus's formula "the common thought of separate thinkers," and Diogenes Laertius's statement "Friendship is an equality made of harmony," which allows her to define the Trinity as the "first pair of contraries" made up of unity and plurality (*IPC* 129).

The parallel can continue with the annotations regarding the World Soul. In her copy of the *Timaeus*, Weil notes that the Soul preexists the body of the universe, which it then envelops rather than itself being contained (so there remains no trace of pantheism).[27] But above all, the World Soul is the "proportional mean" and the "mediator between God and the world" because it partakes of both heavenly and earthly being, a mixture that is cut like a ribbon in an X (the *chi* of 36c) and wrapped around the world. Thus it appears as "crucified on time and space"(149).[28] The correlation between this and her analysis of the "second pair of contraries" in "The Pythagorean Doctrine" is striking. The World Soul, identified with the Son in all previous analyses of the *Timaeus* (*SG* 123–28; *IPC* 25–30), becomes in this instance the "intersection" of a divine person and inert matter, this "wretched flesh nailed to a cross" (*IPC* 131) that brings to completion the union of "what limits" and "what is limited" (the second pair of Pythagoreanism). Weil adds immediately that "if this slave is God . . . we have the perfection of harmony as conceived by the Pythagoreans, the harmony in which there is maximum distance and maximum unity between contraries." Clearly the "Pythagorean" harmony has become "Platonic" harmony, the harmony that Weil sees as incarnated by both the crucified just man of the *Republic* and the crucified Soul of the *Timaeus*.

This is the pinnacle of Weil's Christian Platonism. Yet here again, as with the three phases of Platonism, the process is not yet complete. Another look at her annotations to the *Timaeus* makes readily apparent that the third largest group of annotations (after those on the Trinity and those on the World Soul) concerns the "obedience" of the physical world to the World Soul, which is also the human soul's task to imitate.[29] Weil notes, with respect to the creation of souls by the Artificer and the lower gods (41c–d), that since the divine substance does not reside in the human soul, the latter "can only become one with God through the mediation and the imitation of the World Soul."[30] This imitation is accomplished by contemplating (which is linked to the gift of sight) the celestial rotations (47c) and then through the science of musical harmony (47d–e).

Weil's marginal note on these passages—"mediating role of the World Soul (object of imitation)"—is expected.[31] But the explosion of marginal notes found on the following pages is rather unexpected. There, Plato when he defines the world as a blend of intelligence and necessity introduces the third cause of the world, the *chōra*—the empty space in which creation takes place, which receives creation. After insisting on the fact that the *chōra* is the third type of reality "born before Heaven,"[32] Weil returns, with greater emphasis, to the terms with which Plato defines its "receptive" nature: as it receives the "imprints of all bodies," it is the "matrix," the "mother" of material things.[33] Most important is that, as receiver, it must be shapeless, an "imprint bearer" free of all particularizing influence. Weil notes in the margin: "Absolute virginity of the Mother . . . the Great Mother."[34] The fundamental importance of such remarks is patent if we connect them to *cahier* 8, where she identifies the primordial substance and the Virgin Mary[35] and even more so if we compare them to the central passages of "The Pythagorean Doctrine." There her analysis of the fifth level of mediation, inherent in all material things, derives from a "necessity" composed of fixed relationships whose "bearer/medium" is precisely "what Plato would call the receiver, the matrix, the imprint bearer." She adds: "the words matter, mother, marine, Mary are so alike as to be nearly identical."[36]

Obeying the World Soul not only implies obedience to necessity but also entails, on a deeper level, obedience to "the inertness of matter." This is the condition for receiving all form and for being "begotten of water and spirit" (*IPC* 163). This remark then leads to a final significant group of annotations on the last part of *Timaeus* that is on the "formation of spinal fluid," that is, in Plato, the fluid that flows between the head and the organs of desire. Here she finds the "core of the hidden doctrine of the *Timaeus*," namely, that what flows through the spine is the locus of a "divine seed" (translated by Weil as "supernatural seed").[37] This seed defines humankind as a "celestial plant."[38] Weil then writes: "the supernatural seed is a living, divine being within us, an 'internal' mediator. . . . It is the soul of our soul, our inspiration, the organ of supernatural love."[39] These reflections are the source of some significant developments in *cahier* 9 on the "hidden doctrine of the *Timaeus*," described by Weil as "the [doctrine] of the seed."[40] They also form the third source (after the "World Soul" and the "Receiver") of the doctrine of consent and obedience to the Universe as defined in the last part of her essay "The Pythagorean Doctrine": "consent is supernatural love; it is the spirit of God within us . . . [so] we have this extraordinary privilege to be . . . mediators between God and his creation" (*IPC* 163).

Following these analyses, leading from the Christology hidden in the World Soul to the link between matter, Mary, and the Word, we now broach what should be called, from Weil's point of view, a "Platonic pneumatology." The identification of the divine seed planted in humans with the indwelling of the Holy Spirit clearly relates to the call "to complete creation" that governed her earlier associations of the *Republic* with the *Timaeus*.[41] Thus the sense in which Weilian Platonism is "trinitarian" becomes apparent. My conviction is that after writing "God in Plato," Weil composed her own *Timaeus*, that is, "Divine Love in Creation." In doing so, she continued and clarified what to her is the ultimate meaning of Platonism: the revelation of the two mediations of the Word and of the Spirit.

From *Metaxu* to Trinity: Metaphysics as Metaxology

We see how Weil both assimilates and transforms the classical themes of Christian Platonism. This Christian Platonism, from the church fathers to the twelfth-century School of Chartres, had devoted considerable attention to divine goodness and the Trinitarian analogies they could find in Plato's work. German Idealism later even linked the Passion and the Creation, as Weil did. But Weil sees in Platonism not only the doctrines of the Trinity, Creation, and Passion but also the doctrine of the Immaculate Conception, in which Mary is the image of the primeval obedience of creation, as well as the doctrine of Pentecost, in which humankind becomes a mediator in turn. But this does not sufficiently express the originality and the deepest metaphysical importance of Weil's understanding of Plato. This is what I would like to develop here.

The Sovereignty of Good

We can begin to show Weil's counterproposal to the contemporary plan to overthrow Platonism by focusing on what distinguishes her reading of Plato from Heidegger's. This is necessary because it was Heidegger's interpretation that played a determining role in the perception of Platonism as a metaphysics of "presence" that subjects being to a "principle of reason." For example, in his lecture of 1942, "Platons Lehre von der Warheit" (Plato's Doctrine of Truth), Heidegger glosses over both the *transcendence* and the *descending* movement of Good that Weil considers so essential in Plato. By considering the idea of the Good as an idea whose preeminence can be no greater than that of the greatest "visibility," Heidegger achieves a double reduction. On the one hand, the Good is not defined as good per se but rather as good in the relative sense of "what enables" something;[42] it is reduced to a function of "visibility" and "potentiality" by which each thing is what it is in its own power (*dunamis*).[43] On the other hand, despite Plato's affirmation according to which the Good is beyond being and essence, Heidegger makes out as if it were subjected to what is "within sight," leaving totally aside Plato's assumption of the Good's "incommensurate grandeur."

This double reduction takes Platonic truth as "what is seized from what is torn loose from its concealment,"[44] and also as "precision of perception and language," on which was based the transition from truth as *aletheia* (i.e., revealed truth) to truth as "exact equivalence."[45] Heidegger thus obscures the dimension of the "revelation" of a truth that in fact surpasses pure reason, the locus of Weil's Platonic experience of grace. The contrast between the two readings of the myth of the cave is significant in this regard. For whereas Weil compares walking in darkness, followed by being blinded by the sun to the two stages of a relation with the transcendent Good (i.e., the analogy with the two nights of St. John of the Cross), Heidegger notes a desire for control through which the subject seeks to "settle on the stable limits of things" and to reduce all reality to what can be imagined, that is, to its *quidditas*.[46] Therefore, this reading sets apart the *relationship* of being and its essences to "the Good beyond being and essence." But it also excludes another essential relation: reason with love, *logos* with *eros*. By defining the Platonic essence of truth in the way he does, Heidegger indeed simply "forgets" the Platonic dimension of love.[47] But Heidegger forgets precisely what Weil considers essential: the connection by which the "intellectual path," linked to the transcendence of Good, is subordinate to the "non-intellectual, i.e., ethical and mystical, path."[48]

By insisting on the transcendence of the Good, Weil anticipated the twentieth-century thinker who wrote the most decisive rebuttal to Heidegger, Emmanuel Lévinas. In a recent work the French Plato scholar, J. F. Mattei, has shown the impact of Plato's thought on Lévinas: first, quantitatively, by counting nineteen references to Plato in *Totalité et infini* and twenty-six references in *Autrement qu'être ou Au-delà de l'essence*,[49] and second, and even more important, by noting that his very titles derive from Plato. The "Infinite" that Lévinas opposes to the primacy of "Totality" that reigned from Parmenides to Hegel is the "Desire" for the divine of the *Phaedrus* and the *epekeina tes ousias* (beyond being) of the *Republic* (book VI). The "beyond being" is patently the

"Other" that the *Sophist* opposes to the "Same" of Parmenides, thus forcing Plato to commit parricide with respect to the father of metaphysics. These references are the same ones used by Weil, for whom the desire for Good and the affirmation of divine goodness are the essential truths of Platonism. In contrast to the celebrated formula of paragraph 7 of *Sein und Zeit*, "Higher than actuality stands *possibility*," we might define here a new "principle of principles": "Higher than possibility stands the Desire for the impossible," that is, the Desire for the Infinite that exceeds the possibilities of *Dasein* and of the world. So by declaring that "Weil understood everything except the Bible,"[50] Lévinas demonstrated both his failure to understand Weil's views on the Bible and his profound understanding of the positions they shared: first, an openness to an alterity that rejects the ontology of the Same, the neutrality of the Heideggerian being, as well as every ontology of being as *conatus*; second, and more significantly, the similarity of his theme of the substitution of "the One for the Other" and the rending of the self in Weil's concept of decreation.[51]

Nonetheless, despite the shared reference to a Plato freed from the onto-theo-logical framework, two elements create a distance between Lévinas and Weil. On the one hand, unlike Weil, Lévinas partly shares Heidegger's viewpoint, remaining critical of Plato, reserving, depending on the text in question, an ambivalent attitude toward him.[52] On the other hand, the separation he imposes between being and what is beyond being seems more dualistic, and appears to make the rooting of Good in the world impossible. As Mattéi notes, Lévinas tends to think, with an unbearable tension, about the "hereafter of essence . . . in the mode of the hereafter, as if language could gather momentum . . . and leap *over* being . . . to reach the Good, without the hard springboard of the *ousias* (essences)."[53] But why? It strikes me that Weil offers an answer we do not find in Mattéi's text. Neither Lévinas nor Heidegger properly recognized the essential nature of mediation in Plato, which is at the heart of Weil's interpretation.

Metaxu, Vinculum, *and Trinity*

A strength of Weil's reading of Plato is that she recognized, in the Platonic corpus, that the adverb *metaxu*, which translates as "between," "intermediary," and "mediation," is related to both the essence of love and the essence of reason. As the *Symposium*, the *Republic*, the *Philebus*, and the *Timaeus* show, by using the term *metaxu*, Plato brings together his definitions of philosophy (the intermediary between ignorance and wisdom), Love (the intermediary between the human and the divine), and Dialectics (the intermediary between opinion and contemplation).[54] We can see what is at stake. As opposed to Heidegger's reading, this term reveals truth as a movement of relation (not the grasping of an *idea*) and, at the same time, shows the unity of the two Platonic paths, the intellectual and the nonintellectual. Let us then consider the *metaxu* at a deeper level, whereby Weil, following Plato's example, defines all things of this world as a *metaxu*, as related to the Divine. Every thing is a relation: (a) in the sense that it implies a plurality of unified elements, and (b) in the sense that this plurality is related to a principle of unity not residing within it. Weil clarifies this situation by outlining the Pythagorean doctrine of the union of opposites and the Kantian theory of antinomies whereby the principle of unity always transcends what is unified, with no thing containing in itself the ultimate root of its being. No reality is a closed substance; this is why each thing is as if made of a "hole," containing an internal "void"; this void is the equivalent in nature to desire in the human soul.[55] In such an ontology there is no pure nature. This is as true for nature as it is for spirit. For instance, the wonder of the Pythagorean discovery of the incommensurable numbers shows even in mathematics itself there is no such thing as pure reason (SG 121–26). All reality of this world, whether material or spiritual, thus bears a relation to a transcendent principle whose key defies understanding; this principle, as a unifying relation, functions as a mediator between a thing and itself.[56]

That all reality thus opens to a relation that is a mystery, a relation that must be conceived as both an ascending and descending, leads Weil to connect the philosophy of the *metaxu* on the one hand to the *Timaeus*'s World Soul and on the other to the doctrine of the Word "in whom all things were made" (John 1) and "through which all things hold together" (Col. 1). Such a perspective departs not only from the fundamental ontology of Heidegger but also from the pure metaphysics of the transcendence of Good laid out by Lévinas. By articulating an "analogical" movement of being toward Good, and a "catalogical" movement of Good toward being, she frees herself from the either or choice of immanence or transcendence typifying modernity.

Such a connection makes Weil's thought astonishingly similar to Maurice Blondel's, the creator of a metaphysics of mediation that explicitly rejected this opposition between immanence and transcendence. The initial intuition that inspired Blondel's famous thesis of 1893, *L'Action*, can be summarized by a formula taken from his *Lettre sur l'Apologétique* of 1896. There he declares that for the human condition, "no natural solution is a solution" because "we cannot reach the 'being in nothingness' without at least implicitly passing through the Universal Creator who is the source of all and who links all being."[57] At the end of "Divine Love in Creation" Weil also writes: "God is mediator and all mediation is God. . . . We cannot pass from nothing to nothing without passing through God. God is the only way. He is the path."[58] As I have argued elsewhere,[59] there are at least three levels of similarity between Weil and Blondel. Level one is a philosophy of the relation between nature and the supernatural, rejecting both what Blondel calls *extrinsicisme* (which would separate the two) and *immanentisme* (which fuses or merges them). For Blondel, there is no "pure nature": all voluntary choice is illumined by the "true light which enlightens everyone" and that "came into the world." Through it all are implicitly led to "come to the decision regarding one's salvation."[60] On level two, there is a connection between a phenomenology "of insufficiency" and an ontology of mediation. *L'Action* of 1893 insists unceasingly, as does Blondel's metaphysical trilogy of the 1930s, on the intrinsic incompleteness of being and of acting, as attested to by the "crack," the "gap," the "void" inherent in natural and spiritual being, and at the same time by the fact that being and acting are "intermediaries" whose "mediating role [creates] absolute truth."[61] Finally and most important, on level three, this ontology is related to a metaphysics of the Mediating Word, which is defined as the *Vinculum Substantiale* of all created being. The aim of this metaphysics "to the second power"[62] is to go beyond a purely conceptual or "notional" metaphysics (which ignores the relation of reason to mystery and love)[63] by suggesting that being and acting have a hidden relation to the Incarnation (and not only to the creator God).

The most remarkable element can be found in Blondel's final work, *La Philosophie de l'esprit chrétien*, in which he expresses in its final form "the philosophical enigma of a constant mediatory function and the mystery of the incarnated Mediator."[64] Blondel, developing a new concept of a *philosophia perennis*, viewed the Pythagoreans as the first to sense the ontological mystery whose key would be Christ. This was through the discovery of a suprarational mediation hidden within being founded thereon the discipline of *"philia-sophia."* He also saw in the discovery of incommensurable numbers the supreme example of the "suprarational," of the "presence of the infinite in the finite itself."[65] The full impact of this example becomes clear by understanding that the relation between humankind and God is always defined by Blondel as that between *incommensurables*, a relation incarnated in Christ who, as the one "between the

Creator and the created, makes of himself the bridge, Pontifex, the passage reuniting the extremes."[66] Blondel does not explicitly speculate on the idea of a proportional mean; but the union of incommensurables is its equivalent and corresponds to Weil's concept of supernatural love. This precisely makes the impossible possible, makes unity and love possible across maximum distance. Blondel writes: "God somehow withdrew himself and emptied himself to create nothingness, to leave room for virtual being, and to provide him with the means to recreate, to resuscitate God. It was impossible according to metaphysical appearances[,] . . . but nonetheless, it is the real truth. *Deus seipsum exinanivit*."[67]

Higher than incommensurability, then, stands possibility. And because the metaphysics of the *Vinculum* concludes in a metaphysics of the gift, we can add, paraphrasing J. L. Marion, there is as much giving as there is incommensurability.[68] Blondel and Weil both saw in Creation the expression of an initial divine self-emptying (*kenosis*), in the Trinity the potentialities of the Cross, and in the Cross the pinnacle of Trinitarian love. The mysterious nature of those ideas is the truth revealed in the phenomenon of mediating being and in the Trinitarian principle of the "fullness of being." Nonetheless, it strikes me that Weil's use of the modalities of the concept of the fullness of being seeks to connect being and Trinity more deeply than Blondel's; on this point we return to Weil's reading of Plato.

Being and the Fullness of Being

On a basic level, the concept of the "fullness of being" designates for Weil being and life within the Trinity, the revelation of the essence of Good. Still, we must differentiate here between (a) the level of the divine essence where the uniqueness of the Trinity is the identity between being and relation—here being is pure Relation[69]—and (b) at a higher level, the personal being characteristic of the three divine Persons. Unlike human attachment to the self, divine personal being is "the divine model of a person who transcends himself by renouncing himself." This model is the "creative principle and master of the Universe[,] . . . the fullness of being."[70] This sheds light on the God who "does not feel envy" (*Timaeus* 29e). It only does so, though, by positing an intra-Trinitarian *kenosis* as God, as does Balthasar. Through this *kenosis*, this self-emptying, the divine life is grasped as a substantial ecstasy, a subsisting altruism, where each person is an orientation toward and for the other.

At a second level, the fullness of being refers to the Trinitarian Love that is able to reveal itself and to exist at the greatest distance, from the Creation to the Incarnation and to the Cross. This can be illustrated first by the experience of Beauty. In the *Phaedrus* (250b–c) Plato defined Beauty as the only Idea made "visible and manifest by itself (*auto*).[71] Weil understands beauty to be a figure of the Incarnation, through which the transcendent Good radiates and reveals itself in Beauty without being reduced to it. This is why, in a Trinitarian perspective, "Beauty itself is the Son of God, because He is the image of the Father, and Beauty is the image of God."[72] This relation transforms aesthetics into "the key to supernatural truths."[73] These formulas coincide with what can be called the "principle of principles" as defined by Balthasar in *The Glory of the Lord:* "He [Christ] *is* what he expresses—namely, God—but he is not whom he expresses—namely, the Father. This incomparable paradox stands as the fountainhead of the Christian aesthetic, and therefore of all aesthetics!"[74] This is why since the coincidence of love and distance form "the soul of beauty," Weil and Balthasar see the fullness of beauty in the glory of the Cross, for it is an expression at one and the same time of maximum love and maximum distance, the distance between human misery and divine completeness. "The proof for me, the truly miraculous thing, is the perfect beauty of the accounts of the Passion. . . . This is what compels me to believe."[75] The Cross is the "supreme mediation[,] . . . that of the Holy Spirit unifying across an infinite distance the divine Father to the Son who is equally divine but emptied of his divinity and nailed on a point of space and time."[76] By showing that "the love between the Father and the Son is stronger than the distance between the Creator and the created,"[77] the Cross is the supreme *metaxu*, because it fulfills through an *event* the *essence* of Pythagorean mediation as the capacity to unify absolute distant terms.[78]

To perfect the mediation between God and creation, then, a third level of the fullness of being needs to be defined, where the Spirit's mediation is combined with that of the Word. Here the divine plenitude of being inhabits the world, not only through the Incarnation of the Word, but also through the participation of humanity in the Spirit of love that unifies the Father and the Son.[79] This level is about God's presence in the world, "for which God needs the cooperation of creation . . . not because He is the creator but because He is the Spirit"—a presence, Weil adds, that is "the presence of decreation."[80] This affirmation is essential to understanding the *creative* meaning of decreation and Platonism in Weil. Once again, we have to compare the *Philebus* and the *Timaeus,* this time for the distinction between the perfection proper to divine life and the perfection proper to the "good life" for the human being: "the good life" implies that, as human beings are a blend of spirit and sensibility, their vocation should consist in harmonizing this dual dimension. One formula of the *cahiers* sums up this reading of the *Philebus* and at the same time defines the third level of the fullness of being: "The fullness of the reality of God is beyond this world, but the fullness of human reality is in this world, even should one be perfect."[81] Of course, this does not mean that a philosophy of the world might take the place here of the metaphysical and mystical dimension. Quite the opposite; we must keep in mind the following: (1) the truth of the world and of action only exists as the image of Trinitarian life, the latter being the renunciation and giving of oneself, for only the "non-acting" action of the "decreated" ego (filled with the Holy Spirit) can act in such a way that the divine fullness is transmitted to the world; and (2) the ultimate goal of creation is to reach the perfect unity of the three levels of the fullness of being we already defined, which implies that we should become fully cognizant of the perceivable world as Plato describes it. This is why Christian Platonism must be put into practice in a philosophy of work, of establishing roots, of the body politic, as a systematic link between Good and necessity.[82] (See chapters 4 and 5 in this volume.) Weil's Platonism and Trinitarian metaxology do not lead to ecstasy but to participation here and now in the "non-acting action" of Grace.[83] The events of salvation "are historical events. They are realities, not only in heaven, but also on earth. There is no other reality in this world than what occurs in a set place and a period of time."[84] Thus is defined the Trinitarian structure of the "fullness of being," at levels one and two—"God is only perfect as Trinity, and the love which constitutes the Trinity finds its perfection only in the Cross" (*IPC* 132)—and at level three as the presence of "the spirit of God in us," by which we become "mediators between God and his own creation" (IPC 163).

Conclusion

I conclude by bringing together, in the form of five proposals, certain dimensions that I consider to be the at the heart of Weil's thought.

1. What I have called Weil's metaxology should assist us in breaking through the impasse created by the alternative between the Aristotelian and Thomist metaphysics of being, on the one hand, and the Neoplatonic/Lévinasian metaphysics of "beyond being," on the other, that still structures metaphysical debate

today. The very rich concept of the fullness of being in Weil's thought, too often misunderstood, is a decisive key, for it allows us to preserve an analogical relation between being and the fullness of being, a relation established by Creation, while at the same time Weil's descending metaphysics of the fullness of being (what I call the "cataloghy" of grace) keeps the limits of this analogy flexible.

2. This is so because Weil's philosophy of mediation recovers the double meaning of the prefix *meta-* as found in Greek thought. Its primary meaning is not the traditional "beyond" begun with Andronicus of Rhodes but "between" as contained in the term *metaxu*.[85] Furthermore, releasing "*meta*physics" from its purely literal relation to *phusis* (nature), mediation, which is at the heart of the question of being, redefines the universality of the "*meta*-fonction" (S. Breton), implicated at every level of being.

3. Metaxology, rooted in the phenomenon of mediation that is a relatedness over distance, allows us to conceive of a mode of being beyond the alternative between immanence and transcendence and also beyond the dilemma of presence and absence in which the phenomenological critic of metaphysics risks becoming entrapped. The wavering, for example, between the rejection of "presence" on the one hand (Derrida), and the affirmation of an "immediate" or "saturating" presence of the Absolute on the other (M. Henry's philosophy of Life, but perhaps also the "saturated phenomenon" and the "phenomenon of revelation" of Marion), seems to confirm the significance of the path undertaken in the *Philebus* that Weil makes her own: to develop a philosophy of revelation that avoids "reaching the One too quickly" and forgetting that, since revelation does not suppress mystery, "what is hidden is [always] more real than what is manifest" (C II 273–74).

4. Weil's metaxology reestablishes in an extraordinarily bold stroke the link between Philosophy and Revelation by granting philosophical status, as did Blondel, to the concept "supernatural." At the same time, this link refuses to compromise on the question of the irreducible autonomy of reason. All phenomena of mediation participate, in a hidden and implicit manner, in Trinitarian mediation, while the doctrines of the Trinity, the Incarnation, and the Passion are only manifested as real for "an intellect driven by love." "Of course, this does not imply that these dogmas could have been discovered by human reason without revelation; but once they become apparent, they impose themselves on the intellect with certainty only if the latter is enlightened by love" (IPC 131–32).[86] Thus the self-evidence of revelation and the glory of the Cross can shed light on the intuition of the *logos*, of beauty and of misfortune that so

infused Greece. If so, philosophy as metaxology is the phenomenon of the Trinitarian presence of God in this world. But this presence, as it is, can only be affirmed through revelation.

5. It is therefore only at the level of practical reason that philosophy can purport to meet God as supernatural Good, and ultimately for Weil at the level where philosophy merges with the mysticism of "decreative" charity. Plato is still present in her most mystical texts. Thus, in what is sometimes called the "terrible prayer" found in the New York *Notebooks* (*FLN* 244–45) where she asks God to transform her whole being "into the substance of Christ and given for food to indigents," we find the following passage: "May this body move or be transfixed . . . in uninterrupted accordance with Thy will. May this hearing, sight, taste, touch receive the 'perfectly exact imprint' of Thy creation" (*CS* 204). "The perfectly exact imprint of Creation" is the term with which Plato, in the *Timaeus*, designates the matrix, the perfectly obedient original substance, a term that Weil had underlined in her copy and that she repeatedly compared with Mary, an image of perfectly pure creation, capable of becoming the imprint of all things. Weil's "sin of envy" when she thought of Christ on the Cross was not solely her wish to become Christ on the Cross. It was to see herself at one and the same time as the Word on the Cross (the crucified World Soul of the *Timaeus*) and as Mary at the foot of the Cross (the perfectly pure and obedient "substance" of the *Timaeus*) in a total gift of self, seeking to merge with the Holy Spirit (whose true name is "Gift"). I doubt that this is a sin of envy. I think rather that it was the meaning of her vocation, of her life and death.

Translated by Céline Bally and Chris Callahan

Notes

1. Gilles Deleuze, "Platon et le Simulacre," in *Logique du Sens* (Paris: Minuit, 1969), 292–307.

2. Actually as far as the summary of *L'amour divin dans la création* to Father Perrin (*CS* 30–36; OC VI.3 400–406).

3. The numerous essays on the Greeks that Weil wrote for Father Perrin in Marseilles to illustrate to him the universality of grace are found chiefly in two French volumes, *La Source grecque* and *Intuitions pre-chretiennes*. Most of these are published together in English in *Intimations of Christianity among the Ancient Greeks*. However, a couple appear in *Science, Necessity, and the Love of God.* — Ed.

4. I outline this task in Emmanuel Gabellieri, *Être et don: Essai sur l'unité et l'enjeu de la pensée de S. Weil*, thèse de doctorat d'etat, Université de Nice, 1977, 454–55.

5. SG 72–73.

6. See Emmanuel Gabellieri, "S. Weil, la source grecque et le christianisme," *Études*, May 2001, 641–52 (on her conviction that persistence in loving the good through pain and evil is proof or our relation to the supernatural).

7. See the extensive analyses of *Gorgias* and *Phaedo* in SG 73–76.

8. SG 96–101. The texts that define the path of knowledge of the Order of the World in *IPC* are already mentioned here (SG 98–100).

9. See Gabellieri, *Être et don*, 459 n. 28.

10. I nonetheless point out that a first reference to Pythagorean tradition and to its notion of the being as "relation," source of the Platonic idea of science (SG 97–101), must be viewed as the initial nucleus of "The Divine Love in Creation," which she composed afterward.

11. *Phaedrus* 250a–251c; 108–9 quoted here.

12. Weil had indicated earlier that "the dialogue in which the notion of order of the world appears blatantly and is personified in a divinity called the soul of the world is the *Timaeus*" (SG 101).

13. It is important for the English reader to realize that the essay "God in Plato" (French: "Dieu dans Platon"), which appears in English translation in *Science, Necessity, and the Love of God* (and only the first fifteen pages in *Intimations* under the title "God in Plato"), is followed in *La Source grecque* by numerous commentaries on Platonic texts. "Divine Love in Creation" in French is considerably longer than the English translation by that name and includes in its later portions pages that in English are separated out into separate essays, most notably the long and very significant essay "The Pythagorean Doctrine."—*Ed.*

14. Heidsieck, "Sur quelques problèmes de traduction et d'interprétation du Timée," proceedings of the conference Simone Weil et les Langues, Université P. Mendès-France, Grenoble, 1991, 155–63; reissued in *Cahiers Simone Weil* 18.1 (March 1995): 35–43.

15. *Cahiers Simone Weil* 18.1 (March 1995): 39.

16. See *IPC* 116, 119–20, 129: these references serve, along with those to Pythagoreanism, as the point of departure for the last forty pages, in which Weil leaves behind all references to rely solely on her own inspiration (*IPC* 135–71).

17. See Eric O. Springsted, *S.Weil and the Suffering of Love* (Cambridge: Cowley, 1986).

18. See the general outline of this text given in Gabellieri, *Être et don*, 463 n. 42.

19. See Gabellieri, *Être et don*, 463–81; and the summary for Father Perrin in CS 29–36.

20. Michel Narcy, in "À Propos du *Timée* de S. Weil: Descartes relayé par Platon?" (*Cahiers Simone Weil* 18.1 [March 1995]: 25–34) has already shown what a first set of

annotations, dating from the time of the Cartesian thesis of 1930, revealed the parallel Weil established between Cartesian and Platonic physics. I intend here to make known another set of annotations in which Weil relates the *Timaeus* to Christian Revelation.

21. One such link is that of "proportional geometry" in which, from three numbers, the intermediary being to "the last one what the first one is to the last one, and reciprocally ", "the intermediary becomes the first and the last" (*IPC* 116).

22. Note top of 144, on *Timée*, ed. G. Budé (Paris: Edition Rivaud, "Belles Lettres," 1925), housed in the Bibliothèque Nationale, henceforth cited as *RSW*.

23. From 28a to 34b.

24. He is "Eternally real" (rather than "eternal being"), "true to himself" (and not identical), "grasped by thought aided by relation, and by the intellect aided by speech" (instead of "apprehended by intellection and reasoning") (*RSW* 140–41). See also 143, 147: "the Holy Spirit who orders all things."

25. *RSW*, bottom of 143.

26. *RSW*, 144, 228.

27. *RSW* 147 (cf. *IPC* 37).

28. *RSW* 148, 150–51, 157, 165.

29. What follows elucidates the "two essential ideas" of *Timaeus* defined at the opening of Divine Love in creation": "the substance of the Universe we live in is love" (*IPC* 37); "this world is also the Model *we must imitate*," as "the perfect image which is the only Son of God" (*IPC* 39).

30. *RSW* bottom of 157.

31. *RSW* top of 165.

32. *RSW* 167.

33. On p. 169 Weil underlines and translates twice the formula "Il convient de comparer ce qui reçoit à la mère, l'origine au père, et la nature qui est entre les deux à l'enfant" (It is appropriate to compare what receives to the mother, the origin to the father, and nature, which is between both, to the child) (50d3–4).

34. On p. 169 Weil marks in the margin, with four vertical strokes and four checkmarks, passage 51a–b where Plato writes that the "shapeless" mother participates very clumsily in the "intelligible."

35. For example, "The holy virgin was incarnated in Mary like the Word in Jesus." And this is exactly what Plato calls the "Mother" (*C III* 22, 17, 21, 39, 57, 61,77–78; and the insistence with which she distinguishes between the "substance" understood in that sense and "development" in *C III* 71, 77, 104, 201).

36. "les mots matières, mère, mer, Marie se ressemblent au point d'être presque identiques" (*IPC* 143).

37. *RSW* 201.

38. *RSW* 225: Weil translates *daimon* as "internal mediator," in accordance with the *Symposium* (where love is designated as the mediator between the divine and the human).

39. *RSW* 228.

40. *C* III 252–55, together with *C* III 89, 97–98, 160 ("pneuma"), 217–19, 226–28, 262; the intermediate analysis of the *Timaeus* (*IPC* 33–34); and the theme of the "second birth" in *CS*.

41. The analysis of the fifth level of the consequences of mediation leads to substantial reflections because it deals with the link (through thought, work, action, and love) between the Spirit and necessity.

42. Heidegger, *La Doctrine de Platon sur la Vérité (Platons Lehre von der Warheit) Questions II* (Paris: Gallimard, 1968), 149–50. The same analysis is present in the Courses of 1931–32, *De l'Essence de la Vérité* (Paris: Gallimard, 2001), 128.

43. Heidegger, *De l'Essence de la Vérité*, 130–32. This understanding of "Agathon" as *dunamis*, power and strength (that recurs in the Aristotelian *energeia* as "strength"— *Kraft*) is the opposite of the "descent" of good in the Weilian sense.

44. Heidegger, *Questions II*, 150. Cf. the analysis of passage 516c2–3, seen as the origin of the term "meta-physics" (ibid., 159), as well as J. F. Mattéi's critique in "Lévinas et Plato," in *Emmanuel Lévinas, Positivité et transcendance, Lévinas et la phenomenologie* (Paris: Presses Universitaires de France, coll. "Epiméthée," 2000), 78.

45. Heidegger, *Questions II*, 143.

46. Ibid., 141, 146.

47. For Plato, truth is "relation with sight, perception, thought, and language," a relation based "on 'reason', 'spirit', 'thought', 'logos,'" which foretells the reign of "subjectivity" (ibid., 162–63). "Que le *Logos* ne doive avoir aucun rapport avec l'*eros* se vérifie dans *Introduction à la métaphysique*, où Heidegger oppose catégoriquement le *Logos* (ici chez Héraclite), compris en seule relation avec la *phusis*, à son interprétation religieuse comme 'un étant particulier, le Fils de Dieu': curieusement, la fonction 'médiatrice' du *Logos* est ici référée au seul Philon (la 'parole' de Dieu transmettant 'les commandements et les ordres') et non à Platon" (*Introduction à la métaphysique* [Paris: Gallimard, 1980], 142).

48. One could summarize Weil's Platonism with the following formula: "Good begins beyond will, as truth begins beyond understanding" (*CS* 224).

49. Mattéi, "Lévinas et Platon," 73–87.

50. Oral communication reported by W. Rabi in *Simone Weil, philosophe, historienne et mystique* (ed. G. Kahn) (Paris: Aubier, 1978), 141.

51. Cf. Weil's quote (*CS* 204) in Lévinas, *Autrement qu'Être ou au-delà de l'essence*, Livre de Poche, 217. This matches Raoul Mortley's and William Desmond's analyses, for whom Plato is a philosopher of desire, of alterity, and of difference. See Mortley, *Désir et différence dans la tradition platonicienne* (Paris: Vrin, 1988). For Mortley, reason tends toward the One, whereas difference tends toward the suprarational (18).

52. This criticism is based on the opposition of "meaning" and "science" (rooted in the primacy of Ideality) and on the rejection of the theory of reminiscence, considered as a nostalgia for "totality" (Mattei, "Platon et Lévinas," 83–84).

53. Mattéi, "Platon et Lévinas," 85.

54. See SG 116–18, 124–28.

55. See the index to *OC* VI.1 564 and *OC* VI.2 720.

56. *SG* 151, 165.

57. Blondel, *Œuvres Complètes* II (Paris: Presses Universitaires de France, 1997), 166.

58. *IPC* 165.

59. Emmanuel Gabellieri, "Blondel et S. Weil, une convergence inattendue," *Bulletin de l'Institut Catholique de Lyon* (October–December): 33–51; "Blondel, S. Weil et le Panchristisme: Vers une 'metaxologie' chez Maurice Blondel et la quête du sens," *Bibliothèque des Archives de Philosophie* 63 (1998): 53–65.

60. Blondel, *Œuvres Complètes* II:132 (44).

61. Cf. *Une enigme historique: Le vinculum substantiale d'après Leibniz* (Paris: Beauchesne, 1930), 122–136; and *L'Action* (Paris: Presses Universitaires de France, 1973), 453.

62. Blondel, *L'Action*, 464.

63. Cf. this type of formula, so close to Weil: "Existence is love; one knows nothing if one does not love." *Carnet intimes* I (Paris: Presses Universitaires de France), 222.

64. Blondel, *La Philosophie de l'esprit chrétien* I (Paris: Presses Universitaires de France, 1944), 83–85.

65. Ibid., 85 n. 1, which refers to Blondel's article "La Pérénité de la philosophie et le discernement progressif d'une constante et indispensable médiation," *Revue de Métaphysique et de Morale* 4 (1940): 319–63, in which he writes that "désespérant d'accorder, par quelque médiation que se fût, leur sagesse grecque avec cette irruption de l'infini dans le réel, ils ne voulurent prendre que le nom d'"amis de la sagesse' <avant que> la dialectique platonicienne en sa géniale tentative [reconnaisse] que tout ce qui est vrai, beau et bon est un mélange, une participation, une médiation de l'infini et du fini" (despairing of reconciling, by any possible mediation, their Greek wisdom with this irruption of the infinite into reality, they only agreed to take the name 'friends of wisdom' [before] Platonic dialectics, in its inspired approach, 'acknowledged' that everything that is true, beautiful, and good is a blend, a participation, a mediation of the infinite and the finite). Ibid., 352.

66. Blondel, *La Philosophie de l'esprit chrétien*, 9.

67. *Exigences philosophiques du christianisme* (Paris: Presses Universitaires de France, 1950), 258.

68. See Emmanuel Gabellieri, "Incommensurabilité et médiation: La triple puissance de la métaphysique," in *Penser l'être de l'action: La Métaphysique du Dernier Blondel*, ed. E. Tourpe (Louvain: Peeters, 2000), 101–17, followed by "Les Exigences philosophiques du Christianisme: Une métaphysique du don," in proceedings of the conference Blondel dans l'Action et la Trilogie, Université Grégorienne, Rome, November 16–18, 2000.

69. "God's sole relation to himself. . . . This relation is its very essence. This relation is the fullness of being" (C II 160 and C II 66–70, 244–48, 267–70). This assertion is also found in the passages of St. Thomas Aquinas's *Summa Theologica* on "subsisting? Relations" which Weil copied into the last notebooks (C III 275–80).

70. AD 172.

71. See C III 57–59, 74–75, where Weil notes: "Plato has changed on this point. He has not always seen the *absolute* in earthly beauty."

72. IPC 37: It is not surprising that Weil writes this in her "Trinitarian" commentary of the *Timaeus*.

73. C III 275.

74. H. U. v. Balthasar, *The Glory of the Lord* (ET), vol. 1 (San Francisco: Ignatius Press, 1982), 29.

75. LR 58.

76. IPC 166.

77. CS 201.

78. "God first, then we, must cross the infinite distance and thickness of time and space"; the Cross gives its meaning to "the length, the breadth, the depth of the love of Christ, which surpasses all understanding" (C III 11–12); "For love to be as great as possible, the distance must be as great as possible," which is in "direct contract to Leibniz" (C III 44–45, 261); "1, 5, 25. Unity above distance. 25 is closer to 1 than 24, which is not connected to 1 by a proportional mean" (C III 261).

79. Gabellieri, "Blondel, S. Weil et le Panchristisme," 64; Gabellieri, "Incommensurabilité et médiation," 105–10.

80. C II 253. "Essential level in order to both understand and supersede the distance necessity and good, which shows why the Trinity is indispensable for an understanding of justice and of good" (Gabellieri, *Être et don*, 537).

81. C II 291. This is why Weil could write: "The object of my research is not the Supernatural but this world" (C II 47), or: "Substance, something that is not spirit, something that is not God. How extraordinary. It is the primary substance that we, creatures, are" (C III 17).

82. See on this point, Gabellieri, *Être et don*, 664–700, and the thesis of R. Chenavier, "L'évolution de la pensée de S. Weil sur le rôle du travail dans la vie de l'individu et dans celle de la société," Université Grenoble II, 1997.

83. Here we should reconsider Bergson's critique of the metaphysics of creation (see the end of *Deux sources de la morale et de la religion*) toward which Weil was far too unjust. See the following passage taken from *Entretien avec J. Chevalier* (Paris: Plon, 1925), 222: "If we refer to Christianity, the Greek mysticism appears quite incomplete, for it considers ecstasy as its end, whereas Christianity . . . beyond ecstasy, reaches love and the action of love. . . . Christ. He does not feel ecstasy, but He is complete."

84. C III 176 and its connection with CS 136, 150. Here it strikes me that Vetö's judgment, in his major work, *La Métaphysique religieuse de Simone Weil* (to which I am deeply indebted), concerning the "greatness and failings of [Weil's] Christian Platonism," in which he defined these "failings" as the incapacity to "grasp the historical nature of the Incarnation," must be softened. (*La Métaphysique religieuse de Simone Weil* [Paris: J. Vrin, 1971], 147, 149).

85. My proposal to replace the classic term *metaphysics* by *metaxology* confirms the inspiration of Desmond in his book *Being and the Between* (Albany: SUNY Press, 1995), who, in making the same remark, sees in what he calls "the Metaxalogical" (inspired also by the Platonic Good) an ontological model superior to the other possible models: Univocity, Equivocity, and Dialectic. The "metaxological" model thus seems to integrate, while superseding, the "analogical" model (not named), which confirms my first point. Most noteworthy for me is the fact that Desmond's research owes nothing to Weil's thought and that I first proposed the term *metaxology* (see my paper "Le dilemme phénoménologique/métaphysique: Propositions sur une Métaxologie," given at the 27th Congrès de l'Association des Sociétés de Philosophie de Langue Française, "La Métaphysique," Québec, August 18–22, 1998) before discovering this book (thanks to Prof. Troisfontaines of Louvain).

86. *IPC* 131–32. The connection thus defined between reason and revelation is at the heart of a monograph in preparation: *Être et grâce, S. Weil et le Christianisme.*

CHAPTER 9

Freedom

MARTIN ANDIC

Simone Weil is concerned with the relation between freedom and necessity, and more broadly between religion and science, although it is the reality of justice—the justice of the world and the God who made it and the men who have to live in it—that provides the context in which she reflects on freedom. She arrives at a religious and moral view of freedom that is remarkably similar to that of Boethius, fourteen centuries earlier. I do not know if she read Boethius's great book *The Consolation of Philosophy*, or even refers to him in her writings, but she would have found his name in the works of Thomas and Dante whom she does mention and quote. Had she lived longer, she would surely have read him eventually, and found confirmation of her views. She would have been drawn to him as a righteous man wrongly put to death and as a Christian who loved Plato, as well as a philosopher who wrote poetry of a high order. It is appropriate on this occasion to compare the two thinkers, and to consider how they throw light on each other and on the questions that they raise about freedom and justice and about the meaning and resources of Christian Platonism, questions that remain alive for us today. We should look for differences too; but it may be their congruity that stands out most sharply in the end.

Boethius

Boethius writes as a prisoner awaiting execution. Dishonored, isolated, and lamenting his misfortunes at the hands of his enemies, he is visited by Lady Philosophy herself, who invites him to pour out his woes so that she can help him. As he tells her, he has followed Plato's advice to philosophers to enter politics, and rising to the highest offices he has worked for justice, only to be falsely accused of treason (for defending the prerogatives of the Senate) and of sorcery (for his astronomy and music, mathematics and philosophy) and to be condemned to death. "Here I am, stripped of my possessions and honors, my name ruined, punished because I tried to do good."[1] O God, he prays, why do you not rule on earth as you do in the heavens and everywhere except among men? Lady Philosophy hears him out, and notes that he has forgotten what he is, how the world is ruled, and to what end. For he supposes that he is "a mortal animal with reason," as if he did not also have a moral intellect that can unite him to eternal God; he complains that he is oppressed and made miserable by wicked fools who are powerful and happy, as if the world were not ruled justly throughout; and he thinks that events occur by chance, as if it were not always only as is right and best. It is only his own moral delusion that has made him wretchedly unhappy, however, and because he still believes that God rules the world there is hope for him. (Like Ivan Karamazov he believes in God, but has lost faith in him, granting that God exists but not that God is just.) He is not in his right mind and has forgotten who he is; but help is available.[2] She will use poetry as well as argument to restore him so that he both feels and thinks as he ought.[3]

She begins by criticizing his notion that he has suffered misfortunes that he has not deserved. The goddess Fortune whose faithlessness he deplores *is* deceptive, but the good things that she capriciously gives and takes are not in themselves worth having and seeking and grieving. The worldly riches and honors and power that Fortune gave him were never really his, seeing that he has lost them. They cannot be shared,[4] and they cannot not make him good by coming or bad by going, so that they cannot truly make his life good and constitute his happiness.[5] The seeming misfortune of losing them is really good fortune, because it shows us the worthlessness in themselves of things that can be won and enjoyed by the wicked and lacked and lost by the good; losing them can *turn* us from them to our true goal.[6]

More positively, Lady Philosophy explains, our true goal is "that which, once it is attained, relieves man of all further desires. This is the supreme good and contains within itself all other lesser goods."[7] It is the Good that (in the language of Aristotle) at once is a formal and final cause of all that is good and the totality of its effects, achieving which would leave nothing else to wish for. We seek this fulfillment in all that we do, and agree on its *meaning*—sufficiency, honor, power, brilliance, and joy—but we disagree about its *criteria*, what it consists in; we pursue its worldly images—wealth, prestige, rank, celebrity, and pleasure—because we have forgotten what it really is.[8] These materialistic goods in themselves are *insufficient* and *ambiguous.* Wealth does not make us good and is never enough, and it makes us feel poor by creating new needs. Honors do not give us the honor that is true nobility, and they dishonor us when offered by the base. The command of kings, and friendship with them, does not give us self-command, and whether we mean to keep it or give it up it makes us unsafe and afraid. Celebrity does not give us any real luster and distinction but is trivial and empty because always limited, even shameful among the ignorant and false. Sensual pleasure does not make us better and bring us joy, and to pursue it leads to anxiety and fear, disease and pain. Thus seeking our happiness in these worldly goods is a blind alley, for none of them is all that is good nor always good; we can be unhappy even in having them, and so it is not having them that makes us happy.[9] But perhaps experience is the best and only proof of the falseness of these goods, the only proof necessary or possible.[10] We seek them because we have forgotten the unity of true goodness that alone makes us truly happy, at once rich, gracious, strong, illustrious, and joyful. This goodness, she goes on to explain in the terms of Neoplatonic philosophy, is only in God, and it *is* God.[11] As he is goodness, so he is unity, and being, naturally sought by everything; and that is how God unifies and rules the world. Everything freely obeys him, and anything that tries to oppose him must fail. Our happiness is to become like him, so that a just man is like God, divine.[12]

Now the prisoner's complaints about the injustice of the world can be fully addressed and answered. If God made the world and rules it justly, then why is there so much wrong among men? If he is good and wise and powerful, then why is there evil that not only goes unpunished but even prospers and is rewarded in place of good, while good in turn goes unrewarded and is punished in place of evil? Lady Philosophy assures him that it would be dismaying if this were true.[13] *But it is not.* The good always succeed and have their reward, and they flourish; the wicked always fail and are punished, and they suffer, and their kind of happiness is worthless.

We are likely to think that this cannot possibly be true. But she will say that our criteria of evil and good, weakness and strength, punishment and reward, misery and flowering, are confused. They are, moreover, the criteria used by the wicked, whose success too much dazzles us.

It is the good who have real power, she explains, for that is power to get the good that truly fulfills us, that makes our lives good by making us good; all men desire this, but only the good attain it. If wicked men could get it, they would not be wicked, and the worse men they are, the less they are truly men at all—so that the *worse* they are, the *less* they are—for evil is a loss of being. They exist, but they are not real, living men.[14] So to do evil is not a power but a weakness, and only the good can do what they truly desire. They are always rewarded by the goodness of their lives, by the integrity that makes them like God, while the wicked are punished by the bestiality of their lives.[15] Though the wicked keep their human form, they cannot ruin the good but only themselves, whom they harm far worse than their victims, by willing to do wrong, still more by doing it, and worst of all by evading punishment that alone could cure them if they accepted it as right and good for them. It is they who deserve our pity (*miseratione*), while the good whom they wrong deserve our love.[16]

Granting that men get the happiness and misery that they deserve—respectively the blessed human happiness of doing right, and the demonic misery of doing wrong—Boethius asks, why does God often send poverty and disgrace and exile to the good, and wealth and honors and position to the bad, as if dispensing these by *chance?*

In other words, even if justice is enough for the just man, he would not choose exile, disgrace, and poverty, and it does not seem right to send him these even if they cannot in themselves make him a worse man or his life really worse. For even if the only real good and evil are moral good, his own right and wrong actions respectively, and even if wealth and reputation and public office are morally indifferent, he naturally *prefers* them and it is more fitting that he should have them than the unjust man. (After all, he is much more likely to make right and wise use of them, and isn't that what they are for?) The fortunes of men seem disposed randomly, and that is unfair.[17]

Lady Philosophy replies that this is "one of the greatest of all questions" that can scarcely be explained fully, at least to human reason.[18] We have to contrast Providence, Fate, Fortune, and Chance, and see how they are the same divine agency as they appear respectively to intellect, reason, imagination, and sense: for we know things not as they are in themselves but as they are to us who know them.[19] Providence is the simple changeless eternal vision of God himself, and Fate is the execution of his vision in the world as it changes in time. Whether Fate works by divine spirits, or the World Soul, or the whole of nature, or angelic power or demonic skill, one thing is sure: Fate accomplishes what Providence disposes. Everything fated is providential, but some providential things are above Fate and free of it, as spheres circling a still center escape centrifugal force by yielding to centripetal, so that they no longer stray into orbit. Changing Fate is to changeless simple Providence as reason is to intellect, as time is to eternity, as a moving circle is to its still center.[20]

Lady Philosophy is relying on the contrast between intellect and reason in Plato, Aristotle, and Plotinus. Plato in *Republic* VI makes Socrates say that whereas mathematics uses reason to draw conclusions with constant reference to examples, philosophy uses intellect to explore the meaning and truth of premises and primitive terms and can dispense with examples, working up to the first principle of all by which everything else is explained: the pure form of Good itself, which shows us what things truly are in what good the best of them do. Aristotle in *Nicomachean Ethics* 6 similarly says that intellect grasps principles of proof but also the particulars of analysis and action in the light of these principles. Plotinus emphasizes that intellect grasps simultaneously and surely what reason takes in successively and tentatively. Intellect is thus an intuitive power directed at first and last terms and especially at moral ones.[21]

Philosophy takes this argument up, saying (as we should put it) that intellect grasps the moral *logic* by which right action is fittingly tested or rewarded and wrong action corrected or punished; though only God can see which it does in individual cases while leaving it up to us (though foreseeing) what use we make of events and thus how we fulfill this timeless logic.[22] It is this power that Boethius has forgotten to use and even that he has it (1.6.33–40), and that she now calls back into action. He must see the only *real* good and evil as *moral* good and evil, *his own* right and wrong actions, and events as truly indifferent in themselves except as occasions for practicing justice and the piety of seeing the justice of God, the Providence by which each has what suits him, what improves and benefits him, or can if he attends.[23]

Now he can take a more active part in his therapy and help to solve the great problem that he raised. Is there any such thing as Chance? Yes, but it is an unforeseen incidental result of the necessary operations of Fate.[24] Is there human freedom within these operations? Yes, for rational beings are free to decide between true and false, good and evil; but they can lose their freedom by surrendering to their bodily passions, and regain it by contemplating the divine mind and what it contemplates. For freedom is this, to judge and choose and obtain the goodness that makes us and our lives good, as it were to find the center.[25] This is the decisive move, as we shall see.

Boethius asks, if God sees what our future will be, then is it necessary and not contingent on our own wishes and plans and actions? Of course, our future cannot be the cause of God's foreknowledge; but if what God foresees *must* happen, then what becomes of our freedom, our goodness and wickedness, and our responsibility for them? How can we coherently hope and pray, and unite ourselves to him in humility by asking for the *inevitable?*

Lady Philosophy replies that some events are contingent whether they are foreseen or not, for example, things that depend on our skill in driving a chariot. To understand that things can be *foreseen* surely (by God) that will not *be* surely (for us, by whom they will be done), we must distinguish between reason and intellect, time and eternity. God is eternal and knows things timelessly. "Eternity is the whole, simultaneous and perfect possession of boundless life."[26] *Our* life in time is bounded by a beginning and an end, and is present only in successive parts, always different, some past and gone and some still to come. By contrast *God's* life is infinite, and his possession of it is complete and simultaneous. For he lives in a single identical present that includes the whole of life all at once and forever. He does not foresee what is future to *him,* for to him nothing is still to come; he "simply sees things present before him as they will later turn out to be in what *we* regard as the future,"[27] whether necessarily like the sun shining or contingently like our walking. Our walking has no necessity, only the "conditional necessity" that it will be *if* God foresees it. Our free choice does not change what he sees, for he sees what we will freely choose. Our actions do not cause his knowledge, but it is itself the measure of them and not their result.[28]

> Since this is true, the freedom of the human will remains inviolate, and laws are just since they provide rewards and punishments to human wills which are not controlled by necessity. God looks down from above, knowing all things, and the eternal present of his vision concurs with the future character of our actions, distributing rewards to the good and punishments to the evil. Our hopes and prayers are not directed to God in vain, for if they are just they cannot fail. Therefore, stand firm against vice and cultivate virtue. Lift up your soul to worthy hopes, and offer humble prayers to heaven. If you will face it, the necessity of virtuous action im-

posed upon you is very great, since all your actions are done in the sight of a Judge who sees all things."[29]

That is the closing paragraph of Lady Philosophy's explanation, and of Boethius's book. These seem to be the last lines that he ever wrote, at white heat, as he awaited execution. One reader has praised this conclusion as "a stroke of calculated and wholly successful art. We are made to feel as if we had seen a heap of common materials so completely burnt up that there remains neither ash nor smoke nor even flame, only a quivering of invisible heat."[30] That is well said; but we must make sure that we have understood these last words of Boethius and are not so dazzled by his art, and by his death, that we fail to give the critical attention that he deserves to what he intends to say and whether it is correct.

For, on the face of it, Lady Philosophy has only defended freedom from fatalism, as it is usually understood, that is, from the argument that what is *true* must be, or even more simply that what *is* must be and cannot not be. She does not defend freedom from determinism, the argument that what is *caused* must be, and yet she has herself invited this doubt by emphasizing the necessity of events as defined by the fate that flows from divine Providence and fulfills it.[31] The first argument is a sophism, as she points out, converting a conditional necessity into a simple one. The second argument may be a sophism too, if it is wrong to convert sequence into necessitation.[32] But Philosophy does not protect freedom from determinism in this way. She simply says that human wills are not controlled by necessity, coming from God's foreknowledge, and adds that he imposes a great necessity to behave with honesty (*magna necessitas indicta probitatis*) if you will not lie to yourselves (*si dissimulare non vultis*); and that leaves us to wonder whether this moral necessity is to *supervene* on the causal one or to *replace* it. For on the face of it, that causal one is left in place; and so is the conditional necessity whereby God's knowledge is the *measure* of all things and not the result of them.

Lady Philosophy, however, has been a Socratic teacher to the prisoner in the sense that amid long speeches and encouraging poetry she has asked him many searching questions and reminded him of truth that he has known but forgotten, truth that he has it in him to see for himself.[33] She now ends Socratically by leaving it to him and to us to work out for ourselves what she means and why it is true. But she has provided clues to guide us through the maze of argument that she has composed.[34]

First, if God's knowledge is the *measure* of our actions, it is as their Judge and standard, in that he is the goodness at which we aim in all that we do.[35] Second, to be good is another *conditional* necessity, to be good in order truly to *be*, and be *one* and have integrity, to be fully human and divinely happy and fulfilled.[36] Third, this necessity both supervenes on and *supersedes* the causal necessity of fate, for the more we recognize and submit to it, the less we submit to our bodily passions and the less we see events ruled by fatal necessity, fortune, or chance.[37] Fourth, though this submission to God's will is a passivity, it is our own *free* act, a consented passivity that is the definition of freedom and activity.[38] God does it all, when we freely consent and become free through consent.[39] Even if we refuse, we *obey* willy-nilly, by fulfilling in ourselves his law that right action improves and benefits us, while wrong worsens and harms us.[40] This law is eternal, it is *logic*, ever realized and never falsified, defining the meaning of what we do, that is to say, its value.[41] Fifth, hopes and prayers are not useless, for they cannot fail if they are humble and just hopes and prayers to be raised and united to divine goodness, asking for God's selfless justice to rule *our* hearts and our lives, which is what he himself desires and loves to do in us whenever we consent.[42] Sixth, and finally, our freedom and happiness and humanity depend on *attention* to him, facing this moral necessity, not deceiving ourselves about finding any other fulfillment which would prove worthless. Attention is not simply intellect, the eye of the mind, for all have that even the wicked who neglect it, but exercising it, directing it: negatively, by turning from vice, thinking how we have harmed ourselves by our wrong actions, and submitting to punishment that can heal us; positively, by cultivating virtues, and above all by rising to the divine mind and submitting to it, or rather letting ourselves be raised, asking and consenting that it be done, so that we think truth rather than follow bodily desires, thus conforming our mind to better things and placing ourselves among them.[43] Attentive desire is necessary and sufficient.[44]

Simone Weil

Simone Weil has a similar view of freedom, and for her too it arises in thinking about justice. Like Boethius, she is concerned with the injustice of human beings and their oppression of one another, moral evil; but as her spirituality deepens she is even more troubled by seeming *natural* evil, the apparent injustice of

God himself in allowing affliction that crushes people physically, psychologically, and socially who have done nothing to deserve so much suffering. She comes to see this as only an appearance of the real love of God, who allows it precisely in order to make a world in which there can be the greatest possible love, crossing the infinite distance of affliction.[45] Likewise she is concerned with the role of *chance*, the contingent and accidental, in shaping events (particularly affliction), and she begins with this rather than with Fortune as Boethius does; she comes to read it metaxically as Providence, the love of God; and like Boethius, she conceives Providence more as a timeless supernatural meaning than a remedy intervening naturally in events.[46] Boethius proposed in effect that what *sense* reads as chance and *imagination* reads as Fortune and *reason* as Fate, *intellect* reads as Providence. In a similar way, Weil says:

> We should read necessity behind sensation, order behind necessity, and God behind order. (*NB* 267)

> We do not have to choose between opinions (except in certain cases); we should wlcome them all, but arrange them vertically, and at suitable levels. Thus [e.g.,] chance, destiny [sc. fate], Providence. (*NB* 139)

> It is one and the same thing which, with respect to God is eternal Wisdom, with respect to the universe, perfect obedience; with respect to our love, beauty; with respect to our intelligence, balance of necessary relations; with respect to our flesh, brute force. (*NR* 295)

These sequences do not line up exactly; but in intention they are closely similar to each other and to the Divided Line in the *Republic*, where we more *clearly* see what more *truly* is by higher powers lit by a truer light, the Idea of good, though Socrates also emphasizes the relation between copy and original. What he calls intellect she calls the intelligence lit by the love of God, though for him too our intellect is lit by the good and generous mind of God.[47]

For Weil, intelligence, the loving intellect, sees Providence and grace active in the world wherever there is justice and compassion, in beauty and everything metaxical: as intervening decisively in events, never as force, but always only as love. From below it looks vanishingly small, like the point at which a circle touches a straight line.

The share of the supernatural here below is secret, silent, almost invisible, infinitely small. But it is decisive. Persephone did not think she was changing her destiny by eating just one pomegranate seed; yet from that moment, for ever after, the world has been her home and her kingdom.

This decisive operation of the infinitely small is a paradox which the human intelligence finds it difficult to acknowledge. Through this paradox is accomplished the wise persuasion by means of which divine Providence induces necessity to direct most things towards the good. (*OL* 166)

The true knowledge of social mechanics implies that of the conditions under which the supernatural operation of an infinitely small quantity of pure good, placed at the right point, can neutralize gravity. (*OL* 167)

[True social architecture] consists of disposing the blind forces of social mechanics around the point [of pure good] that also serves as center [of gravity] for the blind forces of celestial mechanics, that is to say the "Love which moves the sun and the other stars." (*OL* 168)[48]

For Weil too, God is our Judge, and more particularly our judgment and measure, in that he does not judge us so much as he leaves us to judge ourselves in the way that we judge one another and him, like a mirror of truth that shows us how we should be.[49] She is not concerned with his knowing what we will do, so much as our acknowledging his will, which is to goodness, and she agrees that this is true being, and our whole and only being is our *desire* for it.[50] What is more, it is our true freedom.

Men can never escape from obedience to God. A creature cannot but obey. The only choice given to men, as intelligent and free creatures, is to desire obedience or not to desire it. If a man does not desire it, he obeys nevertheless, perpetually, in as much as he is a thing subject to mechanical necessity. If he desires it, he is still subject to mechanical necessity, but a new necessity is added to it, a necessity constituted by laws belonging to supernatural things. Certain actions become impossible for him, others are done by his agency, sometimes almost in spite of himself. (*WG* 129)

To be free, for us, is to desire to obey God. All other liberty is false. (*IC* 186)

> Since obedience is in fact the imprescribable [sc. irremediable] law of human life, . . . where obedience is consented to there is freedom: there and nowhere else. (SWW 126)

She writes as if the consent to obey is submission to another necessity added to the causal one, as if now the wheels of the psychophysical mechanism include a supernatural wheel of charity, as if a steel chain were added to a brass one without tampering with it, as if the good doubly causes what is already caused by necessity; but in fact she is speaking figuratively of our turning[51] from lower motives to higher ones, like the selfless humility that willingly descends in what looks like humiliation, where the good purifies and rewards and increases the desire that seeks it. But like Boethius, she considers that all that *we* do is to consent and let the good act in and through us, so that it acts freely and frees us from our lower motives. We do this "almost in spite of ourselves" (WG 129), without wanting to for materialistic reasons. In affliction and despair it may be that all we can do is to desire to desire this, but that is enough: "love is a direction and not a state of the soul" (WG 135), at least a desire for direction, and it is a question of "attitudes inspired by love" (WG 210). When God responds to our desire, the seed will grow and become a tree of life to which the birds of the air come and make their nests in its branches. Weil's talk of a mysterious complicity between our love of the good and the supernatural mechanisms that are providential—the necessities and laws of grace that are evidently conceptual and a priori rather than merely factual and empirical, fits well with Boethius's notion of Providence as eternal and above time and the fate that fulfills it there. Thus, in particular, when she says,

> Everything that has to do with asking is suggestive of something similar to a piece of mechanism. All real desire for pure good, after a certain degree of intensity [and purity] has been reached, causes the good in question to descend. . . . When the conditions have been fulfilled, God never refuses. If we exercise a kind of compulsion upon God, it can only be a question of a mechanism instituted by God . . . at least as dependable as are the laws of gravity (NR 263–64),

it is not a question of placing further limits on our freedom or on God's but of defining it. If we ask for bread, we will not receive a stone, because it is freedom in us to ask and in him to give. Weil likewise considers this desire and consent and prayer for truth and transformation and union to be an act of *attention* at its highest intensity and purity, its most wholehearted and selfless. "Attention taken to its highest degree is the same thing as prayer. . . . Just as [pure good] is God, [pure attention] is prayer" (*NB* 205, 527).

Christian Platonists

In closing I would like to discuss briefly Boethius and Weil as Christian Platonists. We could wonder whether Boethius is a Christian at all, because in his book he never once says that he is or offers any witness to his faith but simply relies on philosophical argument from premises that non-Christians could accept. Certainly Boethius believes in a God of love who created the world and rules it justly, to whom we may offer our hopes and prayers; but we may find his God impersonal and abstract. He explicitly quotes the Bible on the firm rule and gentle disposition of everything by the supreme good, and he falls into liturgical phrasing when speaking of prayer;[52] but one must admit that it is not with the constancy of Augustine and Anselm. However, in addition to all his philosophical and scientific works written and planned, he has written treatises on theology, including *The Trinity* and *The Catholic Faith*, mentioned by his contemporary Cassiodorus. Nevertheless, even if Boethius is himself a Christian, one could doubt if he has produced a Christian book. For he writes that a man who becomes good becomes not only happy but divine, that the truth is in us and we have only to recall it to mind; he mentions judgment and life beyond death, heaven and hell and purgatory, but as something to discuss some other time;[53] he says little expressly of grace, and nothing of Christ the Mediator and redemptive suffering and forgiveness. Lady Philosophy is something supernatural and divine, but she speaks of God as if he were someone else.

But Christians too call people to live an eternal life with Christ and the Father who sent him, by doing what Christ says and entering into his way; in him God became a man so that human beings might become God. God will adopt us so that we are brothers and sisters of Christ. We will be like words of Christ written by the Spirit to be read and known by all, reflecting his radiant likeness to each other and seeing it reflected in one another. This is the purpose of God's grace, as Augustine understood.[54] Weil takes the reward of the good servant in the Gospel parables to be "a total identification with God" (*FLN* 339), a unity and identity in will, that is to say in spirit, love, and desire.[55]

Christians also say that what the law requires is written on our hearts, and what can be known about God is in the creation plain to all, so that it is our fault if we do not acknowledge him. Yet we are so willful that we cannot do this by ourselves without his help. But Boethius for his part constantly declares our need of God's initiative and assistance, his grace; and freedom to Boethius *is* surrender to God;[56] and even if Neoplatonists in general call on a divinity within, it is a God beyond and above the worldly ego that we usually call ourselves.[57] Lady Philosophy sometimes appears as that inward divinity personified, and we could ask if she represents the Spirit of Truth promised by Christ and thus the third divine person. She behaves like a living Providence that appears differently to the different states of mind of the prisoner: to *sense,* when she touches his heart and wipes his tears with a fold of her dress and sings sweet songs to him to raise his spirits so that he can recognize her and hear her; to *imagination,* when she takes the role of Lady Fortune and quotes poetry and history; to *reason,* engaging him in question and answer; to *intellect,* speaking from the viewpoint of eternity and being. He for his part addresses his healer first as his nurse who brought him up (*nutricem meam*), then as the nurturer of virtues (*virtutum omnium nutrix*), next as the best comfort of weary souls (*summum lassorum solamen animorum*), and finally the guide to true light (*veri praevia luminis*). She has come down from Heaven to share his labor for her sake, and she says that she is always *with* the innocent who oppose the wicked. She resembles Sophia.[58]

Boethius does not speak of forgiveness of those who wrong us but only of pitying them, but perhaps pity is alive and active only in forgiveness and reconciliation.[59] He does not explicitly mention mediation and Christ the Mediator who saves us by redemptive suffering, and these are great topics for Simone Weil, as they should be for any Christian writer.

The fact is, he seems to have meant to write a consolation of *philosophy,* supported by classical poetry. There is much truth in these words from a recent critic:

The distinction between Christian and Pagan can hardly, at that moment, have been more vividly present to his emotions than that between Roman and barbarian; especially since the barbarian [Theodoric] was also a heretic [an Arian]. Catholic Christendom and that high Pagan past to which he felt so deep a loyalty were united in his outlook by their common contrast to Theodoric and his huge, fair-skinned, beer-drinking, boasting thanes. This was no time for stressing whatever divided him from Virgil, Seneca, Plato, and the old Republic heroes. He would have been robbed of half his comfort if he had chosen a theme which forced him to point out where the great ancient masters had been wrong; he preferred one that enabled him to feel how nearly they had been right, to think of them not as "'they" but as "we."[60]

Something similar could be said about Simone Weil, in her hesitation to seek baptism into the Catholic Church. She felt a solidarity with so much that was outside it in Greece, India, China, Japan, and all the nonwhite countries, in popular cultures and so-called heretical traditions, that to join would to be to betray and reject the truth that she found living and active in the world and its history, in some details more living there than in the Church. She wanted the freedom for loving intelligence to find it and look for it everywhere.

In two points at least she would resist Boethius. First, she would challenge his remark "You cannot impose upon a free spirit, nor deprive a rational self-possessed mind of its equanimity." Affliction can strike down *anyone*. She would say, however, that we may be prepared for it, and at least desire to go on loving freely, though it may only be with an infinitesimal part of ourselves. Morever, she likes to quote Agathon's words in the *Symposium* of Plato, that "love cannot be forced, nor does it force"; but perhaps this means that you cannot make someone love (nor will a lover try), and not that you cannot stop him, for example, by killing him or driving him mad, though that is not necessarily to make *him* stop. Boethius would say that you can set a limit to a good man's action but that he can find in it a new occasion freely to practice justice and faith in divine providence; and with that, I take it, Weil would agree.[61]

The second point is that she would reject the very idea of a *consolation* of philosophy. Consolation is not good for us, because—or when—restoring balances and filling voids, getting even and softening bitterness, it conceals the truth that we must learn to contemplate without defilement by hatred but with detachment and love: the truth that we are finite, mortal, frail creatures who are exposed to evil, to hunger, disease, humiliation, isolation, and death, and that we can love nevertheless. Boethius would agree, however, that *worldly* consolation is not good, and so far from freeing and healing us, it only poisons us and strengthens our delusions; we need, not compensation by materialistic criteria of goodness and happiness, but the replacement of these by true criteria.[62] We need consolation in our moral intellect, or as she would say, the raising of our loving attention to the true goodness and life of God. That is our whole and only, our highest and best, freedom.[63]

Notes

1. *The Consolation of Philosophy*, trans. Richard Green (Indianapolis: Bobbs-Merrill, 1962), 1.4.164–66. For the Latin text, see Boethius, *The Theological Tractates*, ed. and trans. H. F. Stewart, E. K. Rand, and S. J. Tester; and *De Consolatione Philosophiae*, ed. and trans. S. J. Tester, Loeb Classical Library (Cambridge, Mass.: Harvard University Press, 1973). See also the freer translation by P. G. Walsh, Oxford World Classics (Oxford: Oxford University Press, 1999), with its extensive introduction, bibliography, explanatory notes, and index. Hereafter I cite this text as *CP*, by part, section, and line numbers; poems are indicated by "m" (for meter). I generally follow Green's version.

2. Prayer: *CP* 1.5m.23–29, 42–48. Right mind, forgetting: 1.6.39–55;10.618b–619b, 621b. Help: *CP* 1.3.10–13, 37–39: "How could I forsake my child, not share your ordeal and help bear the burden you carry because my name is hated, but leave you, who are innocent, to make your way alone? . . . It is no wonder that we are blown about by stormy winds on the sea of life, since our main duty is to oppose the wicked."

3. Boethius's text alternates between poetry and prose but contains more prose as the prisoner recovers. Part 1 begins and with poetry, parts 2–4 begin with prose and end with poetry, and part 5 begins and ends with prose. The first two poems in part 1 and the third one in part 5 are the prisoner's; all the rest are by Lady Philosophy herself.

4. *CP* 2.5.10–17, echoing Augustine in *The City of God* 15.5; and anticipating Dante in *Purgatory* 15.49–75.

5. *CP* 2.2.19–21; 2.3.79–91.

6. *CP* 2.8.

7. *CP* 3.2.5–8.

8. *CP* 3.2.52–54. Cf. 3.9.

9. *CP* 3.2–8; see also 2.5–7.

10. Experience is not enough, of course: it must be deepened by moral reflection of the sort offered by Lady Philosophy, that is to say, attention, thoughtfulness. *CP* 3.8m.9–12: "What can I say to show what fools they are? Let them pursue their riches and honors, and when they have painfully accumulated their false goods, then they may come to recognize the true."

11. As she begins this positive account of goodness, she calls on divine help, as Plato also writes that we should in *Timaeus* 27c, and there follows the beautiful epitome of the first part of that work, which proved so influential in medieval thought. Here is a paraphrase:

God makes the world in his goodness, spreading the threefold soul through the well-tuned world to move all things (for him and toward him and with him); and, duly cut, it turns on itself in a double circle, encircling mind and transforming the world into its own likeness. By his law of love the souls he sows through the world turn to him and are called back like leaping flames. May he lift our mind to him, for it is he, or the sight of him, that is beginning and end, leader and way and goal.

This poetic prayer is so much the center of the book thematically and structurally that it is reasonable to believe that the book as we have it is complete.

12. *CP* 3.10.83–90: "For as men become just by acquiring integrity, and wise by acquiring wisdom, so they must in a similar way become gods [*deos fieri*] by acquiring divinity. Thus everyone who is happy is a god [*deus*] and, although it is true that God is one by nature, still there may be many gods by participation." See 4.3.29–31: "the reward of good men, which time cannot lessen, nor power diminish nor the wickedness of any man tarnish, is to become divine [*deos fieri*]"; 4.3.67–69.

13. *CP* 4.1.20–21: *infiniti stuporis omnibusque horribilius monstris*, a boundless wonder more frightening than any bad sign.

14. *CP* 4.2.100–112.

15. *CP* 4.3, esp. lines 44–69.

16. *CP* 4.4.133, 135, 136, 152, 4.4m.12: "love the good and pity the evil."

17. *CP* 4.5.

18. *CP* 4.6.5–7; cf. 124–25, 197–99, 5.4.6–8.

19. *CP* 5.4.75–77, 82–91.

20. *CP* 5.4.22–82; see 3.12.106–7; and Plotinus 2.2.1–3, 3.2.3.28–37, 6.8.18.1–33, 6.9.8.37–45, 6.9.10.17–18. As we shall see, our just actions escape Fate by yielding to a necessity higher than that of bodily passions.

21. Plato, *Republic* 6.507–11; Aristotle, *Nicomachean Ethics* 6.3, 6–8, 11; Plotinus, 4.3.18, 4.8.1.7–8, 5.1.11; cf. Thomas, *Summa Theologiae* 1.1.79.8.

22. *CP* 4.7.52–55: "You can make of your fortune what you will; for any fortune which seems difficult either tests virtue or corrects and punishes vice." It is up to you to do right and to accept what follows as God's doing right.

23. See the so-called *amor fati* of the Stoics, e.g., in Marcus Aurelius 3.16, 4.23, 8.7, 10.21.

24. *CP* 5.1, following Aristotle in *Physics* 2.4–5. A farmer digging for a plant finds buried gold by chance. Intending one result, he met with another he did not foresee or intend, in this case a welcome one he might have intended had he foreseen it. Here chance is an *effect* and not a cause: something Aristotle might well have remembered in treating nature (in 2.8) as a final cause, working to an end like a farmer who always finds what is welcome without ever planning it. We could translate *tuche* and *casus* as "luck," but that is a term of imagination rather than sense; these are powers that Philosophy means to hold apart.

25. *CP* 5.2, 4.6.65–78. Kant wondered whether we know that we are rational and moral and therefore free or only must humanly believe it, and whether this makes us practically free. Human beings are committed to rationality and morality, which leads to the question whether we know that we are human beings at all, and what could prove it once we doubt it. Or can't we know that we are philosophizing and reasoning about it? See *Groundwork* 3 at 448 and 455–56: "It is just as impossible for the most subtle philosophy as for the most ordinary human reason to argue away freedom. Hence philosophy must assume that no real contradiction will be found between freedom and natu-

ral necessity in the same human actions." Philosophy cannot deny freedom, for it cannot deny itself. But who *is* philosophy, and who can do it, knowing that he does? Lady Philosophy avoids this tangle by simply being herself and affirming herself.

26. *CP* 5.6.9–11.

27. *CP* 5.6.82–89.

28. *CP* 5.6.103–6, 161–63.

29. *CP* 5.6.163–76.

30. C. S. Lewis, *The Discarded Image* (Cambridge: Cambridge University Press, 1964), 90.

31. *CP* 4.6.56–60, 82–93: "the simplicity in the divine mind produces an unchangeable order of events." 5.1.55–58: "These causes come together by the order and inevitable connection of things, the order coming down from its source in Providence which disposes all things, each in its proper places and times." 4.6.200–204: "God, the author of all things in nature, governs all things, directing them to good."

32. David Hume asks whether we can clearly conceive and know causes to be more than a regular sequence of contiguous objects, but he insisted that we always *suppose* it to involve a necessary connection hidden from us. For he is a skeptic, and means to show that we naturally and unavoidably imagine and believe more than we perceive and conceive and know; that our best empirical knowledge has foundations that we cannot fully justify.

33. Thus, e.g., 1.4.5–6, 1.5.38–44, 1.6; 3.1, 3.11m, 3.12.1–29; 5.3m.

34. *CP* 3.12.82–86: you are "weaving a labyrinth of argument from which I [Boethius] cannot escape." 4.6.19–20: I will "weave arguments for you bound to each other in due order." 1.1.13–16: She weaves the thread that alone leads to freedom; more exactly, she defines the path and thus the labyrinth itself.

35. See John 3.17–19, 5.22, 12.47–48; See *CP* 4.4.100–103. "But see what eternal law ordains. Suppose you have conformed your mind to better things: there is no need of a judge to confer rewards, you have yourself joined yourself to the greater excellence." At *CP* 4.6.121–23, God "looks out from the high watchtower of his Providence, knowing what is best for each one, causes it to happen," apparently in allusion to Plato's *Statesman* 272e; but the words *ex alta providentiae specula respexit* can also be translated as "he looks into the great mirror of his providence" in the sense of a living ideal showing us both what we ought to be and what we are, as in *Hamlet* 3.1.161: "The glass of fashion and the mould of form."

36. *CP* 3.10–11.

37. *CP* 3.1m.11–13, 4.6.73–76, 5.2.14–27: "In supreme and divine substances [and thus in divinely blessedly people] there is clear judgment, uncorrupted will, and effective power [sc. freedom] to obtain what they desire. Human souls are more free while they are engaged in contemplation of the divine mind, and less free when they are joined to bodies . . . blinded by a cloud of unknowing [*inscitae nube caligant*] and obsessed by destructive passions, by yielding and consenting to which they strengthen the slavery to which they have brought themselves and are in a way freely taken captive."

This crucial point is in the best tradition of ancient and medieval thought. Thus Plotinus 2.3.15.13–22; Dante, *Purgatory* 16.79–81: "You are free subjects of a more immense nature and power which grants you intellect to free you from the heavens' [astrological] influence"; 18.70–74: "All love [sc. desire] that burns in you springs from necessity: but you still have the power to check its sway"; *Paradise* 3.85; 5.19–24. Thus Plato, *Phaedo* 82d–83 and *Laws* 1.644d–645b, we are like puppets made by the gods that can *choose* which string to obey: that is, we should become their puppets obeying always only the golden string of excellence, become their instruments, making their will and viewpoint our own, as *their* toy and their dance.

38. CP 1.5.13–15: "To be governed by this power and obey his justice is true freedom"; 3.12.47–53: "Since God is rightly believed to govern all things with the rudder of goodness, and since all these things naturally move toward the good, . . . they willingly accept his rule and submit freely to his pleasure as subjects who are agreeable and obedient to their leader"; 5.4m.10–21, 5.5.8–10: "how much more do intelligences which are wholly free from all bodily affections use the power of the mind rather than objects extrinsic to themselves in arriving at judgments."

39. CP 3.9.20–21: "when they have [been] turned toward you, by your gracious law, you call them back like leaping flames." See 3.12.47–53 all submit freely to his rule, 4.2.78–79. What would happen if the wicked were deprived of "this great and nearly irresistible natural tendency" toward the good? Sc. we can resist it; but as Socrates says in the *Republic* 1.351–352c, justice unifies, but wickedness disintegrates us.

40. CP 3.12.56–63; cf. 4.2.97–101, 4.6m.40–43, 5.2.110–12. Treason never prospers, for it means ceasing to be.

41. CP 4.6.22–93, 119–23, 199–206. 5.6.59–72, 166–70.

42. CP 1.5m, 3.9m, 4.6m, with 5.3.97–112, 5.6.170–74.

43. CP 3.1.22–26 turn your eyes the other way, 4.3.38–42 the wicked need self-assessment [*sesi ipsi aestimare*], 4.4.141–46 to see the good they have given up, 4.4.95–103 thinking truth and conforming to what is better; 5.5.50–52 "Let us be raised, if we can, to the height of the highest intelligence, where reason will see what she cannot see in herself"; 3.9.22–26 "Grant, Oh Father, that my mind may rise to your sacred throne; let it see the fountain of good, let it find light, so that the clear light of mind may fix itself in you; burn off the fogs and clouds of earth and shine through in your splendor"; 4.6.204–6, 5.6. 172–76. Intellect as the eye of the soul: CP 5.4.88–91, 97–98, 103: "The eye of intelligence is set higher yet, and passing beyond the universe it sees with the clear beam of the mind the pure form itself . . . as though looking down from above. . . . [W]ith a single glance of the mind it regards all these things as it were as Form."

44. CP 1.5.15–20: no one is exiled from the kingdom of God who has chosen to live there, "but whoever ceases to desire to live there has thereby ceased to deserve to do so"; 4.4.101–3: "if you have conformed your mind to better things, . . . you have yourself joined yourself to the greater excellence."

45. WG 117–36, esp. 119–24, 132–36. NB 333, 428–29, 564, 616.

46. WG 124–25: "Affliction would not have this power [to crush us] without the element of chance contained by it. . . . A blind mechanism, heedless of degrees of spiritual perfection, continually tosses men about and throws some of them at the very foot of the Cross [sc. into affliction]. It rests with them to keep or not to keep their eyes turned toward God through all the jolting. It does not mean that God's Providence is lacking. It is in his Providence that God has willed that necessity should be like a blind mechanism"; 167, 177; NB 243, 254, 463, 480, 596: the *metaxu* are providential; FLN 336, 341; NR 269–71, 285, cf. 94, 232, 262–64: supernatural mechanisms are providential. Let us read these mechanisms as an expression of the *logic* of grace, the love of God. NB 386–87: Christianity is great because "it does not seek a supernatural remedy for suffering but a supernatural use for it"; FLN 69: it brings joy that "soars above pain and perfects it" [sc. gives it significance, transfigures it].

47. NB 240, 242; FLN 131; IC 169f., 201: "attention lit by love and faith, knows" how to read the books of revelation in the universe and human thought. CP 3.9m.4–9, 22–26.

48. See NB 464, 466–67, 548, 559, 632. Plato, *Symposium* 196bc; Dante, *Paradise* 33.146.

49. NB 106, 234, 318: "Not to judge. Like the heavenly Father, who does not judge; through him human beings judge themselves. To let all beings come to one, and leave them to judge themselves. To be a balance. One will not then be judged oneself, having become an image of the true judge, who does not judge." FLN 112, 129; WG 97.

50. NB 491: "Every thing which exists is unreal compared to it. . . . [O]ur very being itself is nothing else than this need [sc. desire, longing, aspiration] for the good," 494, 562; FLN 124 , 284, 307, 311.

51. She knows about the monsters in the soul that make so much repression and lying in the psychophysical mechanism of our life (OL 118; NB 84; LOP 96–97), but she insists that there always can be that "interval" of reflection on justice and truth, that luminous moment of grace and light in which we are saved if we let it work in us. IC 35–36, 48. Much of our life *is* consented passivity to base materialistic motives, but we *can attend* to truth and *choose* which motives to act on. We are like a shipwrecked sailor who can grasp and hang on to a rope thrown to him by God from the highest heaven (IC 194; FLN 82). Similarly, Wittgenstein, *Culture and Value*, trans. Peter Winch (Oxford: Blackwell, 1980), 33e: when love *holds on to* religious belief, "you no longer rest your weight on the earth but suspend yourself from heaven. Then everything will be different, and it will be no wonder if you can do things that you cannot do now." It is your heart and soul that holds on, not your speculative mind: "for it is [your] soul with its passions, its flesh and blood, that has to be saved, not [your] abstract mind."

52. Cf. CP 3.12.63–54, Wisd. 8.1; 3.10m.1–4, Mt. 11.28–30; CP 5.3.97–112, 5.6.170–174. See also, e.g., 4.1.2–24 and 2 Tim. 2.20, Rom. 9.21–24; 1.1.32–34; Mt. 13.22, 2.4m.15–22; Mt. 7.24–27, 3.10.86–88; II Pet. 1.4.

53. 2.4.91–94: "You are a man fully convinced by many proofs that human souls are in no way mortal." 2.7.81–86: "If men perish completely in death, a thing which our

reason prevents us from accepting, then there is certainly no glory when the man who is supposed to have it no longer exists. But, if the soul, in full awareness of its virtue, is freed from this earthly prison and goes to heaven, does it not disregard all earthly concerns and, in the enjoyment of heaven, find its satisfaction in being separated from earthly things?" 4.4.16–31, 75–79: "'Do you leave no room for the punishment of souls after the death of the body?' 'I do, indeed,' Philosophy answered, 'and such punishments are severe. Some are imposed as bitter penalties, others as merciful purgation. But it is not now my intention to speak of these.'"

54. See chapter 11 in this volume.

55. Cf. *FLN* 310: "total assimilation to God"; 132: when a man has become a mediator of the love of God, "then Christ is he." This is not "the sin of envy" (*WG* 83, 59), if that is wanting to be God and savior. Here it is a question of wanting to be his living likeness, his fully adequate servant, *a* mediator and incarnation, thus both saved and sanctified. We should desire this, but not with our worldly part (*NB* 149, 273).

56. *CP* 1.4.28–29: God gave you to the minds of wise men; 1.6.49–51: thank the Giver of health that nature has not wholly forsaken you; 3.9.99–101: ask God's help always; 3.9m.20–24: you turn us and call us back to you, raise our eyes to your divine vision; 3.12.100–102: with his help we reached the decisive point; 4.1.25–26: we will find the truth with his help whose kingdom we now speak of; 5.2.14–20: freedom is abandonment to divine providence.

57. We may think that Platonists do not pray, and Socrates says that we should not, because we do not know what will be good for us: 2 *Alcibiades* 138b, 248a; cf. *Laws* 3.668b. But Socrates means that we should not pray for *worldly* nonmoral goods; and he himself prays for wisdom and excellence that make us godlike, e.g., in *Phaedrus* 257bc, 279bc, 278d, 247cd, 249bc; see *Symposium* 202e–203a, *Euthyphro* 12e–13, 14e–15a, and *Laws* 4.716de: prayer is good for the good man and bad for the bad. Plotinus offers prayers, e.g., 4.9.4.7, 5.8.9.8–17; 5.1.6.9–12: "Let us speak of it in this way, first invoking God himself, not in spoken words, but stretching ourselves out with our soul into prayer to him, able in this way to pray alone to him alone," about which Armstrong remarks "his whole philosophy is prayer in this sense" (A. H. Armstrong, trans. *Plotinus*, Loeb Classical Library [Cambridge, Mass.: Harvard University Press, 1966–88], 5:29n.1).

58. *CP* 1.10–11, 16–18, 1.3.1–3; cf. 3.1.1–3; 2.1.18–25, 2.2.1–2, 33–42; 3.3.13–14, 3.3.86 "my pupil"; 4.6.126–27, 196–99, 5.4.6–9, 5.5.51–56, 5.6.1–5; cf. 4.1.35–39: "I will give wings to your mind," with 4.1m. 1.3.4, 2.3.2, 3.1.4, 4.1.5. 1.3.6–15, 37–39. I owe the comparison with Sophia to Dunstan Morrissey, in conversation.

Philosophy does defer to "someone even greater than I" who said that a holy man's body is built by heaven or heavenly virtues, apparently Hermes; but Socrates says this too, that a good man cannot be harmed: *CP* 4.6.144–45, *Corpus Hermeticum* 13.14.9–11, *Apology* 30cd, 41cd. When she goes on to say that she cannot speak of Providence as if she were divine, for no man can understand all that God does, she *may* mean that she cannot explain it as if it were no mystery to human reason as opposed to intellect, which is something that Socrates could say too. CP 4.6.196–97; cf. *Phaedrus* 246a, *Republic* 7.517ab, 533a.

59. CP 4.4.136–52, 4.4m12.

60. Lewis, *The Discarded Image*, 78–79. Cf. WG 75, 77–80.

61. CP 2.6.24–26; WG 121; Plato, *Symposium* 196bc.

62. NB 149, 211, 229, 238, 424: "any form of consolation in affliction draws us away from love and truth"; 483–84: "To turn suffering into an offering is a consolation, and it is thus a veil thrown over the reality of suffering. But the same applies if we regard suffering as a punishment. Suffering has no significance. There lies its reality, which is absence of significance. Otherwise we do not love God." CP 1.1.26–41, 1.4m.

63. Consider the words, so different in appearance yet deeply similar in spirit, of R. H. Blyth in *Zen and Zen Classics* (Hokuseido: Hokuseido Press, 1970) vol. 3, p. ii: "The aim of life, its only aim, is to be free. Free of what? Only to be free, that is all. Free through ourselves, free to be sad, to be in pain, free to grow old and die. This is what our soul desires, and this freedom it must have, and shall have." Blyth does not mention God, but he too intends a deeper, fuller entry into divine vision. As Thoreau says (*A Week on the Concord and Merrimack Rivers*, "Thursday"), the unconsciousness of man is the consciousness of God.

CHAPTER 10

Countermimesis and Simone Weil's Christian Platonism

CYRIL O'REGAN

This chapter reflects on Weil's perspective on the economy of violence. It is especially concerned to show how Platonism and Christianity individually and together provide diagnostic tools for its recognition, suggest sites for its disturbance, and exhibit exemplary figures that break the cycle of violence, a cycle of repetition or mimesis. Crucial to Weil's perspective is the close relation she sees between violence and evil. Unfortunately, it is a relation that seems rendered opaque rather than clarified when Weil identifies evil with non-being on the authority of the Greek tradition. So the questions that need to be asked are, how coherent is Weil's Plato if he sums up perspectives on violence and its rupture in the Greek tradition and is understood to look at evil from a metaphysical point of view, and how consistent is Weil's own broadly "Platonic" position, which yokes together more descriptive and metaphysical discourses on violence and evil?

I argue that Weil's Plato is coherent and that Weil's own constructive "Platonic" position is consistent, and she would never fail to take pride in "Platonism" in any self-ascription. I also argue that Weil relates Greek discourse and the discourse of Christianity in such a way that the Gospels are the *telos* of Greek discourse, which then itself becomes a mode of revelation. Specifically, I argue that for her, Christ is the reality that fully reveals the circuit of mimesis and the recycling of violence while representing its overcoming. Using the language of René Girard, Christ, for Weil, is the figure of countermimesis. Textually and historically, Christ prophetically fulfills as well as points toward all those figures who resist violence and who desire in the name of a vision of a transcendent good or a transcendent justice.

Naming Violence and Evil and Overcoming Them

For Weil, violence can be spoken of in many ways. It has different constituencies: outsiders, select groups of insiders, individuals perceived as threatening. It also takes many forms. Although war is the most obvious, Weil is also aware of institutional forms such as the law, economic forms such as capitalism, and political forms such as Fascism, as well as a variety of interpersonal forms. It is Weil's view that the Greek tradition from Homer to Plato has exposed the dynamics of violence, offered a realistic account of its all-pervasive rule, and soberly assessed the prospects for transcendence.

The *Iliad* enjoys a certain preeminence in Weil's multilayered writings on the Greeks.[1] If violence is a conspicuous theme in Greek tragedy and Platonic texts, in the *Iliad* it is the very subject, specifically, the form of violence directed against outsiders in a war that becomes total. Although Weil suggests the *Iliad*'s preeminent treatment of violence in a number of places,[2] "The *Iliad* or Poem of Force"[3] explicitly names the *Iliad* as the text that names violence (163);[4] it is, she claims, the real subject of the epic. Rather than violence being an accidental (albeit degenerative) relation between groups or between persons in it, people function as the personae of this actor, the predicates of this subject. Not only no text before it, but arguably no text after it in the Western tradition (including Hegel's *Phenomenology*)[5] shows so clearly how violence from the beginning to the end of human life is an essential economy that does not discriminate among its victims, even as it divides human beings into classes, those who inflict and those who suffer violence. If violence is not an economy with absolutely no way out, certainly it is an economy with no obvious way out. A fundamental lesson of the *Iliad*, for Weil, is that violence is blind to nation, ethnicity, and ideology. Neither Trojan nor Greek, German nor French, Communist nor Republican is exempt from its rule.[6] It is blind to gender and generation; its domain includes women, grandparents, and children, people who do not bear arms or who cannot be construed as a threat. Violence maintains itself while the actors are changed and interchanged, while victor becomes victim, victim victor in the dizzying back and forth of the war between Greeks and the Trojans.[7] In its self-reproduction violence is a circle of repetition, a circle of mimesis that is almost but not completely unbreakable.

Naming violence, drawing attention to it as a structuring principle, and determining its forms is the singular achievement of the *Iliad*, later complemented and supplemented by Greek tragedy and the texts of Plato. Those forms include slavery and chattel, the razing of a city as an economy of group memory and well-being, the excising of grief, the body in the throes of fear, the hacked body and the bottomless bitterness of its peremptory leavetaking. More subtly and hauntingly, these include the living death of those who empty themselves of everything human and all not permitted by the master, a sort of petrification.[8] The *Iliad* realizes the epic and transcends it in an objectivity that is not coldly distanced. Its specific genius is that of a "dispassionate tenderness" (SWA 188). It shows how perilous are the domestic economies of love between spouses, between parents and children and vice versa, how exposed are the cultural economies of respect for tradition and the achievements of one's group, and how vulnerable is the personal economy of memory that cannot persist when survival depends on being nothing, on being the shadow of the master who is the subjectivity of emptied self. More graphically than any other text in the Greek or even Western tradition, the *Iliad* does not offer the consolation of limit. There is no structure of human behavior capable of surviving violence's onslaught, no domain of psyche strong enough to resist. The *Iliad* shows how naive it is to believe that violence stops at the body; violence torments the vulnerable body to incise its nihilation on the soul.

Yet the *Iliad* points without nostalgia or staginess to the traces of the leveled domestic, cultural, and personal economies. Conjugal love (SWA 187) and filial love (SWA 186) continue to be recognized when the world is undone in violence. There are flashes of communal memory; shreds of personal memory outline the erased self, providing a kind of monument for its passing. More important, the *Iliad* points to moments in which violence is arrested, when its circuit is ever so temporarily broken. These moments are epiphanies of countermimesis. At the center of the *Iliad*, Weil famously claims, is the figure of Patroclus, the friend of Achilles. Achilles is the killing machine in whom violence is refracted in its purest and, in Greek terms, most "glorious" form (SWA 186). He is violence at its most glamorous in a text that represents, without commenting out loud, the ideology of war, the war provoked by so little that costs so much, whose cause is forgotten and that quickly comes to have no other purpose than war itself. As the friend of Achilles, however, Patroclus makes Achilles vulnerable like other men, and gives him pathos. It is Patroclus who makes Achilles something other than a personification of violence and war and their redoubtable glamour. But in a deep sense Patroclus is Achilles' alter ego, his real other. He sheds a light on Achilles that questions his glamour, and that of the martial, and with it the ideology that made it possible, specifically the ideology of fame, the ideology of immortality of name.[9] Patroclus is for Weil (SWA 184) nothing less than the hinge that unhinges the agreed upon conventions of both Trojan and Greek in which value is tribally assigned on the basis of actions that have the cast of fury and dangerous intensity. The *Iliad* reveals that what passes for action is not action at all but a reflex where the fear of the loss of prestige outweighs the fear of the loss of life.

A person of measure,[10] Patroclus represents a rupture in the unmeasured economy of violence. His measure is also directly related to, indeed dependent on, the "interval," the space of reflection and hesitation in which the hand is stayed, compassion rendered, suppliant respected. This is the interval in which justice happens. Patroclus subverts the economy of violence, and the fury, illusion, and self-delusion that fuel it. He subverts it not because he is invulnerable to violence, or because he effects an alternative. He functions subversively because he is physically subject to violence's economy, yet points beyond violence to a justice that is real, that appears as the breech that cannot be named positively.

The *Iliad*, then, is nearly scriptural bedrock for the Greeks in its diagnosis of violence's omnipresence, its mechanisms of renewal and recirculation, its effects on its victims and victors, and the possibility of transcendence as focused in a figure of countermimesis. Weil also believes that Greek tragedy complements and supplements the *Iliad*. Aeschylus and Sophocles complement the *Iliad* by focusing on particular aspects of violence, for example, political and institutional violence as represented in the *Antigone* by Creon (*IC* 9, 22–23),[11] or domestic and political violence in the *Electra* of Sophocles as represented by Clytemnestra. Greek tragedy in Aeschylus and Sophocles complements Homer's work of genius also by presenting differentiated portraits of transcendence.[12] Whatever the flaws of Antigone and Electra, for example, innocence and stubbornness in the case of the former, *ressentiment* and hate in the case of the latter, they are afflicted figures protesting against injustice and invoking a transcendent justice that holds out hope for a transformation of political, institutional, and domestic economies that otherwise perpetuate violence and oppression.

Greek tragedy also supplements the *Iliad*'s profound unveiling of violence. Although the *Iliad* implicates the gods in the violence that is enacted on the human scene, divine participation is random and unfocused. Not so in Greek tragedy, particularly the Prometheus cycle of Aeschylus that inscribes violence in the very relation between Zeus and Prometheus (*IC* 56–73). Here is a deepening of Weil's reflections on violence. Violence is no longer a force of nature, a nondivine reality that unfortunately the divine cannot curb. What makes violence "tragic" is that it is inscribed in the relation of the divine toward Prometheus who would champion the prerogatives of the human.

Yet, for Weil, the "tragic" account of relation only seems to offer an explanation. She does not impugn the heroism of Prometheus: "Prometheus suffers because he has loved men too well. He suffers in man's stead. The Wrath of God against the human species is entirely carried by him, who, nevertheless, was and is, destined again to become the friend of Zeus" (*IC* 67). Still, Zeus is not a villain, just as jealousy is not an explanation. Zeus and Prometheus are destined for a reconciliation in which human beings will enjoy a mode of existence excluding neither autonomy nor gratitude. Given this reconciliation that Aeschylus presumably fully carried out in the lost segments of the Prometheus cycle, the violence of Zeus might better be construed, Weil believes, as a symbol of the suffering that is undergone to bring a limit to misrule and violence that has its origin in human pride. The suffering of Prometheus is redemptive but mysterious in a double sense. First, it is impossible to capture in a formula how this suffering effects redemption. Second, and even more important, the intimacy of the relation between the apparent antagonists Zeus and Prometheus (*IC* 67–69) is such that one cannot rule out the possibility that Zeus participates in the redemptive suffering of Prometheus, which prefigures Christ as the paschal lamb (*IC* 67, 70–71).[13]

So Weil's reading of the Prometheus cycle is not reduced to an opposition between Zeus and Prometheus. There is nothing inconsistent in her refusal to demonize Zeus and her extraordinary positive reading of Prometheus as the noble representative of humanity who reduces himself to total powerlessness on humanity's behalf (*IC* 67). Like Patroclus, Antigone, and Electra, Prometheus is a figure of countermimesis—but with a difference. Prometheus is immortal. The sacrifice that limits, indeed, undoes the dialectic of crime and punishment, is executed from the divine and not the human side. Overcoming guilt and violence necessarily involves the participation of the divine and not simply the human. The double-sided emphasis on the human and the divine in Greek tragedy provides, according to Weil, one very important reason why Greek tragedy represents a crucial resource for Christianity, for it figures nothing less than the Incarnation that achieves its full revelation in the Cross (*IC* 67–70, 118–19; *WG* 141).[14]

Violence and the Metaphysical Definition of Evil

For Weil, of course, it is Plato who is the culmination of Greek reflection on violence and its counter. Aristotle's evasion of the problem on the political, social, interpersonal, and finally theological levels makes him less than Plato, constitutes him as a mere philosopher, or perhaps even other than a philosopher.[15] Plato's thought for Weil is an extended reflection on violence and overcoming violence. Here the relationship between Plato and Greek tragedy is particularly important, for Greek tragedy shows violence in political and social contexts in which its operations are not as obtrusive as in war and its supports not as obvious. But Plato continues to attend not only to the phenomenon of violence, so richly detailed in the *Iliad* and so finely nuanced in Greek tragedy, but also to its counter. Plato's delineation of the just man in the *Republic* (*IC* 79–80, 139–41) is a general figuration of countermimesis. Plato believes that this figure is historically exemplified by Socrates and assumed by anyone who follows the philosophical path his texts recommend. This mode of life, defined by its orientation toward truth and goodness, will be marked by derision, suffering, and death. Plato thus continues a line of counterposition that begins with the depiction of Patroclus in the *Iliad*.

How is one to relate Weil's diagnosis of violence's economy and justice's otherness, or the good's otherness, with her more general reflection on evil? In the *Iliad* violence and evil are fundamentally coextensive; they fundamentally overlap in Greek tragedy. This is not so in Plato. On the one hand, evil for him includes nonviolent phenomena (e.g., convention, lying, compromise, gluttony); on the other, evil can be spoken of in the metaphysical language of non-being. Still, the relation between evil and violence remains close in Plato. Much of what superficially might be regarded as nonviolent evil is implicitly violent; blindness and self-interest is disregard of others, and fails in accountability regarding the harm oneself or others inflict. So, Plato, who Weil claims invented nothing (*IC* 76), also expresses the Greek tradition of the *Iliad* and Greek tragedy, since for him harm goes all the way down. Human beings are not other than their flesh which bears their history and which is both the point of their vulnerability and their transcendence. Weil speaks on behalf of Plato and herself when she declares in "On Personality":

> Justice consists in seeing that no harm is done to men. Whenever a man cries inwardly "Why am I being hurt?" harm is done to him. . . . When harm is done to a man, real evil enters into him, not merely pain and suffering, but the actual horror of evil. (*SWA* 73–74)

In her analysis of the *Republic* (*IC* 132–50, esp. 134; also *GG* 101, 108), Weil points to Plato's cave to suggest the range of desire and the range of prejudice that have to be overcome for the other to have a human face. The lesson of the *Republic* and other Platonic texts is that other human beings do not necessarily wear a human face: if not a monster, the other is an *it* to whom nothing is owed. This delusion, which encourages absolute licence, finds a complement in illusions of absolute invulnerability. Anyone who becomes an actor in the economy of violence, and becomes intoxicated by it, believes himself invulnerable. In Plato the crowning symbol of the illusion of invulnerability hinted at in the *Iliad*, and in tragedy's portrayal of *hubris*, is the "myth of Gyges ring" (*GG* 191–93). This is the myth of the power of invisibility, that is, perfect unaccountability and invulnerability to consequence for one's actions.

If as war shows violence does not discriminate (*IC* 135–36), it still can be focused on a few who fulfill special criteria (e.g., Jews). Violence can be directed especially toward a philosopher who exposes it and the myth of invulnerability that expresses and legitimates it (*IC* 137–38). Moreover, evil in general, as the potential to engage in violence, appears to share in the glamour of violence, a kind of nonmoral gloriousness that exceeds reality as we normally experience it. Evil is experienced as reality at its most intense, nothing less than a revelation of Being itself. Just as with violence, evil in general is spectacle automatically worthy of representation and narration in the way ordinary lives and the lives of the good are not (*GG* 119).

I will return to the point about the glamour of evil. But for now what is one is to make of Weil's endorsement of the metaphysical view of evil as non-being (e.g., as in GG 119–30)? Weil could not be more explicit about the equation: "The unreality which takes goodness from good, this is what constitutes evil" (GG 127; also 120, 121). Is this not relatively speaking an obfuscation, a notion that, on the one hand, detracts from the seriousness of evil that leads to devastation, to the violated bodies and the only half-alive selves, and, on the other, distracts from the glamour of evil that the good or justice does not seem able to compete with? The answer is complex. It involves reflecting on the way in which "evil as non-being" is existentially contextualized in the *Gravity and Grace* selections as well as on what this contextualization means with respect to who Plato is in Weil's texts and what *kind* of Platonism is embraced there as a lens for reality.

"Evil as non-being," endorsed by Weil, is not explicitly asserted in Plato's texts. Historically "evil as non-being," together with its explicit privative connotation, is Neoplatonic; it is through Neoplatonism that it becomes an essential part of Christian reflection on evil, largely by way of Augustine.[16] Yet if "evil as non-being" is only made explicit much later in Neoplatonism, it is still possible (maybe even necessary) to argue that this is a direction that many of Plato's own texts take. Moreover, I am not confining such a tendency to the more Eleatic-oriented texts such as the *Sophist* and the *Parmenides* but find it even in a text such as the *Republic*, which is primarily concerned with justice and goodness and how they can be made the regulative principles of the self and society. Evil, which has its ultimate source in chronic inattention, and its proximate source in imagination and desire, Plato judges, neither connects with nor reveals reality as such.

There are, I believe, two different but related ways of characterizing the metaphysical or ontological view of evil in Plato's own texts and in Weil's appropriation of Plato without appealing to a Neoplatonized Plato. As evil in Plato's texts gets linked with ignorance and illusion, in contrast to the good which is associated with knowledge and being, the interpreter is forced to acknowledge Parmenides' influence. Since Weil's analysis of evil and good links the same things (GG 120, 121, 127), even her ontological characterization of evil as non-being is at its root "Parmenidean." Even if the actual equation of evil and non-being and its privative framing is a product of a later era, it was the result of a struggle of interpretation over Plato's texts, especially over the *Parmenides* and the *Timaeus*.

Nevertheless, even if the Parmenidean characterization has to be given a certain functional priority in understanding Weil's relation to Plato, it is necessary to entertain another possibility. Weil underscores the importance of Pythagoreanism (*IC* 151–201) in a way few scholars of ancient Greece have. For her, ancient Greece is saturated with Pythagorean ideas, even outside what could be narrowly identified as a Pythagorean school. Plato is no exception to this rule. For example, the concept of the unlimited or the indefinite (*apeiron*) to which Plato recurs in a number of texts is of Pythagorean provenance (*IC* 153). The epistemic correlative to the unlimited, Weil indicates, is ignorance (*IC* 153).

Despite the obvious overlap here between views ascribed to Parmenides and to Pythagoras, Weil does not explicitly connect Parmenidean reflections on non-being and Pythagorean reflections on the unlimited in *Intimations of Christianity*. Matters are different elsewhere, however. Side by side with the more Parmenidean explorations of evil as non-being and illusion, Weil introduces the concept of the unlimited, which suggests privation more overtly than non-being. For example, the idea of the "unlimited" is important enough for Weil to mention a number of times in her notebooks (e.g., *GG* 145, 146). The most telling reference occurs in the context of a treatment of evil where "evil as non-being" is explicit. The second entry under "Evil" in *Gravity and Grace* reads: "Evil is limitless, but it is not infinite. Only the infinite limits the limitless" (119). The phrasing suggests that this passage should be read as a paraphrase of the famous Pythagorean fragment of Philolaus, which concerns the limiting of the unlimited, commented on by Weil in *Intimations* (153). As she does with Parmenidean non-being, Weil associates the limitless with lack of knowledge. This association truly yokes together Parmenides and Pythagoras, for the association of limitlessness and ignorance is one that Weil draws our attention to in her treatment of the fragments of Philolaus in *Intimations in Christianity* (153).

In her own work, then, the Parmenidean "non-being" and the Pythagorean "unlimited" complement and reinforce each other in a complex metaphysical definition of evil. Admittedly, Weil is tempted to simplify things by suggesting that the Eleatic is in principle reducible to the Pythagorean. This suggestion is not only implausible historically, it is also theoretically limiting. Although Pythagoreanism does suggest a correlation between the unlimited and ignorance, this is *the* emphasis in Parmenides' proem. This gives Parmenidean "non-being" a rhetorical power that the Pythagorean symbol does not possess as it is more dismissive of the negative than of the "unlimited." Consequently, not only historically but also systematically, Parmenidean non-being is an irreducible linguistic and theoretical counter in Plato's and Weil's metaphysical naming of evil.

Metaphysical as "evil as non-being" may be, Weil is persuaded that precisely by virtue of its roots in the Parmenidean and Pythagorean traditions neither Plato's characterization of evil as non-being and unlimited nor her own retrieval of that characterization is bedeviled with abstraction. Neither the historical Plato nor Weil's Plato is ever inclined to deny the catastrophic consequences of individual and social pursuits of illusions. For if evil is nothing at all, its effects are superbly real: the war described in the *Iliad*, the sacrifices of the innocent and the just in Greek tragedy, the peril of the just man in the *Republic*, the death of Socrates in the *Crito* and the *Phaedo*, as well as subsequent Western history that gives credence to Hegel's summary image of history as a "slaughter-bench."[17]

What makes Weil's thought here truly compelling is its movement from evil's effects to evil as cause. It is not from evil, first defined in ontological fashion, to effects. These effects are as ramified as they are catastrophic. The lessons provided by Plato's literary predecessors leave no doubt that physical death or the living death of slavery is a real possibility. Greek tragedy leaves the realistic thinker in no doubt that violence is not simply atavism but socially and politically regulated. The context of evil in Weil is, as in Plato, always existential. In this context the question of the cause of evil, defined ultimately—although not absolutely—as harm to others, is generated. The answer is counterintuitive and maybe ironical. Not only, for Weil, is it the case that the cause of evil metaphysically or ontologically is less real than the effect, but one might postulate something like a law of inverse proportion: the more ontologically empty the cause, the greater the scope and intensity of the effect. In speaking of evil as non-being, Weil evinces the need to unearth and discredit a common *fallacy of inference* and, most important, to unearth and discredit what might be called the *fallacy of representation* (GG 103).

One commits the fallacy of inference when one supposes that huge harm requires a cause that is just as big or bigger. Weil's Plato questions this as an illusion, and wonders whether the evildoer is best understood more as a "leaky vessel" than a truly full and active agent (*IC* 72).[18] Extrapolating from the Parmenidean and Pythagorean elements of Plato, Weil herself concludes that ontological privation rather than ontological plenitude is the root of evil so existentially real in its effects (GG 155–56).

By contrast, what I am calling the fallacy of representation is more immediate, although it supports and is supported by the aforementioned fallacy. It denotes the tendency, especially evident in literature, to take the evildoer as glamorous or interesting, precisely because he or she is a source of transgression, which in effect amounts to a source of great potential harm to others: "Imaginary evil is romantic and varied; real evil is gloomy, monotonous, barren, and boring. Imaginary good is boring; real good is always new, marvelous, and intoxicating" (GG 120). Of course, if only the attribution of glamour or interestingness were a purely literary phenomenon,[19] something that occurs when we suspend disbelief, we would be farther from harm than we actually are. But, for Weil, this phenomenon of literary attribution appears to reflect a general tendency of human seeing, and is, therefore, more indicative of the workings of our imagination than constructive of it (GG 101–3). We have much to fear from the tendency of imagination, which after Descartes and Spinoza, as much as Plato, Weil associates with the will (GG 62–65, 91, 93, 99–110, 169–76).[20]

An interesting if merely implicit corollary of all of this is that all too often literature merely reflects and does not correct imagination. Its flirting with the ideology of transgression can even be conceived as a strange form of conservatism. Weil's basically positive relationship with the velvet pornographer Georges Bataille notwithstanding, she critiques, implicitly if not explicitly, a whole line of literature devolving from de Sade, including Baudelaire, Rimbaud, Cocteau, Gide, and Genet as well as Bataille. For Weil, free speech is one thing. Its prerogatives, however, should not be confused with immunity from ethical analysis and critique. With the example of Gide especially before her in *The Need for Roots*, Weil points out it is precisely this immunity from critique rather than prosecution that the apostles of transgression demand.

> Writers have the outrageous habit of playing a double game. Never so much as in our age have they claimed the role of directors of conscience and exercised it. . . . But if somebody called upon writers to render an account of the orientation set by their influence, they barricade themselves indignantly behind the sacred privilege of art for art's sake. (SWA 107)

Viewed from the vantage point of an intelligence that is not in thrall to the imagination, however, evildoers are revealed for what they are. They are not transcendent demigods; they tend toward what they attempt to reduce their victims to, that is, the condition of matter. Weil's examples of evil usually are not the demonic kind. But whether demonic or nondemonic, she judges that whatever the glamour ratio of the evildoers, they are not interesting, if by interesting one implies things such as depth of character (GG 121) constituted by a life of action and suffering and a unique perspective on reality. Rather, evil-doers are boring, their lives monotonous, their acts repetitious:

> Monotony of evil: never anything new, everything about it is *equivalent*. Never anything real, everything about it is imaginary.

> It is because of this monotony that quantity plays so great a part. A host of women (Don Juan) or of men (Célimène) etc. One is condemned to false infinity. That is hell itself. (GG 119)

If such classical evildoers fail to be truly interesting, *a fortiori* this is true of the more ideologically wrought modern literary specimens. Before Hannah Arendt,[21] Weil smoked out the glamour—demonic or otherwise—of the evil-doer as false. The evildoer is banal.[22]

Thus far I have argued that precisely at the point that appears to be its weakest link, Weil's reflection on evil justifies itself not despite but because of its Platonism. Whatever its abstract surface, evil in both Plato and Weil is existentially reducible; evil is traceable back to the phenomena of harm on vulnerable bodies and fragile psyches. This, however, is not the only aspect of the experiential inflection of Platonism evident in Weil's constructive and historical work. Related to the existential redemption of evil as non-being/privation is what, *faute de mieux*, I will call the *tensional understanding* of the self.

At first glance there appears to be a stridently anti-Platonic element in Weil's vision of the self, namely, her insistence on the vulnerability of the flesh and the psyche that is linked to the flesh. How does this square with the palpable "Orphic" element in Plato's texts: the decrying of bodily life, the body-soul dualism, and the arguments that the soul alone defines the self and is essentially immortal? The question is hardly rhetorical, given Weil's celebration of Plato's Orphic dimension and her underscoring of its structural importance (cf. IC 74–88). Any answer is conditional here: a "no" or "yes" verdict depends on whether Orphism in Plato, or Orphism as retrieved by Weil, is read as a concatenation of metaphysical dogmas about the self or as a series of insights—nothing less than revelation—coded in symbolic and mythical language requiring interpretation and existential translation. There are certainly aspects of Orphism that would appear to make it incompatible with Weil's insistence on the importance of the flesh. (i) The self is composed of body and soul, which are two different substances with different properties; materiality, changeability, corruptibility, and vulnerability in the case of the former, immateriality, unchangeability, incorruptibility in the case of the latter. (ii) The self has access to the immortal soul that exists prior to its nonintrinsic connection with the body, the soul's opposite, through acts of knowing. (iii) Ethical judgment of selves is an actual postmortem event that reverses worldly values. If all this is the Orphic dimension of Plato, then Plato is viable only if this element is excised. A Plato that would categorically maintain these ideas is a Plato who reneges on the essential insight of the Greek tradition about a humanity with no reserve of invulnerability, and thus a Plato and a form of Platonism that understands evil and its violence on the self in a more superficial way than the discourses that precede it.

But, of course, talk of excising the Orphic dimension of Plato, or correcting for it, is merely hypothetical. For the Orphic dimension of Platonism should not, indeed cannot, be read dogmatically. In a brilliant analysis Weil proposes a reading in which each of the three above elements are relieved of their thetic components and are made experiential, or experimental, to use Weil's own word (IC 79).

(i) With respect to the body-soul dualism and the attendant vilification of the corruptible and lusting body, a prominent feature of Plato's texts, especially the *Phaedo*, Weil suggests that the implied metaphysical commitment is reducible to the experienced tension between the immanent and transcendent dimensions of the self. This tension need not be substantialized. Indeed, substantializing this tension represents a doctrinaire deformation of Orphism and the Orphic dimension of Plato.

(ii) As is clear in "God in Plato" (IC 83–84) in particular, Weil does not think that either Orphism or Platonism, despite apparently express pronouncements to that effect, essentially involves a commitment to the *anamnesis* of a prior disembodied form of existence, or that amnesia consists essentially in forgetfulness of this separated form of existence. For Weil, anamnesis and amnesia in Orphism, and thus Platonism, refer not to *past* states of existence but rather to *essential* states of existence. *Anamnesis* refers to our attention to the transcendent dimension of our own and external reality. Similarly, amnesia is our ignoring of such reality and our consent here and now to live an unexamined form of life. (On this point, see chapter 11 following.)

(iii) Without indicating any skepticism about the reality of eschatological judgment, Weil contends that the central point of the myths of judgment, conspicuously placed at the end of the *Phaedo*, *Gorgias*, and *Republic*, lies not in their postmortem character but rather in what they say about truth and value

(*IC* 84–88). Plato and his genuine followers recognize the unreliability of human judgment. Good not only goes unrewarded, it goes unrecognized. The bad not only prosper, but they are often seen to be good. Eschatological judgment is the transcendent viewpoint available here and now that judges otherwise than the world, and judges in terms of reality rather than appearance. Judgment, Weil writes, "is nothing but the expression of what each one really is. Not an appreciation of what he has done, but a showing forth of what he is" (*IC* 81).

So the Orphic dimension of Plato's and Weil's thought does not conflict with her commitment to the reality of evil that is existentially guaranteed if and only if there is complex and tensional subject that is at once agent and patient. Indeed, Orphism rightly understood, that is, accepted as a trove of symbols and myths that resist exhaustive conceptualization, enables a deeper grasp of evil because it offers a three-dimensional view of the self that commits evil and suffers it.

Weil's broadly Platonic elaboration of a metaphysical account of evil represents a significant achievement. In a way unmatched by non-Christian and Christian Platonists alike, she shows not only that the language of "non-being" and "limitlessness" is viable, but even necessary for a proper account of evil. Thus Weil does not play down metaphysical analysis but accentuates it. What allows her to do so is that the Platonic metaphysical language, in both its Parmenidean and its Pythagorean aspects, never loses connection with experience. For her, a metaphysical account must match up with, indeed be traceable back to, the phenomenon of harm so superbly rendered in the "literary" discourses of Homer and Greek tragedy. At the same time, Weil's praise of Homer's and tragedy's view of selves totally exposed does not lead her, as one might have thought, to decry Orphism, to deny its presence in Plato, or to excise it in a modern and critical retrieval of Platonism. For Weil, Orphism does not support a substantialist form of anthropological dualism, and consequently does not set the historical Plato or the modern Platonist in opposition to the deliverances of the Greek "literary" traditions.

The very subtlety and incisiveness of Weil's account of evil may, however, have the unfortunate consequence of giving the impression that it is evil rather than the good that commands Weil's attention. Weil's interest ultimately is not evil but the good, not injustice but justice, not the mimetic violence but countermimesis, those acts and those lives that break violence's circuit. Of course, by defining evil as parasitic, and by showing how evil has a hold on our imagination in the way good and justice do not, Weil successfully limits the epistemic privilege of evil. Nevertheless, since the good, justice, and countermimesis are only disclosed against the backdrop of evil, injustice, and mimetic violence, practically speaking, it is difficult not to spend a considerable amount of time on these negative "realities," even if for any Platonist their positive counterparts exist on an entirely superior plane of reality.

Looked at properly, for Weil, the good is both the plenitude of being (GG 127; IC 140–41) and "beyond being" (*epekeine tes ousias*). As with her equation of evil and non-being, these equations also have a checkered history in non-Christian and Christian Platonism. The locus classicus of the equation in Plato is obviously the *Republic* book 6, where the good (*to agathon*) is defined as being beyond knowledge and being and yet their very foundation. Good's transcendence and grounding function, however, are but two sides of the same coin. As the really real that makes all reality possible, as the intelligible that makes all reality intelligible, the good is seen, discerned, but cannot be named.[23]

Considered thus, the metaphysical definition of the good no more represents an *inference* than the metaphysical definition of evil does. As evil is grounded in experience, so is good, and that is also of Greek pedigree, for example, in the *Iliad* and in tragedy, as well as in its consummate expression in book 6 of the *Republic*. There the vision of the good becomes possible in the philosopher who has experienced the "pull" of the good that is responsible for the painful conversion from convention and the false glamour of power and violence fueled by desire, imagination, and representation (IC 135–36). But it is necessary to go one further step. The renunciation of illusion is the necessary but not sufficient condition of the experience of the good. The philosopher must also renounce any comforting naming of the good; the good is not one more object in the world, ideal or otherwise. The experience of the good is thus the experience of the totally other; even if the good is revealed only against the backdrop of evil and illusion, the experience of the good is of a reality that is not correlative to any evil at all. For Weil, there is an important distinction between the good being other than evil and being *essentially* other (GG 120).[24] To say, as Weil does, that "the word good has not the same meaning when it is a term of correlation of good-evil as when it describes the very being of God" captures the semantic space occupied by the good for Weil (GG 152).

As a reality that can only be glimpsed, the good cannot be exhaustively conceived to provide a foundation for a world polity. The good is glimpsed, but the one who glimpses the good does not become the *Übermensch* or a legislator of the world. On Weilian grounds it is a mistake to read, as Popper does,[25] Plato as a totalitarian with Hegel and Marx, as a thinker who has mapped the reality of good and who seeks to lay out an irrefutable utopian program. The philosopher no more in the *Laws* than in the *Republic* offers a blueprint for the modification of society. Society is not infinitely malleable. Indeed, the best one can hope for, according to Weil, is to limit its evil (*IC* 87). Nor in the portrait of the "philosopher king" does Plato suggest that power should be in the hands of a special class. Fascism is oligarchy under a different name. Identified with the "just man," the philosopher king serves rather than rules. Of all people the philosopher king is most vulnerable, the most unaccommodated, the most subject to affliction.

The philosopher who glimpses the good and desires to communicate it also does not fare well in a society that is ruled by prestige and subject to the representational fallacy. Not only is the good dismissed there because it is unknown, and devalued on utilitarian grounds because it "doesn't work," the good man also is an object of ridicule. Under the cyclopean gaze of the great beast, that is, public opinion (*IC* 84–85), the just or good man may not even appear good or just (*IC* 79–80, 138, 140). Indeed, it may be necessary for him not to appear good or just, lest his integrity be compromised by association with one who only accidentally renders just judgment. As does Plato (*Rep.* 360, 361, 366), Weil recognizes that the absence of prestige is a form of suffering touching the self to the quick and, like violence, leads to a denuding of being, unglamorous in the extreme (*IC* 137). This form of suffering when it attends the death of the just man or the true philosopher makes suffering excessive or, as Weil sometimes says, "penal" (*IC* 138; also WG 119, 134–35).

The therapy of attention can and does reverse these judgments. But then it is precisely the philosopher who is arguing for this cure, and it is his very credibility that is in question. Thus the bind: the cure can be taken only if the philosopher has authority, and she has authority only to the degree to which her message is taken to be true, which will not happen unless the philosopher has authority, and so on. So there is a rather high index of resistance to change and to adjusting the equations of evil and good with being and the assigning of glory. But Weil thinks that Plato does manage to persuade some people about the good that is beyond being, its very foundation, and that he provides the contours of a counterrepresentational strategy in which the good is not weightless. But it is a point and a depiction that is extraordinarily difficult to get across, and one must be inspired to be able to do so. For example, Weil thinks that works of art that suggest either or both are exceptions and are the work of genius, not talent.

Neither the "just man" of the *Republic*, that is, the historical Socrates, nor any of the Greek figures of countermimesis solve the problem of evil in the sense of putting an end to it. Plato does not offer an anthropodicy any more than Kant does in the modern period. Nor do matters change essentially when the more theological aspects of Plato come into view in his speculation in the *Timaeus* about the World Soul and in the *Symposium* about Eros (*IC* 65–66), and where more specifically Plato hints at a connection between the divine and suffering. Because it is love that is at the origin of this suffering, suffering is not explained. Despite reminiscences of the more speculative accounts of creation in the Kabbalah,[26] Weil refuses the charms of a speculative theodicy of a Hegelian type in which suffering is necessary if God is to be God. What is called for in suffering is not knowledge but faith, not the ability to account for the ontological necessity of evil but the posture of hope. Hope expresses itself in endurance and fidelity to God precisely in the apparent absence of God.[27] Plato, then, confirms the truth of Job, the affirmation that is wrested from Job in his affliction, the hope against hope on which all theodicy runs aground.[28]

Christianity's Revelation of Violence and Countermimesis

I have argued that Weil offers an existential or experiential form of Platonism that redeems as well as repeats the ontological urgency of Parmenides and Pythagoras and the essential anthropological insights of Orphism. In doing so, I do not wish to overlook that Weil puts Plato at the end of a long tradition in Greek thought, its heir, or that Weil plots Platonism on a trajectory completed by Christianity in general and by the Gospels in particular. These emplottings do not *force* the experiential inflection, but they encourage and reinforce it. I wish to say something about these two plottings here.

First, Weil's plotting of Platonism within the tradition of Greek thought: it is teleological through and through.[29] For Weil, Platonism realizes rather than rejects the wisdom disclosed in the *Iliad* and in Greek tragedy, just as it realizes rather than rejects the insights of Orphism, Parmenideanism, and Pythagoreanism. If Platonic philosophy surpasses the *Iliad* and Greek tragedy, it is only by recapitulating their insights about the vulnerability of bodily selves, the difficulty of attention and insight, and the advent of an unnameable justice and goodness that interrupts the economies of violence and evil. Similarly, if Platonism surpasses Parmenides, Pythagoras, and Orphism, it is only by recollecting their deeply experiential inflection that discloses an overwhelming reality impinging on a frangible subject. Thus, despite all the hierarchical notes struck in Weil, the category "Greek" in her account finally refers as much to a dynamic field of force of mutually modifying poles as discrete discourses arranged in hierarchical order. We need, however, to treat Weil's treatment of Platonism as something completed in Christianity at greater length. Specifically, more needs to be said about how Christianity completes and surpasses Platonism, without making it redundant, particularly on the metaphysical level. Of course, in broaching this issue, it must be conceded beforehand that just as in the case of Platonism, and for similar reasons, we are dealing with an existentially reduced form of Christianity. First, Weil is forever leery of Christianity's institutional and dogmatic aspects.[30] Second, for her, from a textual point of view Christianity is primarily identified by the New Testament texts and above all by the Gospels. Christianity is focused in the figure of Christ who reveals all that the human being is, all that God is, and all that the relation between God and human being can be.

Weil actually operates within fairly standard Christian parameters. In fact, formally her understanding of the relation between Platonism and Christianity operates in terms of the model forged by the Greek Apologists and perfected in the Alexandrian theology of Clement and Origen. Materially, however, Weil differentiates herself from this tradition, with the possible exception of Origen, by her focus on the concrete figure of Christ and in her understanding that Christ's meaning is given in the Cross rather than in the Incarnation. The figure of Christ represents unsurpassably a human being's love for God, a human being's unrestricted desire for the good and justice, which are only real, as she points out in particularly eloquent fashion (WG 139–57), in the here and now, specifically in the service of the broken and marginalized other. Christ possesses no reserve of invulnerability. Thus any portrayals of Christ even by Christian Platonists of the first centuries who emphasize omnipotence, omniscience, and impassibility are for Weil deformations of the astonishing realism of the Gospels and the equally astonishing negativity of the Cross. As the Gospels render him, Christ is not only exposed physically, but also psychically or spiritually. He experiences the abandonment of the Father that wrests from him the great cry of dereliction, *Eli, Eli lama sabathani* (GG 139; WG 88, 121–22). This is the apogee of exposure. All human vulnerability and exposure rests within its parenthesis.

Christ realizes all that is meant and can be meant by humanness. His life is an alternative to life lived in the shadow of power and violence; his giving himself for others is the norm by which our approximations to humanness are judged and our failures exposed. Christ also sums up or recapitulates all previous figures of countermimesis, and includes by pointing forward to those figures of countermimesis, remembered or forgotten, who follow. Certainly, Christ recapitulates Patroclus, Orestes, Antigone, all the suppliant figures in Greek tragedy, the "just man" of Plato's *Republic* and Socrates. Crucially, Christ is the realization of the suffering servant of Isaiah 53. But as the standard by which all past (and future) countermimetic figures are measured Christ also surpasses all these figures: never has a human been so abandoned, never has a human experienced so thoroughly the absence of God while remaining faithful to God in God's very absence.

The parallels between Girard's thought here and that of Weil are unmistakable and extensive.[31] At the same time there are significant differences between Weil and Girard with respect to the content of what Christ's Cross discloses, and therefore, to what the Greeks anticipated and what was later recollected in nontheological discourses. For Weil, Christ cannot be reduced to the anthropological or sociological dimension; there is always a specifically theological dimension.[32] Christ is more than *the* exemplary figure of resistance to violence and evil, just as the sacrifice of Christ is not reducible to its function of social integration.[33]

Asserting the theological dimension of revelation is hardly unusual; it is difficult if not impossible to imagine the construction of Christian doctrine without it. Nevertheless, Weil's support for the theological dimension of revelation is not a capitulation to the doctrinal tradition. For Weil, too often the Church has taken a second-order dimension for the theological one. For Weil, the theological dimension of the Cross is resolutely first-order: it is given in the phenomenon of the Cross itself. As the Cross represents a reversal of priorities and fundamental forms of life, it also represents the love of God for a suffering humanity plunged in violence. The love of God is nothing less than God's presence, even if this presence is hidden under its apparent absence (GG 72, 130, 137, 141–42, 166–67; WG 120–21).[34]

The necessity of a theological reading of Christ as the figure of countermimesis in Weil is supported by her reading of Greek tragedy. It is axiomatic, for Weil, that Greek tragedy has its ultimate end in Christianity. Greek tragedy, however, itself is not reducible to anthropology. A figure such as Prometheus is not simply an exemplar of human resistance to evil. Prometheus also discloses the love of God for humanity that goes to the point of embracing the affliction that besets the human estate. Neglecting the theological dimension of figures of countermimesis distorts the Greek tradition as well as the Christian one. One also cannot simply tack on a theological dimension to a foundational anthropological analysis. What is necessary is a real integration of the two dimensions that is given in the phenomenon of the Cross, as indicated in the ancient Pauline symbol of *kenosis* (GG 48, 139–43).[35]

On the Cross God's love for the human being is defined as a suffering love. The connection between God's love and suffering can no more be explained than can God's love itself. What makes the relation of love and suffering in God resistant to explanation is that both are defined by freedom. Explanation, therefore, would necessarily imply a bad form of metaphysics. As is obvious from her treatment of evil, Weil does not in principle object to metaphysics, although, arguably, metaphysics is always correlative to phenomena given in experience. In this respect Weil again differs from Girard, who tends to think of metaphysics as a spurious form of dogmatism, often ideological in its masking of oppression and violence.

For Weil, however, there is good as well as good metaphysics. Bad metaphysics either avoids the phenomenon of evil and its overcoming altogether[36] or offers reasons where none are available, or can be available. Such bad reason-offering with respect to the relation between God and the world of suffering and violence in particular was condemned by Kant in a famous essay on theodicy.[37] Weil belongs to the Kantian line of opposition, and perhaps might agree with some antitheodicists who argue that attempts at theodicy are nothing short of the intellectually scandalous.[38] For Weil, however, theoretical refusal does not issue in despair or skepticism. Acceptance of God, and God's universe, is actual and possible. It is possible and actual, however, only in the form of an existential and practical stance.

If Weil owes much to Kant, arguably she owes even more to Plato. But whether it is Kant or Plato, philosophy can still illumine reality. To the extent to which it does so, it is nothing less than a fundamental form of revelation itself. Platonism is revelation, as are all its various aspects, whether that of Orphism, Parmenideanism, and Pythagoreanism. But even if this huge claim were to be allowed—and it most certainly will not be allowed by those Christians of *sola scriptura* persuasion—is there not here the danger of syncretism? Worse, is there not the danger that Christianity becomes an aspect of Platonic philosophy rather than philosophy qualifying Christianity? Obviously, contextually as well as genetically for Weil "Christian" qualifies "Greek thought" or "Platonism." Weil not only comes to Christianity belatedly, but Christianity is rendered in a philosophical discourse that owes much to a complexly figured Platonism. From a normative point of view, however, "Greek" and "Platonic" qualify "Christianity," since Christ is the definitive revelation, the one that sums up Greek thought and Platonism. What qualifies what, whether it is more accurate to speak of Weil's "Christian Platonism" or her "Platonic Christianity," therefore, can only be decided depending on whether the focus is on the normative claim or the interpreting discourse. When the normative claim is to the fore, if not explicitly, then implicitly, one is speaking of "Platonic Christianity." When the issue is that of interpreting discourse, then it is legitimate to speak of "Christian Platonism." In my own title I have highlighted both, since my essay is at once about Weil's use of Platonic discourse to expose a phenomenon that is of great importance for Christianity and her teleological model in which all Greek discourse in general and Platonic discourse in particular find themselves fulfilled— if not silenced—in the discourse of Christianity.

Notes

1. This preeminence has been recognized by many scholars. Coming at Weil's texts from very different points of view, Miklos Vetö and Michael K. Ferber are but two of the many scholars who underscore the importance of the *Iliad* in Weil's general argument about the construction of the self and society. For Vetö, see *The Religious Metaphysics of Simone Weil*, trans. Joan Dargan (Albany: SUNY Press, 1994), 80–82. For Ferber, see "Simone Weil's *Iliad*," in *Simone Weil: Interpretations of a Life*, ed. George Abbot-White (Amherst: University of Massachusetts Press, 1981), 63–85.

2. See IC 75, 117; WG 70, 129. See also GG 165.

3. I use throughout Mary McCarthy's translation of "*L'Iliade* ou le poème de la force," first published in 1940, reproduced in SWA 162–95.

4. Of course, the condition of the possibility of saying that the *Iliad* is the text that names violence is the putting in parenthesis of the Gospels. But the purpose of the Gospels is to spell out in a way not realized in the *Iliad* how violence is transcended. And, of course, it is in the transcendence of violence that violence is truly disclosed.

5. I highlight the status of Hegel's *Phenomenology* here, since in the France of the 1930s, due largely to the lectures of Alexandre Kojève at the École Pratique des Hautes Études during the period 1933–39, it came to be read as the text that defines historical reality and thereby human existence as essentially that of the battle for power between

masters and slaves. For Kojève, Hegel's *Phenomenology* interpreted Marx, just as Marx's description of the mechanics of power flesh out Hegel. For a good account of the reception of Kojève's lectures, see Michael S. Roth, *Knowing and History: Appropriations of Hegel in Twentieth-Century France* (Ithaca: Cornell University Press, 1988). Given that Hegel's text was all the rage and that intellectuals such as Bataille attended them, it is interesting to speculate whether in her essay on the *Iliad* Weil was not engaged in dismantling the authority of Hegel's text by appeal to an ancient text that discloses the violence of historical reality while at the same time pointing beyond it in a way that Hegel's text never does.

6. However brilliant Weil's essay is as a reading of the *Iliad*, it is clearly not the work of a mere scholar but that of an engagé. The dynamics of violence, which cannot be controlled by any antagonist, is a lesson that applies to the contemporary world. There may be good reasons to support one or the other side in a conflict, for example, France over Germany in World War II, but a major point Weil wishes to make is that war is as terrible as it is universal, and leaves no one with "clean hands."

7. Weil writes: "The progress of war in the *Iliad* is simply a game of seesaw. The victim of the moment feels himself invulnerable, even though a few hours before, he may have experienced defeat; he forgets to treat victory as a transitory thing" (SWA 175).

8. In emptying itself, the self moves toward a condition of an inanimate object and thus petrifies. Achilles dealing with the prostate Lacoon, and his treatment of Priam are but two of the many examples cited by Weil as evidence of petrification. See especially SWA 167–69. Of course, Weil's reading of relationships in war—which serves as a real image of the world as fallen and discloses it as such—is contestable. It has been contested on more general and more specific grounds. In his essay, "Simone Weil's *Iliad*," Ferber does both. Weil's pointing to petrification represents a real insight, but the theme is not as prominent, Ferber believes, as Weil thinks it is. In addition, situations and relations cited as examples of petrification, for example, Priam coming to Achilles as a suppliant requesting the body of his son Hector, do not support Weil's interpretation. In their meeting Priam shows more autonomy and Achilles more humanity than Weil allows (SWA 70–72).

9. Weil's emphasis in her famous essay on the dynamics of war has been accused of misreading the cultural and ideological fix of the *Iliad*, which is that of the "fame of men" (*klea andrōn*). But in fact, Weil does not misread the *Iliad* on this point. Indeed, given Weil's sensitivity to the ways in which ideologies function in societies, what after Plato she christens the "great beast," she is not a likely suspect for such amnesia. Her point in emphasizing the objective dynamics of war rather than the motivations and the reasons parties offer to go to and maintain war is twofold. First, her vantage point is that of the impersonal narrator of the *Iliad*, who dispassionately unveils how uncompelling the reasons and motivations are in the face of death and petrification. Second, whatever the intention of the author of the *Iliad*, the distance taken by the narrator from his subject means that the ideology of immortality of name becomes implicitly at least an object of critique. For a clear statement of connection between war and social prestige, see IC 135–36.

10. At one level, the characterization of Patroclus as a person of "measure" functions as one side of a descriptive contrast. Most—if not all—of the other personae in the *Iliad* are in one way or another "unmeasured" in the sense of given to excess, especially to excesses of violence, being mastered by it, thereby becoming mere expressions of its totalizing reality. At another level, the characterization obviously bears explanatory freight, since *measure* is a technical term in a variety of Greek traditions but especially in Weil's beloved Pythagoreanism. At such, therefore, "measure" or "limit" functions both phenomenologically and metaphysically. It is interesting how in the war situation in which *measure* gets applied to a person, the term does not evoke in any way Aristotle's ethical man who most certainly is a person of limit. In fact, the measure illustrated by Patroclus, and after him by Antigone and Electra among others, functions critically with respect to Aristotle's ethical man, who if virtuous also functions more calculatively and does so in a nonagonistic situation that if real, in Weil's view, is likely to be merely temporary.

11. For further reflections on the figure of Creon, see Weil's essay "On Personality," *SWA* 49–78. See esp. 62–63.

12. At one level Weil tends to share the influential view that Euripides represents something of a deformation of Greek tragedy. Consistently in her specification of Greek tragedy, Euripides is excluded. Thus Weil's view bears a family resemblance at least to the views of Hegel and Nietzsche, both of whom in their different ways thought of Euripides as surrendering essential aspects of Greek tragedy. Certainly, compared with Aeschylus and Sophocles, both agree that Euripides is more rational and more ironical. Weil would probably not disagree. And in general, whatever the literary virtues of Euripides—and they may be similar to those of Virgil—he lacks the genius that can be ascribed to his two predecessors. In the end, however, the exclusion of Euripides in Weil by contrast with nineteenth-century German philhellenes is relative rather than absolute. Euripides' *Hippolytus* can be spoken of in the same breath as Sophocles' *Electra* and *Antigone* (see *IC* 79, 100). At the same time, it is not at all evident that Weil is suggesting that every work attributable to Aeschylus and Sophocles is an expression of genius. For her, genius is an objective rather than a subjective category. It refers not to its origin in the mind of an author but to the perfection of a rendering of the terrible beauty of reality. And perfection ratio may vary from text to text even of the same author. Not all of Aeschylus's and Sophocles' dramas are brought forward as examples of genius.

13. Weil takes the risk of being speculative, and suggests that the figure of a suppliant Zeus (*IC* 71), at the fore of Aeschylus's play of the same name, be used to interpret the Zeus that torments Prometheus. Here Zeus is not the object but the subject of supplication, identified with the cry of the suppliant, as Prometheus is with a humanity bereft of the human flourishing that comes with *technē*.

14. In the cited passages Weil is particularly anxious to underscore the close connection between the figure of Prometheus and Christ. It should be noted that in pointing to the connection between Christianity and Greek tragedy, Weil promoted a view that had little currency in her own day among those that either favored Christianity or abjured it. In a situation in which Enlightenment critique sets the terms, especially with

respect to the idea of revelation, the association tends to reduce Christianity to drama and its fictions. Thus depending on aesthetic judgment, Christian texts succeed or fail judged against the Greek paradigm. But in any event, Christianity loses the absoluteness and self-authentication of revelation. The other side of the coin is to dissociate Christianity and Greek tragedy and think of Christianity as good or bad philosophy, depending on one's antecedent inclinations. In the case of Christians, the emphasis will fall on rationales for the uniqueness of Christian discourse and at the same time its fundamental translatability into rational discourse. Weil's proposal of fundamental connection between the discourses of Greek tragedy and Christianity remains fecund for contemporary theology. The value of this connection, as well as the harm that is done to Christianity by neglecting this association, is underscored in the theology of Hans Urs von Balthasar, who retrieves both Homer and Greek tragedy in this magisterial theological aesthetics, *The Glory of the Lord*, and makes drama foundational for his systematic theology. See especially, *The Glory of the Lord: A Theological Aesthetics*. Vol. 4: *The Realm of Metaphysics in Antiquity*, trans. Brian Mc Neil C. R.V., Andrew Louth, John Saward, Rowan Williams, and Oliver Davies, ed. John Riches (San Francisco: Ignatius Press, 1989), 43–154.

15. Most often Weil will simply accept that Aristotle is the basic figure of philosophy as a rational and argumentative enterprise. Thus Plato is something different, a religious or mystical thinker. See especially *IC* 74, 85. But this difference is not indifferent: To be the kind of thinker that Plato is, is to be more than Aristotle. At the same time, there is something of an undertow as to what counts as authentic philosophy, the kind of "love of wisdom" that defines Plato, as it defines Weil's own work. On this standard, Aristotle and the rationalists fail to be philosophers. Specifically, they fail to respond with the requisite kind of urgency toward the good and the beautiful as well as the true.

16. The classical Neoplatonic rendition is to be found in those texts in the *Enneads* where Plotinus refutes the Gnostic interpretation of Plato. See especially *Enneads* 1.8 and 2. 9. Augustine, of course, famously availed of Plotinus's work to refute the Manichaeans. The trope of evil as non-being and privation is deployed consistently throughout Augustine's approximately twenty-year battle with the Manichaeans. It enters into Augustine's discourse in *On Free Will* (389). Perhaps the most known avowal of this view is to be found in Augustine's recollections of what led him to leave Manichaeanism behind in the *Confessions* (bk. 7). Augustine's metaphysical characterization became the standard one of the Western theological tradition, and was adopted by Aquinas. But Augustine is not the only patristic thinker who supported such a view. Gregory of Nyssa has his own version of the trope, although it plays a much less central role in his theology than it does in the case of Augustine.

17. See Hegel's introduction to *Lectures on the Philosophy of History*, trans. J. Sibree (New York: Dover Press, 1956), 21. For a treatment of Hegel's philosophy of history precisely as a theodicy, see my *The Heterodox Hegel* (Albany: SUNY Press, 1994), 310–23.

18. As a specification of this fairly formal view, see Plato's scatological reference to the evildoer as like "dirty bird" in the *Gorgias*. Here Plato is underscoring the insati-

ability of the appetite for pleasures and the short half-life of the pleasures consumed by the bird that continually excretes.

19. This is the tack of Michael Ferber in his essay "Simone Weil's *Iliad*," (79), where citing the same passage that I have, he upbraids Weil for thinking that the "literary" fiction belongs only to literature and is not an essential phenomenon of human judgment and evaluation. This seems to misunderstand totally the point of Weil's concern with the "literary," which is that it reflects our social imaginations while also educating imagination.

20. Weil's knowledge of Descartes is exceptional. In the *Meditations*, of course, the critique of knowledge is fundamentally a critique of imagination, which, Descartes argues, does not render reality but influenced by desire and will projects it. This critique is fundamental to Spinoza's *Ethics*. Weil's debt to both Descartes and Spinoza on this score is clear. At the same time, it is this set of conceptual relations that announces the extraordinary close relationship between the work of Iris Murdoch and Simone Weil. See *The Sovereignty of the Good* (London: Routledge and Kegan Paul, 1970), where having as her proximate target the voluntarism of Sartre, Murdoch argues for a Platonic vision of ethics in which the good and evil are not so much approvable and disapprovable free choices of the will so much as attention and its lack. Murdoch leaves the interpreter in no doubt that Weil is a major influence on her thought. See Murdoch's last major philosophical work before she died, *Metaphysics as a Guide to Morals* (London: Penguin, 1992). This text is replete with references to Weil. Note in particular Murdoch's reprise of Weil's notions of attention and affliction, 52–54 and 498–503, respectively.

21. See Hannah Arendt, *Eichmann in Jerusalem: A Report on the Banality of Evil* (New York: Penguin, 1963).

22. For Weil, then, the metaphysical, or more particularly, the essentially Parmenidean-Pythagorean equation of evil and non-being, is ethically and existentially redeemable in Plato's work and can be recommended to all who dare to think the question of evil. Here Weil differs from a philosopher such as Paul Ricoeur, who in an influential essay on Augustine commented on the impossibility of existentially redeeming "evil as non-being." According to Ricoeur, Augustine's appropriation of the trope plays havoc with both the specifically Christian and existential bases of his thought. Weil would not disagree with Ricoeur that Christianity provides an opportunity for considerable deepening of the existential or experiential dimension of evil. Still the trope of evil as non-being is existentially redeemable even within the Platonic domain, and because it is, it is redeemable in principle within Christianity. She believes that the depth of the Christian view lies in its grasping clearly that what is so little causes so much damage, that what is intrinsically so unglamorous, because so empty and weightless, causes havoc represented in a way that inevitably glamourizes what is vacant and hollow.

23. In both Plato and Weil the good is not named in the full and proper sense. Rather than a determinate entity, even a determinate intellectual entity, the good is the foundation of all entities. Of course, Weil does not have the historical Plato's compunction about identifying the good, as absolute metaphysical principle, with God.

24. Weil's thought here can be translated into a more technical idiom, specifically the Neoplatonic idiom of "not other." God is "not other" to evil. The great Renaissance Neoplatonist, Nicholas of Cusa, used the technical term *non aliud*, or not other, to indicate the noncontrastive relation between God and all created being. Cusa's precise concern was to combat the finitizing of God he thought was the inevitable result of thinking of God as one term of the binary opposition of God and world.

25. See Karl Popper, *The Open Society and Its Enemies.* Vol. 1: *The Spell of Plato,* 3d rev. ed. (London: Routledge and Kegan Paul, 1957).

26. The relation of Weil's notion of decreation (see GG 78–89) to the Kabbalah, especially the concept of *tzimzum,* is long-standing. The relationship is a critical one from an interpretive point of view, since as Vetö points out, the Kabbalistic view is taken up in modern philosophical thought, especially in German Idealism. For some interpreters of Weil, this association indicates the speculative *Tendenz* of Weil's thought—a speculative tendency that secretes itself into her reflections on the Trinity. For others, such as myself, the association with the Kabbalah provides Weil symbols rather than explanatory concepts that would map ultimate reality in an adequate fashion.

27. The symbol that captures the complex of endurance and fidelity is, of course, the Greek notion of *en hypomene* that is so central to "Waiting for God" (76, 82, 86).

28. The figure of Job is a pivotal one in Weil's great essay "The Love of God and Affliction" (WG 117–36; see also WG 173, 177; IC 59, 102; GG 166). The antitheodicy function of Job in Weil's texts is remarkably similar to the role Job plays in Kant and Ricoeur. For Kant, see "On the Miscarriage of all Philosophical Trials in Theodicy," trans. and ed. Allen Wood and George diGiovani, in *Religion within the Boundaries of Mere Reason and Other Writings* (London: Cambridge University Press, 1998). For Ricoeur, see "Evil, a Challenge to Philosophy and Theology," in *Figuring the Sacred,* trans. David Pellauer, ed. Mark I. Wallace (Minneapolis: Fortress Press, 1995), 249–61. But, importantly, there are any number of Greek exemplars of affliction. For Electra, see IC 8; for Prometheus, see IC 67–68, 100. It is obvious, of course, that throughout Weil's Platonism is supplemented by her Stoicism. See especially "Forms of the Implicit Love of God" (WG 137–215, esp. 160, 175–76).

29. What is evident in *Intimations in Christianity* is confirmed in *Waiting for God,* especially in "Forms of the Implicit Love of God." The use of the word *implicit* here does not mislead. Plato realizes in a fully explicit way what is implicit or merely intended in pre-Socratic "literary" and "philosophical" texts.

30. These reservations are everywhere. See especially *Waiting for God.* For Weil's reservation regarding the Church as institution, see esp. 52–54, 75. For her reservation regarding the dogmatic tendency in the Catholic Church, see esp. 79–80.

31. Interest in the relation between Weil and Girard is long-standing. For a review and estimate of this interest, see Jean-Marie Muller, *Simone Weil: L'Exigence de non-violence* (Paris: Éditions du Témoignage Chrétien, 1991), 185–99.

32. For Weil, the theological dimension is basic in a way it is not for Girard. God is proper name and grammatical subject of creation and redemption in a way that is not

the case for Girard. From a strict Girardian perspective, Weil illicitly posits divine realities, and compounds the problem by making God the only real actor in history, which indeed is the history of salvation.

33. In the Girardian scheme of things Christ's sacrifice serves this function by focusing antagonistic desire and covering up the agency of the crime.

34. The relation between Weil and Luther here is remarkably close. However Catholic her orientation, Weil seems to recapitulate Luther's trope of the *sub contrario*.

35. See also Weil's reflections on decreation (GG 78–80).

36. To the extent to which philosophy follows the disciplinary model of Aristotle — and much of the Western tradition does — it is guilty of this avoidance.

37. For information on Kant, see note 28. In her antitheodicy stance, Weil has appropriated the lesson of Dostoyevsky's embargo on theodicy. See Weil's remarks on Dostoyevsky at GG 131.

38. See in particular Terrence Tilley, *The Evils of Theodicy* (Washington, D.C.: Georgetown University Press, 1991).

CHAPTER 11

"I Dreamed I Saw St. Augustine . . ."

ERIC O. SPRINGSTED

It would, in the strictest sense, be a mistake to call Simone Weil an Augustinian. Though she quotes Augustine directly and cites him with occasional frequency, her citations are often mixed. If, on the one hand, she points to his saying, "God is a good which is nothing else but good," as a positive example of Platonism (SN 104), on the other hand, not only does she cite his canonization as the ironical proof that the Church had replaced genuine faith with "the doctrine of an idolatrous state" (SN 145), she also criticizes him for making doctrine and ceremony the condition of salvation, not its grammar and symbol,[1] and finds his consignation of unbaptized infants to the nether regions particularly loathsome. On the whole, though, she does not seem to have delved very deeply into him. Augustine, for Weil, was chiefly to be cited—positively and negatively—as an authority of official Christianity, and was not somebody whom she herself read as a guiding intellectual and spiritual master the way she read Plato or St. John of the Cross.

Nevertheless, Weil shares something at a very deep level with Augustine, as she did with Pascal whom she treated similarly, namely, Christian Platonism in general and more particularly the "inward turn" of Augustine's Christian

Platonism. This, of course, is a point on which Augustine is most frequently misunderstood and most criticized. For example, his search for the inner self in *Confessions* is often claimed to be the beginning of our unholy individualism and our obsession with the self and with personality as the ultimate expression of ultimacy. Weil had much to say about *that*. Moreover, the "inner self" is just as often criticized as an example of the sort of wrongheadedness that lies at the heart of metaphysics, the need to posit an inner entity to explain the outer workings of the world, or a privileged place of vision in which luminosity guarantees truth.

Augustine is easily and now regularly defended from these sorts of charges. His invention of the inner self is not individualism but a discovery of an inner place where God, where otherness, is met.[2] It is not a private, lonely place at all, a place where one is isolated and insulated from the world; on the contrary, it is the space where our isolation from the world is actually overcome. The world of the senses is actually the most private world—who else can feel what we do?—the inner world is where we discover ourselves, ourselves as sought by and grounded in God, where God's own Word becomes our inner word welcoming and, for once, open to all that God has wrought.[3] Here doctrine is not a replacement for the movement of the heart for God but teaching meant to form a character and to focus the wandering mind, as well as a discipline meant to order outer life precisely so that one can proceed inwardly, a movement from *scientia* to *sapientia*.[4] It is, in Weil's terms, a *metaxu*. Indeed, how else could one fairly read a work such as *De Doctrina Christiana*?

But if this is Augustine, if Augustine can be defended, then the real question that his authority poses is not whether he is guilty of being a baleful influence but whether he is right even when read accurately. If he is, then his Christian Platonism, which is at the heart of his "inward turn," stands against and diagnoses our spiritual malaise, and may well be an alternative to it. That by itself, however, may not make Augustinianism more welcome or understandable to the modern mind, which is individualist, isolated, and distanced, even imperialistic and dogmatic, although it tends to be dogmatic about its own relativism. For what is Christian Platonism to us any longer? It may still simply be an alternative rooted in an outmoded metaphysics of the self, and hence no real alternative. Here is where the Christian Platonism that Weil broadly shares with Augustine is particularly important. It is at the very heart of what she thinks ought to be inherited from the past, and what ought to be pursued in the future, for it is not a philosophical doctrine but a way of life and an alternative way of doing philosophy. What she therefore sees in Christian Platonism is something that may allow us to recover that tradition, including Augustine as a real authority, in a meaningful way. But I also suggest that Weil herself may be one who actually is able to distill and present that in a way that is even purer than Augustine's.

The Inner Element of Christian Platonism

What, then, is Christian Platonism? Within Christianity, Platonism has actually been two things. In the first place, it has been regarded frequently as the mother of all heresies, chiefly heresies of the Gnostic variety, as Hippolytus of Rome argued in the third century. This is a Platonism that is a speculative doctrine and that encourages and begets speculative doctrine, an attempt to say a final word. It is frequently at odds with orthodoxy. Second, however, it is a very different sort of tradition, one in which philosophy is assimilated to contemplation and contemplation is assimilated to prayer and the life of prayer. Assuming this assimilation, Cassian, for example, without any trace of irony or being metaphorical, could call the desert hermits Christian philosophers. In a similar vein, Evagrius of Pontus claimed, "If you are a theologian, you pray truly. If you truly pray you are a theologian."[5] This is a Christian Platonism in which the foundational story of Platonism, namely, the allegory of the cave in *Republic* book 7, is likened and assimilated to a foundational story of Christianity, the Exodus and Moses' ascent of Mount Sinai.[6] Here religious life and the philosophical life are united, and united in such a way that philosophy and theology flow from and are rooted in the fullness of religious life.

Now, to be sure, these two forms of Christian Platonism were not always distinct in either the ancient or the medieval period. Evagrius himself is an excellent example of mixing the two, as he both assimilated Platonic contemplation to the life of prayer and managed to get himself into serious trouble for speculative excesses that were rooted in his Origenism. Origen, for that matter, is another example of their combination, and there are elements within Augustine that on occasion put him under a similar cloud.

If, however, these forms of Platonism often overlapped within Christianity, in good part it was because thought and life were not regarded as distinct as we often make them. That they were not, is in fact the most positive aspect of the second type, and suggested its basic criticism of the first type; that is, it had separated life and thought too easily, and proceeded with religious life as if it were a matter of uncommitted thought and speculation alone. It was not only Christian Platonists who voiced this criticism, non-Christian Platonists did as well. For example, in arguing against the Gnostics, after showing how silly their pseudo-Platonic speculations really were, Plotinus goes straight to the heart of the matter by pointing out that the real problem at its root was that their Platonism was strictly a speculative doctrine that had nothing to do with the amendment of life and that offered no *way* to the God who was so glibly spoken about. Thus Plotinus complains: "they have never made any treatise about virtue . . . nor how the soul is tended, nor how it is purified. For it does no good at all to say 'Look to God,' unless one teaches how one is to look. . . . In reality it is virtue which goes before us to the goal and, when it comes to exist in the soul along with wisdom, shows God; but God, if you talk about him without true virtue is only a name."[7] Similarly, when criticizing the Manichaeans, Augustine echos Plotinus's criticism of the Gnostics when he confesses that his problem as a Manichaean was that he believed Manichaean intellectuality made him look more clever and sophisticated, and thus actually prevented him from learning or improving in virtue. It made him smug and arrogant.[8] What the Gnostics and Manichaeans lacked was a deep sense of an inner life, a life of self-reflection and consciousness of the self with respect to the demands of religious life.

It is precisely *this* sort of inner element that Augustine found attractive in Platonism. Augustine recognized it in Socrates and Plato and saw it as akin to Christianity. For example, Augustine notes that Socrates saw that the causes of things are "reducible to nothing else than the will of the one true and supreme God — and on this account he thought they could only be comprehended by a purified mind; and therefore that all diligence ought to be given to the purification of the life by good morals, in order that the mind, delivered from the depressing weight of lusts, might raise itself upward by its native vigor to eternal things, and might with purified understanding, contemplate that nature which is incorporeal and unchangeable light, where live the causes of created natures."[9] Similarly, Augustine says, Plato followed Socrates on this score, emphasizing that the conduct of life and contemplation of truth were inseparable.[10] Thus Plato perfected philosophy "by combining both parts into one." Recognizing this combination in his predecessors was a good part of Augustine's own genius. Straight thinking alone will not save us; the problem with us is usually our wills. They even distort our thinking — and vice versa.

So it is important to bear in mind how the two forms of Christian Platonism are distinct. They are *not* two ends of the spectrum. One does not represent a more intellectual approach to Christian philosophy and theology and the other a more affective one, a mysticism of experience. To suggest that they are related this way would be to impose a modern distinction, a very Cartesian or even Kantian one, on ancient Christianity that did not exist in its own period At their heart these are two types of Platonism that are opposed, for the difference between the two is not between reason and faith, or reason and affectivity, and one cannot split the difference. Rather, there is a distinction in how one reasons. One can speculate by unaided reason, without grace, or one can reason in the context of a moral and spiritual life that sees the moral and spiritual reformation that is an integral part of faith at the heart of understanding. In this sense, if desert monks with little learning can be appropriately called Christian philosophers, so too can people such as the Cappadocian fathers and Augustine, who not only wrote works that are recognizable as philosophy to us but also wrote more devotional works and worked out much of their own theology and philosophy in sermons. They themselves probably did not see a lot of difference between the two forms as ways of thinking. Surely there is more to be said about this distinction; nevertheless, it ought to be clear enough to give some sense of what Christian Platonism is, and the role of the inner in it. It is the "inner" in this sense, I suggest, in which Simone Weil was most interested in Platonism, that she thought really was at stake in Platonism and why Platonism was so very important. It is also this sort of inner sense that she actually recovers of Platonism and reformulates.

God in Plato

When Weil wrote her numerous essays for Father Perrin about the Greeks, she did so to prove to him the universality of grace. It is important to note that she would have had no hope of convincing him of this (and she seems to have convinced him) unless she could somehow show that thinkers such as Plato really were Christian in some important sense. This is the goal of her essay "God in Plato." But it cuts the other way too. In uncovering what is most important in Plato's thinking, Weil is also trying to show what is most important in Christian thinking, and the essay therefore goes to the deeper point about the nature of Christian thinking itself—and the nature of philosophy in general. In going to that point, I want to suggest that Weil explicitly embraces and recommends a Christian Platonism of the second type given above. Plato's teaching—and Christianity's—is not speculative doctrine but a way of life and a way of thinking. Specifically, then, she wants to argue that if Platonism is not a doctrine but a mysticism, and is an intimation of Christianity, then by parity of reasoning, Christianity itself is not a doctrine but a mysticism. But this mysticism is not a matter of gaining *an* experience; it is the development of a certain sort of inner sense that permeates and configures our knowledge.

At the outset, and throughout the essay, Weil argues that Plato is a mystic. His wisdom "is not a philosophy, a search for God by means of human reason. . . . [It] was nothing other than an orientation of the soul towards grace"(SN 99). Weil here is obviously drawing a sort of Kantian distinction about philosophy, but prescinding from that, if we still are willing to call Plato a philosopher, she is then saying he is a very different sort of philosopher from that which Kant had in mind. The reason is that the knowledge that Plato was after was from beginning to end a spiritual knowing. But what exactly does this mean?

Weil argues that Plato's spirituality contains these things: (1) that we are children of heaven, children of God; (2) that our lives are lives of forgetting this, and the supernatural truth; (3) that the condition for salvation is thirst for this forgotten truth; and (4) that "if we thirst sufficiently for that water and if we know that it is for us, as children of God, to drink it, then it will be given to us" (SN 91).

Let us begin by considering what she has in mind in calling present life a forgetting, and therefore what remembering actually amounts to. While Weil does not spend a great deal of time analyzing Platonic memory, her few comments are striking. Platonic memory is not, as a naive reading of the *Meno* might suggest, simply remembering some past fact gathered in a previous state of existence that we have now forgotten. Plato himself drops that sort of imagery after the *Meno*. Rather, if the thought has any meat, it is that the mind has a natural affinity to know, and that natural affinity lies at the mind's very roots. The point is not so much one of where we have gained knowledge, then, but one about the very personal nature of knowledge. It is also about *how* we gain that knowledge.

Weil observes what the phenomenon of memory is like in relation to "remembering" the supernatural truth. If there is some fact of which we have been in possession but forget it, then we direct our attention for a few moments to an empty space. Suddenly the thought is there. Two things are striking about this phenomenon. The first is that although we have forgotten, in directing our attention to an empty space, we somehow want and desire to know, even though we cannot exactly say what it is that we want to know. Memory comes from this sort of attention, and here it is attention in her own highly developed sense in which Weil is interested. This is *her* inward turn. Second (although Weil herself does not draw this conclusion out) is that in remembering like this, when the thought does come back to us we have a sense that it is familiar, that it somehow belongs to us.

This is what it is like with the knowledge of God. To come upon it is like remembering. We first have to wait for it with attention for it to come to us. Second, even if it is startling and puts everything in a new light, there is a sense that it is at home with us, and that in knowing God we are more at home than we have ever been. It is like "the smile on a beloved face" (WG 69). It gives a sense of self-possession and self-consciousness that we did not have when in a state of forgetting. The knowledge of God that we now remember is not knowledge of a new fact but a familiar one. So it often comes to us not only as a knowledge of some thing but also as a matter of self-knowledge. So even if this is a supernatural knowledge, and comes about only by grace, as Weil adamantly insists, it is not the sort of knowledge that conquers our minds and wills, but actually makes them more fully what they are. To know God is to know, as Nicholas of Cusa put it, an other that is not other (*aliud non-aliud*).

Thus we begin to see where the suggestion that we are children of heaven might arise. It is not the result of giving human beings an a priori metaphysical status that elevates them and the importance of their projects above the rest of creation. It is as Weil puts it, an "experimental truth." Indeed, it cannot be otherwise, since to know God is inseparable from knowing one's own self. To have any true sense of God one has to have within that very conception a sense that somehow we, and the creation, belong to God. Furthermore, since God is good and nothing but good, as Weil quotes Augustine, one cannot come to know God without moral and spiritual self knowledge and reformation. Thus Weil points out:

(1) THERE IS NOT AND THERE CANNOT BE ANY OHER RELATION OF MAN TO GOD EXCEPT LOVE. WHAT IS NOT LOVE IS NOT A RELATION TO GOD.

(2) The appropriate object for love is God, and *every man who loves something other than God is deceived, mistaken; as though he ran up to a stranger in the street, having mistaken him for a friend.*

Further, it is only in so far as the soul orients itself towards what ought to be loved, that is to say in so far as it loves God, that it is *qualified to know and understand.* Man cannot exert his intelligence to the full *without charity,* because the only source of light is God. (SN 104)

Herein, of course, lies precisely the problem that Plotinus and Augustine saw with the Gnostics and Manichaeans, respectively, and the problem that Weil imputes to Aristotle: their search for God by reason alone is a distanced search, one that is not self-involving, a search wherein the thinker stands apart from what is known. This, of course, is not simply an ancient problem; it is the obsession of the modern world from Descartes to Locke and onward. Its quest for neutral reason is not simply stoic detachment in order to cultivate *amor fati* but ultimately involves a sense of foreignness and alienation.[11]

This then gives form to the Platonic claim that we have forgotten. Even if the name of God remains within a culture or within philosophy, once the sense of self-involvement disappears, once the sense of who we are in relation to God disappears, so too does any genuine knowledge of God. It becomes knowledge not of an Other, but is just other than the knowledge of God. This can be seen in Weil's linking of falsehood and unconsciousness (SN 109), as the chief characteristics of the inhabitants of Plato's cave. Because we are unconscious, what we think is therefore false. Because knowledge involves the knower, real knowledge involves treating the world and standing in front of it in a very different sort of relation. Judging shadows and seeing in the light of the sun are very *different* sorts of activities. The difference is not simply a matter of right or wrong information but a very different way of thinking.[12] Thus Weil aptly suggests that the opinions of the great beast are not necessarily wrong. Since the beast's opinions are formed by chance, it is likely that they will be on occasion correct. Nevertheless, she continues, "even where its opinions are *in accord with the truth they are essentially alien to the truth*" (SN 100).

It is equally important, however, to understand just why Weil claims that "the precept 'Know thyself' is not practicable in the cave" (SN 108). How and why we live in a state of unconsciousness and forgetfulness helps to draw us closer to what she is ultimately getting at in the positive case.

The problem she argues, characteristically, is the social, which she never tires of claiming kills real thought. It makes us passive, for in the social world, "[i]t is not we who move, but images pass before our eyes and we live them"

(SN 108). Weil certainly has here in mind the great degree to which our very sense of the self is shaped by the images of life that we are given in social life. For example, young girls raised on *Marie Claire* come to think of themselves and their roles in life in a very particular way that leads them to adopt, usually uncritically, those same roles. Similarly, it is no surprise that boys raised on stories of Roman glory want to be warriors. Ironically, everybody thinks they are wholly autonomous in doing so. But of course they would, since autonomy is one of the most powerful of these images. As Augustine might have pointed out, they have come to live their lives entirely by the "outer man."

But if passivity is the face of the problem, paradoxically, that passivity results from human activity. The deep problem is that the world of the cave is, she says, "an artifact"(SN 108), by which she means it is a world that we construct, and that it does not "emanate from the supreme Good" (SN 108). The problem is that in constructing a world for ourselves, a world in which we are protected from the outside and in which we set out our own space, we lose both the world and ourselves. It is precisely in asserting ourselves in trying to construct a human space that we lose ourselves and are passive. In good part this is because that the more successful we are in making this world *ours*, in making it self-contained, and making ourselves masters of it, the more it then, in turn, makes us, as it is the sole source for our sense of self and value. Far from actually making us autonomous, free, and open, it isolates us from any larger world and from each other. Moreover, to the degree that we are successful in making the social world self-contained is also the same degree to which we will lack any awareness of, that we will forget, a larger good.[13] So "[w]e are unaware of being under punishment, of being in falsehood, of being passive, and, of course, of being unconscious" (SN 109). The effect of constructing a world, particularly when the construction is all-embracing, is to lose the sense that it is constructed. The only way out, of course, is some sense of otherness that can either break the walls of or somehow limn the artificial world so that we can see it for what it is. Without such an other, one might well think the world perfect. As Weil notes, affliction often plays this role: "If there were no affliction in this world, we should be able to believe ourselves in Paradise. Horrid possibility" (NB 294).[14] So too do the Platonic ways; first, of contradiction, which forces one to face the limited nature of the images by which we think and then to resolve them on a higher plane, and, second, the contemplation of the beauty of the world a priori, a promise of a greater good that beckons the soul on. Both incite an important dissatisfaction with the constructed world and direct desire to a something larger; both, by actually changing the soul's thought, change the soul and can cause it to remember itself.

On one level, of course, this process is one of deconstructing the unconscious, amnesiac self that has invested itself so passively in the images it has been given and false senses of presence. Appropriately Weil cites St. John of the Cross's "dark nights of the soul," nights that are not mere low spots in the spiritual journey but moments of the deep disorientation that the self experiences as it loses its familiar polestars, first in giving up dependence on the senses for life, and then, when all other values, including some good ones, disappear, in the blinding vision of the sun. But more important, this process is a matter of opening oneself to pay attention to the world, and to take it into oneself, a process of remembering in which we actually do "direct our attention for a few minutes towards an empty space." It is a process of coming to identify with the world as a whole, in which the world becomes our body, and we feel each and everything in it as our body. In commenting on the *Symposium*, Weil notes, "Our vocation is unity. Our affliction is to be in a state of duality"(*IC* 110).

Contemplative Philosophy

Thus Weil's reading of Platonism, and her own Platonism, which in its broad outlines sets her thinking squarely within the Platonic-Augustinian tradition of the inward turn that discovers itself in God, stresses the practice of philosophy as a learning to die and as a wisdom that is self-involving. This much may be obvious enough. But what bears further investigation is how this is philosophy at all. Weil, of course, in "God in Plato," wants to call it mysticism and not philosophy, but this is really more a bow to the way these terms tend to be used now. The issue really is one of what philosophy is and ought to be, of what it means to love wisdom. Thus it is especially worthwhile to look at what sort of point Weil is ultimately making about philosophy, for in writing about Plato the way she does, she is deliberately pushing for an alternative to present practice.

What this alternative is might be approached by what I take to be a similar attempt made by Josef Pieper several years ago. Pieper pointed out in reference to Kant how we tend to look at philosophy. For Kant, he argues, philosophy is exclusively discursive, not contemplative, and is therefore a form of work. Plato, Kant claims, is that "Father of all raving enthusiasm in Philosophy" while "Aristotle's philosophy is truly work."[15] Now while Kant's criticism may be aptly directed against the Romantic vision, which it in fact was originally, it is also highly revealing of what we think philosophy is since Kant. Reason is exercised on things, and since it does not mirror nature but constructs the impress of the world into something thinkable, not only are we barred from any direct knowledge of God and ourselves, the most reasonable world we can have is a constructed world, a world always mediated by our representations. Thus it is always our world, but our world is not necessarily the world as it is. Kant, of course, has much more to say than this, and it would be puerile to make him into somebody who thought we make up the world according to whim and want. Nevertheless, the Kantian world still remains the cave, even if it is a very sophisticated cave.

Just as important, though, to Kant is that therefore philosophy is work, indeed a "herculean labor." In commenting on Kant's saying, Pieper argues:

> [I]n this laborious aspect, [Kant] saw a kind of legitimation of philosophy: philosophy is genuine, *insofar* as it is a "herculean labor." The fact that "intellective vision" didn't *cost anything* is what made it so suspicious to him. Kant expected no real gain in knowledge from intellectual vision, *because* it is the very nature of vision to be effortless.
>
> Would not such a viewpoint bring us to the conclusion, or at least close to the conclusion, that the *truth* of what is known is determined by the *effort* put into knowing it?[16]

This conclusion, of course, is thoroughly in keeping with Kant's own highly Pelagian theology.

Pieper's contrast highlights two very different ways of thinking philosophically (and theologically). It also sheds direct light on the commonly understood division between philosophy (and again theology in the modern world) and mysticism. Philosophy on the one hand is rational, that is, strictly discursive, public, propositional, and determined by method and universal canons of rationality. Or, at least, if it is not yet determined by such canons, it would like to uncover them and despairs when they are not forthcoming. Mysticism on the other hand is affective, experiential, and generally defies formulation, and is therefore strictly private, and hence not rational, or a matter of knowing, although assessments of that are both positive and negative. Pieper, however, suggests that knowing *is* vision. Indeed, to know what is really worthwhile, one has to stop working, one has to stop constructing, in order to look and listen.

Now Weil certainly knew her Kant and admired him. She particularly admired his moral philosophy, its stoicism that demanded utter altruism and the need to discard a heteronomous imagination. But in the end she uses those moral elements in a very different way from Kant and what she is driving at is ultimately far closer to Pieper. For example, if she is deeply interested in the spiritual value of labor, it is not because labor constructs a world but because it deconstructs one, because it can wear down the self-centered imagination and erase the screen that keeps us from the world. For Weil, the result that comes out of this altruism and effort of the will is purgation, and a having to face the void and our own nothingness. It is not until then that the light can break in upon us—but it must break in upon us. So the role of the will is not only a negative one of suppressing natural desires (and so Kant would have believed) but is undertaken so that a much deeper desire—a supernatural one—may be freed. The will's effort is an effort in the void.

Knowing, at least the right kind of knowing, is then decidedly *not* a construction but vision. But for that reason it is also always a matter of grace. It can only be given, and no amount of effort can achieve it. After all, Weil thinks, if it came from us it would be no better than us. It is something for which we have to wait. We have to look and we have to listen without imposing ourselves on what is revealed. This waiting and openness is what Weil claims is the heart of faith; this is also at the heart of the Christian mystical tradition itself, the tradition in which contemplation is the acme of the Christian life, the *telos* toward which it tends.

This, however, is to put matters very sharply and probably somewhat misleadingly with respect to what the problem really is that Weil is driving at. Vision and construction are not quite sharp alternatives, for they continually interact for Weil. The problem as Weil saw it is a perpetual one of how they interact and are ordered. We *do* continually construct. Kant was right in seeing this, she thought, and his insight is underlined more boldly by thinkers after him that saw this construction depends on historical factors. The problem, then, is and always has been how to transcend the solipsism of this construction, and to let the world penetrate our minds. But even to put it that way for Weil would also be misleading if by talking about transcending this construction we were to talk about that transcending as another way to what the ancients and medievals called *scientia*, that is, the knowledge of the empirical world, in order to replace it with knowledge of an inner world of essences. Rather, for Weil, the question is not whether *scientia* is possible or not, or even how it is possible—construction or vision. The question rather is one of *sapientia*, that inner quality that for Platonism defines understanding and sets it apart—at least for thinkers like Plato and Augustine—from mere *scientia*. The question is then one of how the two are related. For Weil, I would suggest, this is the deep issue, for the key to Platonism lies here. It is also where her contribution lies.

For Weil, in the strictest sense we never transcend construction in this world; even the philosopher who leaves the cave returns, and indeed must return as a direct consequence of whatever vision of the Good she has had. On returning even she has to deal in representations. As Weil notes, the *Timaeus* is the book of one who has returned to the cave; so its value is not as physics per se but in what it points the reader toward. Vision and understanding never leave the world. Rather we are always "reading" the world. As bodily creatures we handle the world through media—first, through our bodies and the sense of pleasure and pain, and then later through symbols. We feel it through the end of a blind man's stick. But if we are always reading and always have a perspective (God alone does not read), nevertheless for Weil there are levels, and one can move up through them. One, for example, can move from the thoroughly egocentric world of pleasure and pain that reads the world from the highly individual perspective of one's own body to a world of symbols that is at least indifferent to our narrow desires and that is impartial. From there Weil thinks that one can move to a point where the world is my body, where we feel and think from a perspective that takes in as its own whatever goes on in the world, with consent and without resentment. We are not gods in doing so, but have a sense, a memory, that whatever God has ordained belongs to us intimately.

But if we never stop reading, then wisdom is not an alternative to knowing, nor is it the vision of a private and otherwise hidden world, similar but distanced from this one, a world of separable and separated essences. Rather wisdom is an underlying moral stance from which we read the world. It is, for example, to look at the world justly—as it is and not as we would like it to be. It is what we do with our knowledge, which is not itself a separate knowledge but the very configuration of our knowledge; although, to be sure, the facts that we pursue and the facts that we come up with may look very different given different moral levels. This was Weil's point in the essay "Classical Science and After." If then there is a problem with construction it is not that it tries to represent the world, and such representation is not the true world, but that it represents the world with an eye to using it in a certain way. In this sense the problem is not just our construction of the world, but that our construction of the self and the world is something that is no longer the world as God intended it but the world we have willed. It is the outer expression of our inner being. But inner and outer here are not related as cause to effect but are inseparably linked. Similarly, the knowledge of God is contrary in spirit to that of construction. As *sapientia* it infuses itself into whatever *scientia* we might possess.

So vision never leaves the world, nor is it meant to do so for Weil. As she points out, "To love God, to think on God, is nothing else than a certain way of thinking on the world"(*NB* 25). And similarly:

> [A] bride's friends do not go into the nuptial chamber; but when she is seen to be pregnant they know that she has lost her virginity.
>
> There is no fire in a cooked dish, but one knows that it has been on the fire. . . .
>
> It is not the way a man talks about God, but the way he talks about the things of this world that best shows whether his soul has passed through the fire of the love of God. In this matter no deception is possible. There are false imitations of the love of God, but not of the transformation it effects in the soul, because one has no idea of this transformation except by passing through it oneself. (*FLN* 146)

Thus it needs stressing that for Weil the mysticism that she sees at the heart of Platonism and of Christianity is not *an* experience. It may well depend on experience—one cannot just think oneself into it but needs an apprenticeship, and apprenticeship for Weil is not simply a training of the body (but it is that too) but something that succeeds only when we pay attention to what we are learning. It results in the way we experience the world, that is, the way we take it in. It takes in the world, and does not rest in itself. It is salutary to remember here Weil's most explicit definition of attention as consisting in "suspending thought, leaving it detached (*disponible*), empty and ready to be pentrated by the object" (*WG* 111).[17] To be *disponible* is to be open, and ready for use. It is not a blankness but a desire that does not reach out to grab the world, but which desires to be filled and used by the world.

Vision—or more properly, looking and listening—then, as distinguished from construction, is something like a habitual practice or attitude of the soul. It is a sort of *lectio divina* in which self-will is silenced, wherein one is radically open to a world that strikes her—particularly as it does not cooperate with her cherished individual projects—as alien and other, but yet which is also beautiful and beckoning. This openness has as its heart's desire the desire to know, to see things simply as they are and as God intended them. In order to know the beloved, it waits and does not press, and it waits even in absence and darkness. This is a moral stance, and is itself born out of love and desire.

Here the Platonic-Weilian philosopher does not *intend* to construct a world, although construction may be coincidental and unavoidable. Philosophy is rather an education and an apprenticeship on the one hand, and a willingness to teach, on the other. But it is not and cannot be a doctrine, a final word. What defines it is precisely that it is a love of wisdom, which, of course, is itself already a sort of wisdom itself.

What Is Important about Christian Platonism

This is to look at the "inward turn" of Platonism, taken so clearly and definitively in Augustine, in a very different way than it often is. It is not a movement of the soul toward an alternative, private world, a movement that is fascinated by and dwells on "inner experience," although it necessarily engages the individual fully and concretely. Nor does it involve gazing upon metaphysical objects. Rather, as Denys Turner has argued, within the tradition of Augustine, Dionysos, Bonaventure, Eckhart, St. John of the Cross, and others—which is the tradition of Christian Platonism—the distinction between "inner" and "outer" ultimately is a distinction belonging to the one who remains in the "outer." The one who dwells in the inner is the one who has actually overcome the distinction. Her "spiritual knowledge" is the way she looks at the world as a whole. This does not mean that the knowledge of God is nothing more than a way of looking at the world; but it does mean that it is linked and inseparable from it. Looking at the world attentively and wisely, one participates in God. That is why it is linked and inseparable.

It is clear that Weil belongs to this tradition, which is not surprising since she was indebted to many of its chief figures, particularly St. John of the Cross. Insofar as she does belong to it, she ought to be read in such a way that she draws our attention to it—and helps us to see what was really at stake in it and what was not. Once one realizes that what Weil is talking about really is what is at the heart of this tradition, one should begin to recognize its seeds in thinkers such as Augustine. For example, one should begin to recognize in Augustine's own intellectual and spiritual growth a trajectory from his early very intellectual-istic project of designing an *ordo studiorum* that would propel the mind by think-ing alone to the highest knowledge to the point in his later works, such as the *Sermons on the Gospel of John*, where knowledge and righteousness are related far more intimately. There, for example, in an image strikingly similar to Weil's suggestion that "there is no fire in a cooked dish, but one knows that it has been on the fire" (*FLN* 145), Augustine claims:

> By forsaking God the soul becomes unrighteous; by coming to Him, it be-comes righteous. Does it not seem to you as it were something cold, which, when brought near the fire, grows warm; when removed from the fire grows cold? A something dark, which when brought near the light, grows bright; when removed from the light grows dark?[18]

Here the reformation of one's inner word, which comes from the indwelling of the Word, *is* the gifts of wisdom, godliness, righteousness, charity, and all active virtues. It is the ability to give the quality of justice to what one says and sees and says. It is not a flight from the outer to the inner.

Similarly, we arrive at a reading of *De Trinitate* very different from the mis-taken one we are frequently given. In exploring the analogy between the human mind and the Trinity, Augustine is *not* trying to use the former as a way of con-ceiving the latter in order to write doctrine. Instead he is using doctrine in order to contemplate the perfect unity of the three persons of the Trinity in order to heal *our* inner fragmentation. But even in doing this, he fully understands that he is at best presenting us with an image of the Trinity. Yet, in doing so, he be-lieves, he is simply following Christ's own pattern. Christ, in his incarnate life and death, sets a pattern for the outer person, so that once the outer person is healed she may go inside, and have an inner life. But to have an inner life, to be healed of our fragmentation, is then to overcome our alienation from God; it is the point at which understanding, will, and memory are united and work as they should.

If, however, Weil is at all a help to recovering and rereading the tradition of Christian Platonism, it is well worth stressing that she really is a help because in the end in her own work she has brought that tradition to one of its highest points and has put in focus its key elements. In one sense, she is as severe a critic of the sorts of inner-self metaphysics as any postmodern such as Derrida, with perhaps an even sharper eye than most for the ways in which we do construct an inner self, and with sharper tools for deconstructing it. She does not believe we enjoy presence fully here. Her own journey from Descartes to St. John of the Cross is decidedly a move toward deconstructing the belief that we do. But if she makes this move and voids our inner self of any comforting images, she is also an important example of what Christianity and especially Christian Platonism can say in response to other attempts at this deconstruction. For if, in, say Derrida, all we are ever left with is virtual persons, in Weil there still remains in the human soul "[s]omething that goes on indomitably expecting, in the teeth of all experience of crimes committed, suffered and witnessed, that good and not evil will be done to him. It is this that is sacred in every human being" (SE 10). This "something" is not a some *thing*, however; it is the human itself.

This is no begging of the question but the very outcome of Weil's method of attention, and utter consistency. If Derrida, for example, has deconstructed the self, he has also exposed in his own work the nihilism of modern philosophical method, especially its lack of ability to say anything about that good that we expect, and that everyday people, nonphilosophers, live out. For it is surely two different things to be able to squint at the paintings in a museum and see nothing but patches of paint and to see in paint patches or no, beauty, and to use that to live. If the words on the page are nothing but ink and not the presence of an author or a subject, yet by reading them we do somehow, in not touching the world because they obscure, actually touch a world to which we can have access no other way. As Kierkegaard once pointed out, when attending the theater the person who is not taken in by the actors on the stage is actually worse off than the one who is. It is in this sense that attention is the most important core of Weil's own Platonism. Attention is not founded on the supposition of essences, or any argument therefrom, but is the root desire for good. And for her it is not to be argued to but is the very beginning of philosophy.

But as the heart of wisdom, it is religious. For as she makes clear time and time again, the radical *disponibilité* of attention is the very image of the Word's Incarnation and Passion.[19] In its Christlike desire for perfect good and in self-*kenosis*, attention receives its form (as one can particularly see in "The Implicit Forms of the Love of God"), as well as its contemplative and moral sustenance, and finally its completion. The seeds of this analogy of participation are certainly in Augustine, but nevertheless, it is something that was left to later thinkers such as Bonaventure, St. John of the Cross, and Simone Weil to draw out consistently and explicitly.

Notes

1. For example, in talking about the degradation of an ancient ceremony of cremation, which she thinks must originally symbolized how supernatural fire transports a thing from this world to the next, she comments acerbically: "As the result of a decadence of thought, this ceremony came to be taken as the condition of the thing for which it was a symbol; exactly as baptism became, for narrow Catholics like Augustine" (*FLN* 248).

2. See Phillip Cary, *Augustine's Invention of the Inner Self: The Legacy of a Christian Platonist* (New York: Oxford University Press, 2000).

3. On "inner and outer" in Augustine, see Denys Turner, *The Darkness of God: Negativity in Christian Mysticism* (Cambridge: Cambridge University Press, 1995).

4. See Ellen Charry, *By the Renewing of Your Minds: The Pastoral Function of Christian Doctrine* (New York: Oxford University Press, 1997). Also, Eric O. Springsted, *The Act of Faith: Christian Faith and the Moral Self* (Grand Rapids: Eerdmans, 2001).

5. *Chapters on Prayer*, No. 60.

6. See Turner, *The Darkness of God*, chap. 1, "The Allegory and the Exodus."

7. Plotinus, *Enneads* 2.15, trans. A. H. Armstrong (Cambridge, Mass.: Harvard University Press, 1966), 285.

8. See *De Utilitate Credendi* 13.

9. *De Civitate Dei*, bk. VIII.3.

10. Ibid., bk. VIII.4.

11. Cary, *Augustine's Invention of the Inner Self*, argues that unlike Augustine's "inner space," which is a place of light and vision, Locke's inner space is dark, and we are locked into it with little chance of escape. E.g.: "Plato's picture is intellectual vision, pure and simple, Plotinus's is intellectual vision construed as inward turn, Augustine's is intellectual vision resulting from a turn first in then up, and Locke's picture is of a self with no direct intellectual vision of anything but its own private inner world, seeing only the images of things outside" (5). Also see 122–24.

12. This essential self-involvement also gives a very different way of understanding what exactly the Platonic search for "essences" amounts to. It is not an attempt to peer behind the phenomena to discover a permanent something that is more really the thing than its appearances suggest, a something that can then be treated in much the same way as the appearances were treated. It is to stand in front of and take in things in a very different way, in the light of a necessarily self-involving good.

13. One can see this illustrated, for example, in Huxley's *Brave New World*. Often regarded as a velvet version of oppressive totalitarianism wherein controlling authorities efface real individuality, it in fact portrays the most individualistic world of all—and in that lies its totalitarianism and passivity. Everybody gets everything he wants, and by genetic manipulation is fortunate enough to not want anything he cannot have. Social control and the loss of soul are not achieved by external forces bearing down on the inhabitants of this utopia but by guaranteeing the parameters of choice. Here is the nub of

Weil's point about the world we construct being passive. In choosing in certain ways, particularly ways that avoid the pain that openness to others might bring, we lose the self, and any sense of familiarity with a larger world. But once those inner resources disappear, so too does the possibility of any real originality. Our images, our goals and aspirations, are what we grasp from the outside. This is also a point Tocqueville made about the philosophical effects of equality. When everyone believes himself self-sufficient, and nobody else's opinions as of any more worth than his, he will never consult another. But where then does he get his principles, the indispensable beginning points of thought? From the mob, which alone is big enough to command his respect, Tocqueville suggests.

14. In *Brave New World*, imagine how impossible it would be to discern the artificiality of that world, at least from the inside, if there were not characters like Mustapha Mond who do live in a different world and who can limn the artificial one. Although Mond is hardly a figure of grace, nevertheless his otherness is the only thing that can bring one to consciousness of the problem. Without him, anyone who felt himself out of joint with the world might well think himself the problem with such a perfect world.

15. Josef Pieper, *Leisure: The Basis of Culture* (1948) (South Bend, Ind.: St. Augustine's Press, 1998), 10–11.

16. Ibid., 15. On Kant's rejection of any passivity, or submission, in moral philosophy, see also Eric Blondel, *Le Problème moral* (Paris: Presses Universitaires de France, 1999), 11–15.

17. "L'attention consiste à suspendre sa pensée, à la laisser disponible, vide et pénétrable à l'objet, à maintenir en soi-même à proximité de la pensée, mais à un niveau inferieur et sans contact avec elle, les diverses acquises qu'on est forcé d'utiliser. . . . Et surtout la pensée doit être vide, en attente, ne rien chercher, mais être prête à recevoir dans sa vérité nue l'objet qui va y pénétrer" (AD 92–93).

18. *Tractates in Ioannis* 19.11.

19. I argue this at some length in *Christus Mediator: Platonic Mediation in the Thought of Simone Weil* (Chico, Calif.: Scholars Press, 1983). The point is also elaborated by Emmanuel Gabellieri in chapter 8 of this volume.

CHAPTER 12

Simone Weil: The Impossible

DAVID TRACY

Simone Weil as Mystical-Political

Is there unity in Simone Weil's religious thought? I do not see that there is. It is difficult if not impossible to propose a single unity, even Christian Platonism, for a thinker who wrote so much on such varied topics and in such largely fragmentary forms in so brief a life. That Weil was one of the major religious thinkers of the twentieth century is surely true. If I were forced to try to claim unity in her thought, I would choose political-mystical philosophy. Indeed, she was the foremost predecessor of all the recent attempts — in political and liberation theologies and more recently in many other new forms of Christian thought — to reunite the mystical and prophetic strands of the Christian tradition into a coherent mystical-prophetic philosophy and theology. Of course, her thought cannot be reduced to her life. But her life itself, so multiple and united only by her tenacious sensibility, provides some signal clues to her remarkable flashes of pure thought. Consider, for example, her three famous mystical experiences. Here we find clues to some tenuous unity to her thought and life and to their uncanny power to lure us into her extraordinary presence and demands. In her first mystical experience, while hearing some Portuguese fishermen and their wives sing their songs of sorrow and joy, Weil sees the heart of Christianity: it is the religion of slaves and cannot live except by that insight. For Weil, this is Christianity's most distinctive trait: what will later be called its "preferential option for the poor" in the midst of a radical egalitarianism ("God rains on the just and the unjust" as she loved to quote from the Bible).

In her second mystical experience at the church of Santa Maria degli Angeli at Assisi yet another element of her thought showed itself: the light of the Good in the poverty and purity of God's fool, Francis, and the light of the Good radiant in the necessity disclosed to intelligence by the beauty disclosed in the play of geometric shapes and light in Giotto's frescoes on Francis at Assisi.

Then, while reciting George Herbert's classic metaphysical-theological poem "Love" during the singing of a Gregorian chant at Solesmes and suffering from another of her migraines, she experienced even more intensely in mystical terms her central vision, at once Platonic and Christian; first, as with Giotto, the play of light and mathematical geometric forms yielding the harmony and proportion heard in the West from Pythagoras through Plato through Gregorian chant and Giotto to Simone Weil (whose name well deserves to be mentioned in that list); at the same time and pervading all this light and intelligence in thought, beauty, and religion for Weil was what George Herbert articulates in his great poem—the reality of the Good, Love, God as the Ultimate Reality if we could but pay attention (her favorite spiritual exercise).

These three famous visions were neither random nor arbitrary. She stated, in *Gravity and Grace*, that the meaning of life often depends on which word one uses to describe what happens to one: chance, fate, or Providence. These three mystical visions of hers (perhaps like the three allotted to Plotinus if we only knew what his were) can provide some central clues not only to her exceptional life (which is from beginning to end a mystery) but also to her thought. That thought is, again from beginning to end, a search for an order of the relationship of the Good and necessity in all its forms; an order of the relationship of the Impossible order of charity to the actual order of human wretchedness; the relationship of Creation and Incarnation to the Cross. That order of intelligence, charity, and action for the poor might, if conceived and practiced by others, help to heal the three great disorders of modernity: passion separated from intelligence (never in her); practice divorced from theory, a modern insult to this Platonic activist who insisted on the importance of manual labor for the purity and accuracy of thought itself; form separated from content. Indeed, the union of form and content in her work is stunning from her form of "essays" and her form of "treatises" on oppression and the need for roots. These Weilian forms are part Descartes-like in the form of logical, rigorous meditations and part Montaigne-like in her form of essays as attempts (*essais*), forays, thought experiments. Platonic thought for Weil also needed new forms to prove adequate to its new modern content—work, history, body, that is, matter. Indeed, Weil is more materialist than any other Platonist even as she shares Plato's love for the purely intelligent forms from mathematics to dialectics to mystical thought (the *Republic*). She is often as materialist as Lucretius and as dialectically materialist as Marx and the later revisionist Marxists of Frankfurt. Walter Benjamin is, for me, her explicitly Jewish Marxist other and may prove her best modern conversational counterpart. Would that Weil had learned from Benjamin, as he learned from Scholem, and thus spared herself and her admirers her narrow, willful, and ignorant reading of Judaism. Emmanuel Lévinas, who both shared and praised the force of Weil's insistence on the Other, not the self, as the proper starting point (a prophetic-ethical one) for contemporary thought, was nevertheless entirely right in his anger at Weil's mistreatment and misreading of Judaism when he uttered his violent charge hurled at her like a fist: "Simone Weil, you understand everything except the Bible!"

The Montaigne-like form of Weil's essays and the Descartes-like form of her treatises in her studies of work, body, and politics made it possible for Weil to find new non-Marxist forms for leftist thought and actions of the radical left in the period between the wars. Her other preferred form we can perhaps call *pensées* in honor of Pascal. She shared so much with Pascal that she seemed obliged to criticize him frequently even as she rethought and critically reformulated some of his greatest insights into her own: insights on the wretchedness of the human condition; the centrality of the Cross in Christianity; the centrality of suffering for understanding the Cross—physical, psychological, and spiritual agony—what she brilliantly renamed "affliction"; the importance of the category "order"; above all, the need to acknowledge the Pascalian three orders of existence and to consider their relationships. The first order is the order of the flesh. Force and its rule for Weil is, as she argued in her essay "The *Iliad*: Poem of Force," that kingdom of the necessity of force that affects all human lives as we all must one day die. But force affects some (slaves) for their entire lives, not just at death. Second, the order of intelligence, from logic, mathematics, and science through metaphysics, where most genuine thinkers live their entire lives as much as possible. She typically said that *intellectuals* is an ugly word, but we deserve it. The third order for Weil, again with Pascal, is the order of charity—an order as different from the order of intelligence as the order of intelligence is from the order of the flesh; an order as difficult to sense for those only in the order of intelligence as it is for those only in the order of the flesh to understand those in the order of intelligence.

More than Pascal, but in his spirit, she showed how intertwined these three orders are even for those in the order of charity. The order of charity is one where body—flesh—is still very much present (even for Christ) and to be made real. Her mysticism is, in spite of the perhaps true charges of anorexia against her on her own body, also one of intelligence and body working together. That vision is the central reason why for her thinkers need manual labor. Theologically, for Weil, there is a vision of an overwhelming reality of a kenotic understanding of real bodily incarnation as well as a deeply embodied understanding of Cross as crucifixion. The crucifixion, for Weil, is both bodily and spiritual humiliation. It is the *personal* suffering of Christ as a slave, a criminal, a reject from the body of society. Jesus—stripped, scourged, naked, and in overwhelming pain—must suffer not merely in spirit but also in body so that his soul may suffer in affliction. Jesus, for Weil, undergoes the horror of human and decisive abandonment: Jesus' cry from the Cross, "My God, my God, why have you forsaken me?" she paradoxically insists, shows the divine character of Christianity. The order of intelligence, she also insists, must find a way to be attentive and active in the order of charity as well. She never called her own thought "theology." Perhaps she had good reasons for that refusal. But she always insisted on the need for the keenest use of intelligence (logical, rigorous, demanding, speculative) in reflecting on the order of charity. And surely that *is* theology at its best. Recall her brilliant suggestion that John of the Cross developed a *scientific* account of the stages of the spiritual life. Only high intelligence participating within and yet, as intelligence critically must, distancing itself from the order of charity could count for Weil as the right kind of theology. Recall her references to Teresa of Avila and to John of the Cross rather than to officially designated theologians. She did not admire even Thomas Aquinas: he was too Aristotelian on reason and not sufficiently mystical in spirit for her.

As any attentive reader of Simone Weil soon notes (how rare those readers are, she writes in her brilliant reflections on *attention* as the most needed and nearly lost spiritual practice for true reading), Weil's prose forms—treatises, essays, *pensées*—achieve the lucidity, rigor, clarity, and elegance of the classical French tradition. She does so not only on questions of the body, on mechanical necessity, and on the structure of society but also on the divine mysteries understood *as* mysteries in the order of charity. Weil's is a prose and thought of limit even for the best thought. Hence her admiration for Kant on the limits of reason and perhaps, in Kant, tragedy and philosophy together. Weil left us forms appropriate to her content, perhaps even, in one of her favorite words, necessary for that content. She left thought that never, as in the Enlightenment or the Romantics, divorces passion and intelligence anymore than Pascal did. She left a form of Platonism that, by its insistence on a theory of work, changed Platonism into no less an idealist position while also becoming insistently materialist. She insisted on body, social conditions, history, matter far more than most forms of Platonism usually do.

Which leaves us what, then? A thinker whose very forms of thinking often act like searchlights amid our contemporary confusions. A thinker who articulated better than anyone else of her time why Christianity must be a mystical-political religion of and for the oppressed. A thinker who, in my judgment, stands with Benjamin as the thinker between the wars (and like him, finally destroyed by that war) who dared to expose the self-delusions of most thinkers of that and our period. For me, Weil and Benjamin will one day be recognized as the crucial thinkers between the wars who fragmented the ego of that age and ours just as, in postmodern thought, Nietzsche and Kierkegaard are now acknowledged as the thinkers best suited to expose and smash the self-deluding modern systems of the nineteenth century and of ours.

And yet I cannot claim that even this suggestion of a mystical-political reading does justice to the multifarious character of Weil's thought. Some other focus is also needed. Here, reflection on her as a Christian Platonist advances the discussion of a possible (only one possible) manifold unity of her thought. For Simone Weil was clearly Christian and she always loved Plato. Therefore, it is just to call Weil a Christian Platonist as long as this title is not placed above the wider category of mystical-political and as long as we acknowledge that even Christian Platonism does not account for the full range, originality, and power of Weil's thought. For what a strange Christian and odd Platonist Simone Weil actually was.

Weil's Christian Platonism: The Sea Change of Tragedy

Simone Weil was neither orthodox in some of her Christianity nor was she, on her Platonic side, like most Platonists. On the Christian side, she was reticent when not silent on certain central doctrines or symbols of the Christian symbol system: especially the resurrection, perhaps because of her acute fear of any Christian triumphalism. She was also reticent on the eschatological tradition, perhaps because of her fear of how quickly any imagination, including the eschatological when literalized, can delude us by trying to fill the void with fantasies.

This double reticence on resurrection and apocalypse in the New Testament became fierce when she turned her attention to the Hebrew Bible, which is also Christian scripture, that is, Christians' First or Old Testament. To be sure, she accorded some parts of the Old Testament more attention than many Christian thinkers do to this day: above all, the Book of Job, certain Psalms (especially the Psalms of Lamentation), the Suffering Servant of Isaiah, and, more surprisingly, the creation accounts of Genesis. But it remains a puzzle why this exceptionally attentive mind and soul, so prophetic in her person and thought, would prove so deaf to the great prophets and their demand for what she most cared for—justice for the oppressed. It remains a puzzle why Weil did not read more attentively the Book of Exodus and not just as another book of triumphalism by the victors over the Canaanites (although that is there). For Exodus, as oppressed peoples throughout the centuries readily sense is above all a book of liberation of and for the slaves and victims of history. Even the more Hellenized wisdom literature of the Old Testament does not receive the attention one would expect from the Hellenophile Simone Weil.

Whatever the peculiarities of her own history—born to a highly assimilated, indeed secular Jewish family and open to Buddhism and Hinduism, Confucianism and Taoism—her closedness to and willful ignorance of the riches of the Jewish tradition, even in its biblical form much less its later history (the only exception is that Weil may have read some readings of kabbalists), remain a mystery. That mystery is not solved, in my judgment, by deciding, in prosecutorial style, that Weil was a "self-hating Jew." She did, like Pascal, find the "I" the "moi"—her own—hateful and in constant need of decreation. But she was surprisingly (given her character) insensitive to the massive suffering of the greatest victims in Europe of her day, her fellow Jews.

Her problem here—and it *is* a grave problem for those of us who have learned so much from Weil in her insistence that Christianity should always be on the side of the oppressed in any period—consists, I suspect, of psychological and historical reasons beyond our reach but not our disrespect. After all, she never allowed such excuses to others. She denounced Christianity's involvement in the Crusades, the Inquisition, the treatment of her beloved Cathari, the indifference of the rich and of cultured "Christians" of every century toward the poor in their midst. She despised Corneille on the grandeur of France of the imperialist and, for her, revolting *grand siècle* of Louis XIV. The list of those historical figures she judged harshly could easily be expanded. Her only equal here is Nietzsche.

Weil's intellectual-spiritual problem with some versions of Jewish "exceptionalism" or "election" was shared by some Jewish thinkers (as she should have known) in her own day. It is even more widely shared in our day (e.g., the Orthodox Jewish theologian, David Hartmann) by many Jewish thinkers who never cease fighting the problems of some triumphalist interpretations of election, including those in the Bible, especially the slaying of the Canaanites. This cruel strand of the Bible is for many Jewish thinkers—as she should have known—as deep and troubling as the exclusionist triumphalism and complacent sense of election and supercessionism of many Christians. But why did she not see this? She clearly saw that *Christianity's* temptation to triumphalism and totalitarian thinking is a betrayal of its own inner principles, of the stern reality of the Cross and vocation to privilege the oppressed, the victims of history, and *not* the victors of what even Hegel called the "slaughter-bench" of history.

But Weil somehow refused to see how the same prophetic principle, the same liberationist drive for the victims of history that she found in Christianity, is central to the Hebrew Bible and the Christian reading of it as Old Testament. The Hebrew Bible is not, as she sometimes thought, a long book of Joshua. The ancient Hebrews, driven by their prophetic and legal traditions alike, were not the ancient Romans as she thought. Indeed, even some of the ancient Romans— Virgil above all—were not the vulgar triumphalists she makes them out to be. Her reading of Judaism is a sad exercise in a life and thought otherwise driven by a sense of justice and a demand for compassion.

The real Simone Weil, I continue to believe, is elsewhere than in her readings of the Hebrew Bible. The real Simone Weil is in her readings of the ancient Greeks (whose writings effectively function as her Old Testament) and in her partial but extraordinary readings of the New Testament. Who, except Weil, could move so subtly between two profoundly different gospel accounts of the Passion of Jesus: the gospel of Mark whose afflicted Jesus (as Weil never tired of reminding Christians) screams from the Cross the shattering words of physical affliction and spiritual abandonment: "My God, my God, why have you forsaken me?" Second, the Gospel of John where the very lifting up of Jesus on the Cross discloses God's Beauty and Glory in the last words of John's Jesus: "It is consummated." Weil affirms both gospels as she affirms how beauty in the *Iliad* is seen most clearly on the other side of intense suffering. She affirms both Mark and John as readily and as subtly as she affirms (contra Nietzsche) both tragedy and philosophy, both Sophocles and Plato, among the Greeks. The key to Weil's readings in both cases—Christianity and Platonism—is her unerring sense of necessity, justice, and the Good—in a word, her insistence vis-à-vis both Platonism and Christianity that a tragic sensibility must be maintained. Otherwise Platonism is one more totality system (incorporating, as historically Neoplatonism did, elements not only of Plato but also of the Stoics and the Aristotelians). Otherwise Christianity is a triumphant Christendom as it so often has been. Weil insists on this over and over, for example, in the orthodox Christian triumphalist cry against the Cathari and anyone else unlucky enough to live among them: "Kill them all; God will know His own."

Far more clearly than Pascal, Weil understood that the true wretchedness of humanity must include not only sin (she is always clear how real and pervasive *that* is) but also tragedy, that is, fate as (in her words) the necessity of suffering in life. She sometimes refers to the consequences of sin as tragedy—the curse of fate in Oedipus and even, in the way of innocent substitionary redemption, the fate of Christ.

Simone Weil's thought is a profound Christian theological reading that affects her interpretations of all the central doctrines of Christianity. God becomes at times for her, as much as for Luther, the awe-ful Hidden God of the Void. The Incarnation becomes, in the light of the Cross, deeply kenotic for her and even a cleavage as she believed is suggested by the implication of the Cross and the saying in the Book of Revelation, "The Lamb is slain from the foundation of the World." Even more, Weil's curious speculations on the inner-Trinitarian relationships of Father and Son suggest such speculation as that of Hans Urs von Balthasar or Jürgen Moltmann. Above all, her Christian anthropology becomes one formed neither by traditional (e.g., Thomist) interpretations of nature and grace (although she too affirms our essential goodness, our natural attraction, in spite of our egoism, to the Light) nor by the traditional Reformation interpretation of sin and grace (although she affirms, as strongly as the later Augustine or Luther or Pascal, the power and reality of sin in our personal, social, and historical lives). Weil is ruled by neither the nature-grace paradigm nor the sin-grace paradigm. She is somewhere else: the wretchedness of humanity is seen by her (almost more like Racine than Pascal) as comprising these realities. First, there is our greatness (our intelligence, our intrinsic drive to the light, our graced ability to love, our sense of justice). Second, there is our tragic sensibility: the necessity of force that must eventually invade every human life, and thereby the need for justice, an equilibrium emerging from tragedy's sense of hubris, the sense of beauty as deepened by a tragic sense of fate and its curse on us. As she insists, "If this be my last day—as in the *Iliad* for so many of its characters—the beauty of the sunset or the beauty of family, friends, life itself is more intense and more beautiful than ever." Such a sense evokes compassion toward literally all—not only toward the victors, but toward victims and victors alike as she sees in her beloved *Iliad* or in Aeschylus's *Persians.* This tragic reality comprises for Weil aspects of our greatness and not only our wretchedness: justice, compassion, and intelligence as well as sin (ours and the consequences of others' sin, our fate, our curse). She affirms, I repeat, the reality of sin. She also affirms that sin, both as personal and as a consequence of the actions of others, is there for all Christians to attend to by attending to the kenotic Incarnation-Cross of Christ (including in its social structural form), the only purely innocent, sinless human and the one and only God at one and the same time.

This reading on the centrality of the Cross and the reality of the tragic (as something like a paradoxical medium *metaxu*, between our greatness and our tragic wretchedness) frees Simone Weil's Christian vision from the sin-pessimism of the later Augustine or Calvin or Pascal (we are "lumps of sin" for Augustine) just as the Cross and the tragic freed her from any optimism about humanity or much Christian humanism. She arrived, in my judgment, at a deeper Christian vision of God as hidden, of Christ as incarnate and crucified, of ourselves as wretched (i.e., as great, tragic, and sinful at once), and even of creation as sparks of the Good let loose in the world. Hers is an exceptional and powerful Christian vision, and one that can be understood partly as a revised, that is, tragic, form of a Christian Platonism. Her Platonism, transformed by a tragic sensibility and her insistence on work, is perhaps her deepest philosophical formulation of her Christian vision. But Platonism is not Weil's only option for a usable past. Witness her love for the Stoics, her deep respect for the logical, rigorous, and meditative power of Descartes, her reverence for Kant's thoughts on reason acknowledging its powers and, through that very acknowledgment, the limits of reason. Indeed, she called the greatest use of reason an acknowledgment, like Kant's, of its limits. Recall as well, Weil's sometime sympathy even for the Manichaeans. Did any other twentieth-century Christian thinker share these diverse sympathies? Outside Christianity recall Weil's love of certain texts of the Buddhists, the Hindus (especially the Bhagavad Gita), and the Taoists (especially the understanding of religion as a "way" of nonactive action). If Christianity had traveled East rather than West, Weil, in spite of her love of the Greeks, would not have been deeply disturbed: Buddhist thought would have strengthened her kenotic Christology; the Gita would have become her new *Iliad*; and Taoism would have shown her a way to understand Christ as way, truth, and life.

But that historical possibility, like Pascal on Cleopatra's nose, is merely a great "what if": Christianity did not move East. It entered the Hellenistic world. For Weil, that meant that Christianity entered the luminous world of classical Greece. In sum, she was a Platonist but one with a difference. The difference again comes about through her joining Plato, unlike the Plato of other Christian Platonists, not only to philosophy (Socrates and, for her, the so-called pre-Socratics, especially Heraclitus and Parmenides) but also to tragedy. This was a remarkable achievement in her interpretation of the Greeks.

Since the Romantic rediscovery of the Greeks and the seemingly endless debates especially in German thought on *which* Greeks (Aristotle and Neoplatonism for Hegel; tragedy for Nietzsche; the pre-Socratics for Heidegger), the interpretation of the Greeks by Simone Weil is a singular one. For her, the greatness of Greece (which, like many before and after her she partly romanticized) included not one singular choice but practically all the great forms and expressions of the ancient Greeks: the folklore; the myths, especially the Christlike myth of Prometheus; the poems of Pindar; the epics and especially the *Iliad*, the poem of force; the pre-Socratics, especially Heraclitus; the tragedies, especially Aeschylus, Sophocles, and the *Hippolytus* of Euripides; Plato and his Socrates; and the later Stoics. The almost sole exceptions to her praise of the Greeks were, for distinct Weilian reasons, the *Odyssey* and Aristotle. Even here, however, for Weil, the *Odyssey* is partly good, and Aristotle is acceptable when like Plato. On the later Platonists she is more reticent but, especially on Plotinus, approving.

Unlike most Hellenophiles, she did not look for which part of Greek culture can serve as *the* clue to Greece's greatness. She embraced almost all. And therein lay her genius as a kind of Christian Platonist with a difference. For she consistently reads Plato as related not only to the Pythagoreans and their religious and ritualistic desire for the world of intelligibility in mathematics and music (proportion and harmony) but also to the excessive and transgressive, not harmonious, religious ritualistic (for her mystical) Eleusinian mysteries. Both these sources, mathematics and the mysteries, influenced her reading of the rational *and* mystical Plato. Moreover, she reads Plato as not simply against "the poets" as he famously called Homer and the tragedians but as himself possessing a tragic sensibility. Witness her reading of the speech of Agathon in the *Symposium*, her reading of the tragic theme of the *Republic* and the *Timaeus* long before other scholars argued for the harmony of the tragic-hopeful sensibility between Aeschylus's *Oresteia* and the *Timaeus*. For as in the *Timaeus* intelligence persuades (*peithō*) but never compels necessity (*anankē*).

With all their extraordinary achievements, the early Christian Platonists reflected too little on the tragedies and the tragic sensibility in either the Greeks or Christianity. But they saw clearly the rational texts and mystical character of Plato in the texts that we possess—the *Dialogues* (which Weil dared to name Plato's popularizations of his discoveries). At any rate, Simone Weil's singularity as a Christian Platonist is, I believe, partly occasioned by her use of tragedy to rethink Christianity (especially the Gospel of Mark as contrasted to the Gospel of John) just as she rethinks the relationship of Homer and the tragedians (Marklike) to Plato (Johnlike). I do not know why the early Christian Platonists were so right on the Christian theological relevance of Greek philosophy, especially Plato whom they cherished, developed, and when necessary challenged (e.g., through the Christian notions of Creation and Incarnation) and at the same time so reticent, even wrong, on the Christian theological relevance of the tragedies. A partial exception is Augustine. His Platonism is clear and never abandoned (as the *De Trinitate* shows and the *Retractions* make ever clearer). His later tragic sensibility gave rise to his late in life profound anti-Pelagian reflections on the effects of "original sin." But so convinced was Augustine that the ancient tragic concept of fate denied God's omnipotence that he never developed what he could have for his own Christian Platonic anthropology: a Christian Platonist *tragic* sensibility on our weird human combination of essential goodness and sinful and tragic actuality.

Simone Weil did what Augustine might have done but never did. She restored tragedy to *a* prominent place in both the reading of Plato and the reading of Christianity. She accomplished this remarkable feat without exaggerating the claims for the range and power of tragedy over philosophy (as Nietzsche did) and without denying our drive to justice as natural to us (indeed, she finds a sense of justice *as* equilibrium in the *Iliad* itself). Weil strongly affirmed the power and goodness of our intelligence (as in the worlds of intelligibility opened by mathematics and philosophy). She affirmed the power and essential goodness of our rare experiences of love not as ego-love but as love of the *other* (the neighbor), especially the oppressed other in the order of caritas. She never flinched from a vision of the all-pervasive reality of sin—both personal sin (the ego as she interprets its dilemma is Augustine's ego *"curvatus in se"*) and the societal effects of sin. Here Augustinian concupiscence is not her category but *fate*—always, as she insists, with the sense of *curse* for past sins, our own and others: the family (Aeschylus and Sophocles), history (Thucydides), the entire race (Augustine).

That Weilian anthropology is consonant with, indeed analogous, to her Christology. There Incarnation and Cross (always thought together) play such central roles that she is reticent on resurrection—although, as far as I can see, she need not, in principle, have denied it. A Weilian anthropology is consonant as well with her willingness to name God both Love and Hidden as Void. That anthropology is also consonant with her highly speculative understanding of a certain cleavage in God at creation where "the sparks of the good are let loose in the world" and her even more speculative reflection on the incarnation as so kenotic that it suggests a cleavage in God, that is, in the Trinity.

Even when one disagrees (as I basically do with her "cleavage" metaphor as distinct from her "kenotic" metaphor for creation and incarnation) one cannot but be stunned by the purity of her intelligence, the power and the courage of her Christological speculations—at once Christian and Platonist and something more. That "something more" in her odd Christology occurs again through her unique readings of both Plato and Christianity. Nor did she stay intellectually and spiritually with Platonism and Christianity alone. She found the same kind of Weilian vision of our situation in her readings of Taoism, the Bhagavad Gita, Buddhism. She allowed these traditions to be other and yet reconcilable with her Christian Platonism. She neither simply Christianizes nor Platonizes. Rather she shows how those other traditions too can aid, develop, *and* challenge aspects of both Platonic and Christian self-understanding. She did this in the same spirit as she elsewhere insists that atheism as the real thing, not merely a relaxed intellectual hypothesis, for example, the atheism portrayed in Dostoevsky, not the atheism of the Enlightenment, may be a *necessary* ascetic purification of any authentic faith in God.

This Weilian vision sounds—even to many traditional Christian Platonist eyes—too radical, even excessive (as her critic Bataille sensed), even impossible. In an exact sense, her vision is impossible. Like Kierkegaard, Simone Weil implicitly understood faith, in his words, as a passion for the Impossible. Like Lévinas (her fierce critic and admirer), Weil understood the Impossible to be a category for both the limits of our reason (Kant) and the *es gibt*, the sheer givenness and *gift* of the Impossible. For Weil, the Impossible is best but not solely discerned in the kenotic Incarnation and Cross of Jesus Christ.

Implicitly, Weil understood God as the Impossible. Explicitly, she named humankind not merely as the Pascalian paradox of greatness and misery but as Impossible. Above all, she clarified the Impossibility of Jesus Christ as not only the kenotic Incarnation and not only the Cross, but, impossibly, as both together—each understood properly only through the other. Many contemporary thinkers now involved, both philosophically and theologically, with recovering the category of the Impossible as their major initial category for genuine thinking on God or the Void (Lévinas, Derrida, Meltzer, Caputo, Kearney, and my own recent work) can find Simone Weil a great ally as well as a radical intellectual and spiritual challenge. Like Kierkegaard, she was an early apostle of the Impossible. Moreover, unlike the rest of us, even Kierkegaard, Simone Weil was not only an "apostle of the Impossible." In her strange and unnerving thought and her even stranger and most unnerving life, Weil herself was impossible.

MARTIN ANDIC studied philosophy at Dartmouth College, Princeton University, and St. John's College, Oxford, and has taught at Reed College and the University of Massachusetts in Boston. He has published essays on Simone Weil, Kierkegaard, and Plato and edited *Simone Weil and the Intellect of Grace* by Roy Finch. Andic retired early to devote himself to writing on supernatural knowledge and on Weil and the Greeks. He has been active in the American Weil Society for many years.

ROBERT CHENAVIER, Professeur agrégé de philosophie and Docteur en philosophie, teaches at the Lycée du Mont-Blanc in Passy. He is president of l'Association pour l'étude de la pensée de Simone Weil, editor of *Cahiers Simone Weil*, and president of l'Association Simone Weil, the group of Weil scholars preparing the *Oeuvres complètes* (Gallimard). Chenavier is the author of *Simone Weil: Une Philosophie du travail* and *Découvrir Simone Weil* and also prepared and annotated the new edition of *La Condition ouvrière* (Gallimard). He has published many articles on Simone Weil, Hannah Arendt, and André Gorz in English, French, and Italian scholarly journals.

FLORENCE DE LUSSY is Conservateur Général in the Département des Manuscrits at the Bibliothèque Nationale de France, where she is in charge of the Fonds Simone Weil. Her specialty is poetry and philosophy. Her two-volume work on the origins of Paul Valéry's "Charmes" stemmed from her thesis for a doctorat d'état es-lettres granted in 1984. She recently edited *Oeuvres de Simone*

Weil (Gallimard) and is currently director of the group of Weil scholars preparing the *Oeuvres complètes* of Simone Weil (Gallimard).

E. JANE DOERING received her Ph.D. at Northwestern University. Her dissertation topic was "The Social and Political Thought of Simone Weil." She has been a co-initiator of multidisciplinary courses on Simone Weil at the University of Notre Dame, including "Simone Weil: A Perspective on Justice and Compassion" and "Simone Weil: Justice, Grace and Creativity." She presently teaches in the Core Program "Ideas, Values and Images" at Notre Dame. Her articles on Weil published in *Cahiers Simone Weil* include "Simone Weil: Le pouvoir des mots," "Jean Jacques Rousseau et Simone Weil: Deux théoriciens d'une politique moderne," and "Déclaration des droits et des devoirs: Problèmes contemporains à la lumière de Simone Weil."

LOUIS DUPRÉ is Riggs Professor Emeritus at Yale University, where he taught philosophy of religion. He has published mostly in the areas of modern philosophy of religion, social ethics, and culture. His best-known books are *The Other Dimension* (recently reissued in part as *Symbols of the Sacred*), *Passage to Modernity*, and *Light from Light: An Anthology of Christian Mysticism*. He has just completed a study on the Enlightenment to be published by Yale University Press and is preparing a work on Romanticism.

EMMANUEL GABELLIERI, Agrégé de philosophie and Docteur d'état en philosophie, is Professor of Philosophy at the Université Catholique de Lyon. His recent publications include "Incommensurabilité et médiation: La triple puissance de la métaphysique," in *Penser l'être de l'action;* "Creation as the Retreat of God: The Anthropic Principle and Divine Love," in *Studies in Science and Theology* 8; "S. Weil between Paganism and the Bible: A Dialogue with Ricoeur, Lévinas, Schelling and Pascal," in *Between the Human and Divine: Philosophical and Theological Hermeneutics;* and three books, *La Métaphysique du dernier Blondel, Simone Weil*, and *Être et don: Simone Weil et la philosophie*.

VANCE G. MORGAN is Professor of Philosophy at Providence College in Providence, Rhode Island. He has published numerous articles in scholarly journals, on topics ranging from Simone Weil and Iris Murdoch to the metaphysical foundations of naturalism. His most recent articles are "The Metaphysics of Naturalism," "Humility and the Transcendent," and "Cognitive Science,

Naturalism, and Divine Prototypes." His book *Foundations of Cartesian Ethics* was published in 1994.

MICHEL NARCY, Directeur de recherche au Centre National de la Recherche Scientifique, has written *Simone Weil: Malheur et beauté, Le Philosophe et son double,* and numerous articles for *Cahiers Simone Weil.* Narcy was secretary-general of l'Association pour l'étude de la pensée de Simone Weil and editor of *Cahiers Simone Weil* (CSW) from 1988 to 1997. As editor, in cooperation with the American Weil Society, he began the practice of publishing articles in English in *CSW.* He has contributed to the critical edition of Weil's *cahiers* in the *Oeuvres complètes.*

CYRIL O'REGAN is Professor of Theology at the University of Notre Dame. He specializes in modern theology, philosophy of religion, and hermeneutical theory. He is the author of *The Heterodox Hegel, Gnostic Return in Modernity,* and *Gnostic Apocalypse: Jacob Boehme's Haunted Narrative.* In addition, he has published many articles on hermeneutical theory, Augustine, Newman, nineteenth-century German theology, Heidegger, and Hans Urs von Balthasar. He is currently working on two book-length projects, one on von Balthasar and postmodern thought and one on Romanticism and the problem of God.

PATRICK PATTERSON recently celebrated the twenty-fifth anniversry of his ordination into the Anglican priesthood for which he trained at Oxford University. He is presently reading for a doctorate in systematic theology at the University of Toronto. Like many Canadians, he was introduced to Simone Weil through the work of the Canadian philosopher George Grant. Weil's reflections on human and divine agency and obedience to God figure in his dissertation, which treats the mutual implications of the Church's doctrine of the two wills of Christ and the Gospel accounts of Christ's agony and prayer in Gethsemane.

MICHAEL ROSS is Assistant Professor of systematic theology and philosophy at the Pontifical College Josephinum, a major and minor Roman Catholic seminary in Columbus, Ohio. He recently completed a Ph.D. in theology at the Catholic University of America with a dissertation on Weil's lifelong reflections on the good and its active pursuit. Ross also has a Ph.D. in political philosophy from Columbia University. He is a regular contributing member of the American Weil Society.

LAWRENCE E. SCHMIDT is Professor in the Department for the Study of Religion at the University of Toronto. His published articles include "Simone Weil on Religion: A Voegelinian Critique," "George Grant on Simone Weil: The Saint and the Thinker," and (with Scott Marratto) "The Measure of Justice: The Language of Limit as Key to Simone Weil's Political Philosophy." His current research focuses on ethics in a technological society.

ERIC O. SPRINGSTED is cofounder of the American Weil Society and has been its president since 1981. In addition to more than twenty articles on Weil in French and English, he has written and edited nine previous books, including these on Weil: *Christus Mediator: Platonic Mediation in the Thought of Simone Weil, Simone Weil and the Suffering of Love, Spirit, Nature and Community: Issues in the Thought of Simone Weil* (with Diogenes Allen), and *Simone Weil: Writings Selected*. His most recent book is *The Act of Faith: Christian Faith and the Moral Self*. He has taught at Illinois College, Princeton Theological Seminary, and General Theological Seminary in New York.

DAVID TRACY is Andrew Thomas Greeley and Grace McNichols Greeley Distinguished Service Professor of Catholic Studies and Professor of Theology and of the Philosophy of Religion, the Divinity School, and the Committee on Social Thought at the University of Chicago. He teaches a wide variety of courses in philosophical, systematic, and constructive theology and hermeneutics, along with courses dealing with issues and persons in religion and modern thought. He also teaches Greek classic texts with David Grene. His books include *The Analogical Imagination: Christian Theology and the Culture of Pluralism* and *On Naming the Present: Reflections on God, Hermeneutics, and Church*. He has been a Gifford Lecturer. He is currently writing a book on God.

INDEX

Achilles, 17, 183, 184, 202n8
action, 4, 6, 47–51, 54–55, 60, 64, 65,
    66, 69, 87, 108, 184
Aeschylus, 33, 136, 184, 185, 203nn12,
    13, 237, 238, 240
affliction, 14, 21, 72, 78–79, 83, 109,
    167, 169, 172, 177, 179, 197,
    231–32
Alain, 9–10, 25, 26–30, 32, 35–37,
    38n15, 39n29, 44, 57n4, 61, 63,
    65, 117, 121, 134
Alexander, I., 57n5
algebra, 66, 113
amor fati, 216
Andic, M., 57n8
Andronicus of Rhodes, 151
Annas, J., 3
Anselm, 170
Antigone, 184, 185, 199, 203n10
apprenticeship, 222
Aquinas, 156n69, 204n15
Archimedes, 97
Arendt, H., 192
Aristotle, 1, 4, 26–27, 30, 44, 51,
    54–56, 59nn20, 21, 60nn27,
    29, 30, 161, 163, 174n24, 203n10,
    204n15, 207n36, 216, 238

art, 62, 64, 85, 112, 191, 196
attention, 5, 45–46, 84, 88, 90, 110,
    126, 166, 170, 177n47, 197, 214–15,
    218, 223, 225
Augustine, 2, 6–7, 170, 173n4, 204n16,
    205n22, 209–10, 212, 214–17, 220,
    223, 226n11, 237, 239–40
autonomy, 217

balance, 97–98
Balthasar, H. U. von, 149, 204n14, 236
Bataille, G., 191
Baudelaire, C., 191
Beaumier, S., 39n28
beauty, 5, 9, 13, 19–20, 22, 73, 81–82,
    90, 92, 109, 111, 112, 115–16, 123,
    138, 129, 149, 151, 217, 230
being, 1, 5, 14, 77, 116, 144–45,
    147–51, 195
Benjamin, W., 233
Berger, G., 36
Bhagavad Gita, 22, 238
Biran, M. de, 44, 58n10
Blondel, M., 5, 15, 147, 151, 156n65
Blum, L., 11
Blyth, R., 179n63
Boehme, J., 16

248   Index